Journey To Sexual Wholeness

The Six Gateways To Sacred Sexuality

Kypris Aster Drake

California

Published by Yabyummy Press, San Diego, CA

Yabyummy Press also publishes its books in electronic and audio formats. For more information, and for general information on other products and services, please visit www.yabyummy.com.

Library of Congress Cataloging-in-Publication Data:

Drake, Kypris Aster, 1962-
Journey to Sexual Wholeness: The Six Gateways to Sacred Sexuality / Kypris Aster Drake.

ISBN 978-0-615-19941-2
1. Spirituality 2. Sexuality 3. Shamanism

Printed in the United States of America

This book is dedicated to Steven Jay,
the first person to ever share the fullness of my dreams.
This book would not have been possible without
his loving support and unfailing belief in me.
The divine goddess in me honors the divine god in him.

Table of Contents

Acknowledgements

Before writing this book, I thought that the creation of the written page was a lonely, solitary effort. The reality for me has been that a number of people have contributed their time and energy toward this book's creation. Huge thanks go to my healing partner, Steven Jay, for giving me the time and space to do the writing, as well as editing every inch of this book with a fine-toothed comb and being brave enough to say what he really thinks. I also have huge gratitude in my heart for my teacher, Mellissa Seaman (heartwisdom.net), who cracked the armor off my heart, and brought me on an e-ticket ride into the worlds of shamanism and sacred sexuality. I feel deepest gratitude to my teacher Kamala, (openinghearts.com) for showing me what was possible in partnered tantric work. To Cynthia Taylor-Lambourne, I am eternally grateful for her mentorship and support. This book would never have gotten out of my heart and head and onto the page without Kamala Devi (blisscoach.com), who is an amazing life coach and author in her own right. Jenny Ward, Betsy Crimmins, Jordi Heguilor, and Joy were my readers, and all contributed very useful suggestions. Jennifer Masters (new-moon-design.com) is the incredible artist and designer who created the book cover, illustrations, and layout. Rachel M. Moore (http://elysiumediting.weebly.com) was my copyeditor and friend during the last stages of the book birthing process. Betsy Crimmins (http://photobetsy.com/) also created the back cover photo, and captured my essence with her brilliant eye. Last, but definitely not least, I want to thank my son, Drake, for believing that his mom is the best writer ever.

Glossary of Common Tantra and Shamanic Terms

Aho: Native American expression, used to mean "yes!" or "right on," or "Amen!"

Amrita: The female ejaculate, considered a powerful blessing in sacred sexual practice

Animal Guide: An animal in non-physical form, who comes into relationship with a human as a guide and protector

Chakra: An energy center in the body, associated with different parts of our psychological lives

Earth Mother: The Divine Feminine force embodied as the planet Earth

Lingam: Sanskrit word for the penis, meaning "wand of light"

Namaste: A greeting, meaning "the divine in me honors the divine in you"

PC muscle: The muscle you use to stop yourself from peeing; used to move sexual energy up and down the body

Polyamorous: A lifestyle that embraces multiple relationships that are both loving and sexual

Sky Father: The Divine Masculine force embodied as the Sky, Sun, and Stars

Spirit: The animating force behind the universe, present in every living and non-living thing

Yabyum: A Tibetan term meaning "Mother/Father." In this book, yabyum refers to a position for tantric practice where the woman is sitting in the man's lap.

Yoni: The Sanskrit word for the vagina, meaning "sacred temple"

• Introduction •

Healing the Sexual/Spiritual Split

How does tantric awakening manifest in my daily life? For me, the awakening is most powerfully obvious in the changes in my body. I am more sensitive to each touch, to each look, to each scent, to each smell. With a slight touch, my entire body begins to shiver, and lovemaking travels to heights of pleasure where my old orgasms are only the warm up to new energetic ecstasies. These states I can only describe as pure bliss mixed with primal sexual pleasure. At times, I prowl through my life like a giant black jaguar, seeking pleasure and reveling in the pure sensual bliss of a touch or of a meal. But even in this state, I hold an expanded awareness of my spiritual being, and my spiritual and sexual sensual selves are inseparable. Every lovemaking can lead to enlightenment, and every meditation can lead to sexual bliss.

Juicy aliveness and ecstatic joy are the goals of shamanic tantra, to create a life where sexuality is no longer shut off from the rest of our soul. To embrace our sexual power and carry it with us as an integrated part of our being is a gift, and a gift that all of us were born to as human beings. Sexuality is at the core of so much of human life, of creating children, of dance, of art, of music. It's in Beethoven's Moonlight Sonata, and in Monet's water lilies, and in Baryshnikov's leaps. To deny our sexuality leads only to deadness and a sense of emptiness. The more we open to embracing our sexuality, to living a sex-positive life, the more alive and joyful we begin to feel, because sex breeds these feelings in us. How many of us have had that secret smile throughout the day after a beautiful sexual evening with our partner? And if we haven't, then why not? Sex is beautiful when the heart is open. It is no longer something shameful and dirty, but is instead an ecstatic sacred act that moves us to tears, and even to communion with God.

The Six Gateways to sacred sexuality came into my life through intuition, experience, and a deep connection to Spirit. Their creation came partly in answer to many requests from students for a systematic set of practices they could bring into their daily lives. As they have evolved, each gateway has taken on a life of its own, becoming not only a set of tools, but a true opening in my soul. As I have moved through each gateway I have gone deeper into the mystery, wholeness, and ecstasy that is sacred sex. These practices are shamanic in origin, working with the energies in our bodies, and guided by our spiritual connection to our guides and to Spirit. The gateways are best traveled through in the order they are given here, the last three gateways revealing themselves through patient practice to be deeper levels of the first three.

The first gateway is called "Connecting to Spirit," and is a practice of cultivating safety. It took me many years to feel safe enough to embrace my full power and allow myself to open to connection with others. Attending a pagan conference, I was frustrated by a feeling of wanting desperately to connect, but having no one approach me. And then Spirit stepped in, and I lost a contact lens. Suddenly I was seeing the world with softer edges, and I shifted my energy with my gaze. My whole body became softer, and people began to approach me because I was no longer surrounded by insurmountable walls. Instead, I was forced to find my spiritual and emotional safety through connecting to the Earth and Sky and trusting that they would keep me safe. My first gateway had opened. Through intuition and the wisdom of Spirit, I let go of the huge energy boundary I had been carrying around. I dropped the bubble, and let Spirit take care of me.

A few months after this conference, my tantric partner, Steven Jay, came into my life. Meeting him at a party, the connection between us was instant, electric, and so solid that I had a feeling of being totally connected to the Earth when he put his hand on my leg and sat next to me. I felt pulled into the center of myself and my femininity. There were many obstacles to our coming into relationship together, and yet I stayed uncharacteristically calm most of the time as we grew into knowing each other. My connection to Spirit kept me in the present and unconcerned about what would happen next. Every time I would start to feel afraid for the future, wondering where our connection would lead, Spirit wrapped me in a warm blanket to soothe me, and the fears would leave. It wasn't until we had known each other for a few months that I remembered a profoundly affecting dream that I'd recorded four months before meeting Steven.

In the dream, I entered a cave in the jungles of Bali, a cave lit with flickering candles, and lined with dark shining rock. In the cave was an altar with a Shiva lingam standing in its center, proudly proclaiming the power of the divine masculine. Suddenly, out of the shadows, a priest appeared, with shaven head, and nude to the waist. He had the most penetrating eyes I have ever seen, which he turned on me. Those eyes bored straight into my soul as he said, "Now you're ready for me." Steven has the face, eyes, and body of the man in my dream, and as I grew to know him, I learned that he was also practicing sacred sexuality. We set about creating a partnered sacred sexual practice in which we met once a week for four to six hours to practice together. We explored breathing, connecting, eye gazing, dancing the elements, and aligning the chakras. It was my first experience of working with a partner who was as committed as I was to the practice. From that spiritual union our partnership has grown, until what remains is a purity of purpose, each of us on our individual paths, united in a common cause of creation, manifestation, and pure spiritual joy.

It was in my partnership with Steven that I first practiced the second gateway, "Breathing Love." I knew that breathing was important in my solo practice, and often calmed me and brought sanity into my day. Breathing with Steven was a whole different exploration. I learned to be totally present to the nuances of each moment, to drop into a place of timeless surrender. In this surrender I became truly vulnerable for the first time in my life, and my heart began to open wide.

I learned that being present in my heart and loving unconditionally were the greatest gifts I had to offer a man. I have come to a soft and sweet openness of heart through this unconditional love, which feels like I am carrying pure joy in my soul. This joy leaks out from me wherever I go and in everything I do. Even in life's challenges, when fear and anger course through me, their visit is many times shorter. If I spend a few hours of attention on my breath, the sweetness returns again. Love and gratitude have come to roost in my heart like a standing water bird, and I love the feeling of peace and beauty that they bring.

Becoming present to a lover who is available to catch and contain the feelings that tumble out of me lets me go into the deep, dark emotions hiding in the caverns of my soul. In the third gateway, "Soul Gazing," you will explore these caverns, mapping what is there, and deciding what you will carry up into the light for Spirit to heal. Awareness of buried emotion lets you move toward release, and leads to a relaxation of the Spirit. Enormous amounts of energy are freed by emptying our emotional caves. Using the tools of Soul Gazing to release old feelings makes space for you to welcome in joy, happiness, and ecstasy. Amazingly, as you do this the genitals and the heart become more sensitive and alive. When you let go of what you've been holding, you become more awake, full of energy, and you begin to experience the true meaning of bliss, and of tears that come from joy instead of pain.

The fourth gateway, "Waking the Dragon," opens a deeper layer of being present, moving into an opening of the physical body and the energy body overlaid on it. Waking up sensual and sexual energy as a spiritual practice showed me once and for all that sexual energy was spiritual, because I began to see God while I was climaxing. Every touch from Steven awakened my whole body, and I began to crave this experience of aliveness.

The only other place I had felt this current of ecstasy running through me was in movement, and I still love to feel the ecstasy and arousal that can come with moving my body and energy. Movement helps me to tune in and let go whenever energy is stuck in my body. When I move I am healthier, more sensual, and more alive. Movement shifts negative emotions and physical malaise, leaving me cleansed and vital.

Moving is also an important part of the fifth gateway, "Weaving the Elements." Here I found balance, through moving into a much deeper connection to Spirit. Balancing your body, emotions, creative/sexual self, and mind leads to peacefulness and an ability to have a balanced life.

The fifth gateway has been a very rewarding solo practice that has helped me to balance out the many activities in my life. But it is even more phenomenal in its power to balance a relationship. In my practice with Steven, we often used the partnered elemental dance to show us where our relationship needed attention. If dancing an element together was difficult, then we presumed that element was showing us a place to work on in the relationship. Doing this work is one of the most rewarding and healing practices a couple can do to grow together and create deeply satisfying connection.

The sixth gateway of "Divine Union" is a deeper level of Soul Gazing, and the culmination of all the gateway practices that have come before. In solo practice this is where we go within and find a sense of wholeness in our center or purpose. In partnered practice you bring that wholeness into connection and create something that is greater than the both of you.

Coming into connection with my lovers in this way creates a powerful bond, as I stay present, connect to Spirit, allow my emotions to flow, feel my body connect deeply with my lover, and drop into my feminine to mirror his masculine polarity. This polarity practice of being deeply active or receptive in lovemaking and in the world is the culmination of my current practice. I am learning to let everything that I need come to me as I rest in my center, just as Steven is learning to let Spirit direct him to all that he needs while he journeys on his path.

Accepting that I am gifted with the calling and abilities of a tantrika, I have given my life over to the miracles that occur in this work. Over and over there are unforeseen benefits to the private healing sessions I do with my partner, Steven. Years of sexual wounding drop away, old patterns suddenly become obsolete. I see how there are both healing and sexual paths in the work, that the needs of some students may be only for healing and not for learning to move their own sexual energy. Other students may need the healing that only full acceptance of their sexual nature can provide. And no two students are alike. Even though there is a pattern to the work, the intuitive awareness, the shamanic acceptance of Spirit's direction, is always essential to the healing. And as time goes on a framework emerges. My knowledge deepens with each student, with each miracle, and I create patterns of light, stored on my computer, to remind me of the paths that many people seem to tread in tandem.

On all of these paths, "You must be present to win" is the common thread for tantric work. Sacred sexual practice is not just about learning to have better sex, it is about living all of life with fearless joy. It is about being here now, with every fiber of your being. It is letting go of fear, because fear can only live in the future. It is a skill, and that is why we practice. We practice the art of letting go, of dropping into the moment so deeply that time stands still, and suddenly we see the true nature of all things. Tantra is one path to enlightenment. It is different from most other spiritual paths in that its road leads directly through the body and all of those things about the body that most of us learned to reject and ignore as children. Now as adults we can choose to heal our lives through becoming aware of our bodies, through learning to consciously breathe love into ourselves, through learning to be fully present to ourselves and our partners, through creating a balanced life, and through exploring deeply what it is to be masculine or feminine, and to bring all of this to partnership to lovemaking, and to life.

✦ The First Gateway ✦

Connecting to Spirit

• Chapter 1 •

Creating a Spiritual Practice

Sitting on the edge of an active volcano, I feel the gritty black rock warm under my feet as lava flows beneath it and out into the ocean. Surrounded by a darkness lit only by my headlamp, I gaze out to the sea and watch red molten rock push itself out of the ground and fall into the water. A vast cloud of vog (volcanic fog) rises into the air and drifts over the stark black landscape, instant death to any hapless human or animal who inhales it. A few feet in front of me, a crack in the earth reveals the liquid fire of lava running beneath it. I shiver in fear and in awe as I sit on this point of the creation of worlds, and feel the place where Earth, Water, Air, and Fire come together to create. Goddess Pele's power flows through me, soothing my fear and initiating me into a fiery wisdom that I will carry back from the Big Island of Hawaii to my life at home in San Diego. I breathe Her in and feel my sexual self open and unfold with a deep fire that feels like lava flowing within me. Back safe in my bed later that night, I open in lovemaking to a deep and fiery connection with my lover, and in that connection I am like the volcano, fiery and vast and strong. The fear has left me, and in its place is the utter certainty that the power of Pele and the burning rock now live within my soul.

Longing for connection to God underlies much of human activity. Not longing for religion, but specifically a desire to be connected to the divine force that is behind the magic of the universe. In my connection to the volcano, I felt a simultaneous ecstasy, awe, and peace. When I am fully connected to the divine in this way, my body fills with energy. In this state I am whole and complete and in my power. Spiritual practice feels empty to me without the life of spirit to infuse it. I could do the same practice I do every day, to sit in meditation, and without my connection to Spirit, to the grand animating force of the universe, I would begin to feel bored and stagnant. My connection to Spirit is like a connection to a lover or friend — it contains energizing variety as well as calming familiarity. Only in relationship can I find this alchemy of difference, whether it is relationship to God or to another person. This is the essence of sacred sexuality, to open yourself to this connected bliss, to allow your heart to be ecstatically open as it connects to nature, to the divine, and to other humans. With spiritual practice, you learn that closing yourself off does not protect you, it only breeds sadness and isolation. I have learned instead that I can create safety by trusting spirit, and following its direction. In aligning with spirit this way, my open heart creates joy in me as I am able to receive the gifts that others share.

Beginning

In spiritual practice, the thing that I wish to create above all is a sense of ease. I want my spiritual practice to flow easily, to not to have to think so hard about my behavior, but to have it flow naturally from within. I work at cultivating this by establishing certain habits. For instance, I sit at the same time and the same place every day. Establishing this practice makes it natural for me to meditate, and I begin to look forward to the daily time alone and to the sense of peace it creates in me. I notice a tremendous difference in my behavior and my emotional reactions when I skip my morning meditation. My fuse is short, and I lose my ability to think before I speak. With regular meditation, my habits of negative thought and emotion shift easily because I am able to surrender and accept the situation at hand. It is a powerful learning experience for me to meditate with my son trying to sit in my lap and my cat sharing that same space with him. I find that after years of cultivating inner peace, I can find a place of love within myself and acceptance that they both want to be close to me when I am running large amounts of spiritual energy, as I do in my meditation. Breathing into my connection with them becomes an extension of my meditation practice, and I become a buddha meditating in the midst of a whirlwind.

Even if you feel like you are not "doing it right," continue to sit each day. If boredom begins to creep in, add beautiful objects to your practice. Burn incense, or read a beautiful poem or piece of spiritual wisdom before you begin. Keeping the practice itself fresh helps us to keep doing it, and establishing the habit makes it easeful.

Creating Space

Creating beauty with your spiritual practice is nourishing to your soul. A space for your practice, even if it is just a tiny table in your bedroom with a candle on it, states to your subconscious mind, your inner child, that you are committed to this practice, and that you intend to do it every day. You can engage the child through the beautification of the space, adding meaningful objects. Perhaps you might have a representation of what Spirit is for you, or a symbol of your tantric practice, or symbols of the elements of Earth, Air, Fire, and Water. Perhaps you just like to have a place to light incense. Or perhaps there is a beautiful piece of art or writing that inspires you. Whatever it is, add it to your space.

When searching for spiritual space, be inventive. For years I lived in a one-bedroom apartment with my husband and three cats, and creating a space was tough. I finally realized that the balcony was the best spot, simply because I could go out there to be alone. I wrapped myself in blankets during the winter and wore warm clothing to do my meditation. These days my life has shifted, and I live mostly alone with my very elderly cat. My entire apartment is a shrine to my spiritual life now, with the focus being a small altar set up on top of an old army footlocker painted to represent the Celtic God of the Forest. Your spiritual space is a reflection of you, and the only requirement is that it be inspiring to your deepest soul.

Peace and tranquility are the goals of most spiritual practices, learning to be in a place of great contentment no matter what whirlwinds are wailing around you. This peace is also at the core of shamanic tantra, and for me it is a peace laced with joy.

Solitude

To learn the practice of inner stillness, it is first helpful to experience outer stillness. Solitude is the first step. When I remove myself from the proximity of others, my thoughts quiet themselves and I fall into myself. Solitude is a gift, although often in our culture we do not value it. Quiet alone time allows buried feelings to well up, and thoughts kept at bay to flow through my mind. Eventually, these things pass through me and I find my way to quiet.

I recommend that you begin establishing your spiritual practice by finding a place and a time for solitude. Turn off the phone, tell the kids, the dog, the husband, the wife, that you are not available for the next little while. You only need 5-10 minutes each day to begin. Over time, if it feels right to you, you can increase your meditation time to a half hour or more. In my experience, the longer you meditate, the more powerful the benefits will be for you in your spiritual life. For many of us, getting this quiet time requires that we rise early and greet the sun, or that we stay up late to breathe in the stars and the moon. Either practice is beautiful. In my life as a corporate technical diva, I used to meditate in my car at noon and commune with the sun. Use your imagination to create this still time in your daily life. Whatever works for you, do it.

Quiet

Noise is a powerful distraction from the peaceful serenity that we seek in meditation. Music is a powerful aid to inner stillness, a special friend to city meditators, or meditators with a family. Let's face it, conditions are not always ideal, and you cannot always find a place that is totally free of the noise of the life that exists all around you. What you can learn to do is allow music to shift you into a place where your awareness is no longer focused on anything but the music and your breath. This is the beginning of meditation, to surrender to music flowing through you, to the feeling it creates in you. Select music that creates an unwinding inside you, and helps you relax into what is, as you do your spiritual practice. Beautiful music can so easily create a beautiful mood inside me, and I use it often to shift myself if I am wanting to reconnect with spirit in a moment of despair or anger. Brainwaves begin to shift the moment you hear music. Music takes us into the side of our brain that is not rational and allows us to let go of the mental chatter that most of us carry in our heads every day. Listening to music, I shift into a place of spiritual beauty, and I am enlivened and enriched.

Dropping In

Once I have created a space for my practice, found the time to do it, and searched out beautiful music, I add practices that allow me to go into meditation quickly by telling my mind and body that it is time to let go of the everyday world. This is especially helpful when I only have a small amount of time to meditate. Cleansing myself by smudging with sage is always the beginning to my daily spiritual practice. Over the years the smell of the sage, and the action of passing its smoke over my body, has become a trigger to my awareness that I am entering sacred space. I am pulled immediately into presence in the moment, breathing out deeply and imagining that I am releasing any emotions or energies from my body that do not serve me. I feel refreshed after this process, as if I have showered. Clearing the energy body of thoughts and emotions that are negative and distracting frees up space for Spirit to come in. It allows you to feel lighter and more joyful. You may clear not only your body, but also your space with sage or other fragrant burning herbs like cedar, sweet grass, or tobacco (not cigarettes!). Incense is also used for this, and sandalwood has special properties that both clear the energy body and open the chakras for tantric work. If you cannot abide smoke, then you may choose to clear your energy field with sound, using a Tibetan singing bowl, finger cymbals, a bell, or a chime. All of these produce powerful sound vibrations that enter the energy body and clear it. If sound is not an option, you might try water as a way to clear your energy field. You can do this by symbolically drinking water from a special goblet or cup, by anointing your body with water, or by sprinkling your space with the same water mixed with salt.

Power Objects

Richer connection to Spirit can come from the beauty of power objects that we use in our daily practice. Anchored in my power objects are qualities like playfulness, fiery kundalini healing, grounding, ecstasy, joy, and heart healing. Each power object and crystal that I work with has a purpose. A power object can be anything — a rock, a feather, a candle, even a small box. Holding a power object in my hand, I can meditate or focus on a particular quality I would like to bring into myself, like a more open heart, or more centering. Touching a power object to my chakras, I can bless myself and align with that object's energy. Magick with power objects is another possibility, to let them hold my intention to manifest something in my life, to be a daily reminder of that quality or experience that I am longing for. And healing old emotional wounds is another use for power objects, to place them on my body or my lover's body.

Strong power objects come from the earth and the animals that walk upon it. On my altar are seed pods, leaves, rocks, feathers, and crystals. I use each of these objects for different purposes. A hawk feather reminds me of my commitment to soar above life's obstacles, and to strive for clear perception. A rabbit's foot recalls my awareness of the sensuality and softness of my being. A snake's skin echoes my continual transforming, shedding old behaviors and beliefs through my tantra practice. Each of these objects is a gift from Spirit and must be treated with reverence. Any object that I collect from nature is always collected with permission from Spirit, with thanks, and with an offering of cornmeal, hair, water, or saliva. To ask permission, I simply go into a meditative state and ask the question, "Is it right for me to take this object from its natural home?" I pay attention to my first and immediate reaction when I ask this question. That reaction tells me all I need to know. When I give my offering, I do so with reverence, and with presence, bringing myself deeply into the moment and into a sense of gratitude to the plant or animal or land for the gift. When I have finished my time working with a power object, I return it to nature, or gift it to another human who will benefit from its energy.

Power objects will catch your eye as you are out enjoying time in nature, or in the world, or when you are needing support from Spirit. Recently I was in a state of sadness about a relationship that was ending. As I walked from my front door to my car that morning, I found a raven feather on the ground. The raven is symbolic of endings, and is also seen shamanically as a great benefactor to humankind. This feather, wrapped in yarn and laced with power beads, has become a ceremonial tool for me to use in facilitating shamanic healings that center around endings. The act of passing it over the body becomes a spiritual act because of the power I have given it with my mind.

When you first bring a power object home, spend time with it in meditation, and get to know its energy. Once you have done this, you will know when and how it is appropriate for you to use that power object in your practice. Power objects are full of beauty and magic, and each one has a story to tell you.

I cannot create a spiritual practice from discipline alone. Moving me from within, Spirit takes hold of me again and again to push me into places I would never have the discipline or courage to go to on my own. It is challenging to create motivation for anything in my life without this inner urge of spirit. I have seen over and over again that using my will to force myself to do something that is not motivated by this deep inner urge of Spirit does not serve me. In the end I find that doing anything because I think that I "should" does not help me to grow or be happy. A practice of sacred sexuality, like any other practice, must come from a place of longing inside you — longing for a better sexual connection with your partner, longing for more joy and ecstasy in your life, or longing to commune with God.

Keeping it Flowing

Instead of using force of will, muse and map your way into time and space for your spiritual growth by combining the feeling of what is right for you in the flow of your day, and what is practical. I usually do this practice through grabbing a box of markers and a sketch book anytime I want to add a new thing to my life. I draw the week and fill in all the things I normally do, then in a bright bold new color, I feel into where I should put my new activity. Sometimes I have to start over because the first or second map I create doesn't feel right to me once I've created it. It is important to sit with your little map and see how it feels inside. Does it feel hard? Like duty or obligation? Then it will never work! Look to create a map that excites you, that revs you up, that awakens a "yes! I can do this!" inside you. That is when you know that you have the perfect map. Once you've completed your map, hang it up somewhere you will see it every day as you are beginning your new practice — the refrigerator, the bathroom mirror, your dresser, your altar. Make it important and real to yourself. Then spend some time in meditation imagining yourself doing the new activity at the time you have mapped out each day. Imagine how you will feel as you are doing it. These feelings are the key to success.

Create your spiritual practice also through setting a strong intention. Once you have decided to make the commitment to daily practice, focus your mind on the thought and the vision of yourself doing your practice. See yourself sitting in the sacred space you have created, see the altar, see the room around you, feel in your body how it will feel to have this meditation in place in your daily life. Know that you will succeed. Once you have done this, you will probably find that your practice becomes anchored in your awareness, and that it becomes easier. Setting intention is a form of prayer. It is asking Spirit to help us create what we want in our lives through a strong desire for something. I often picture myself doing my morning meditation as the sun rises and in my visualization I see the sky and how it changes as the sun gets higher in the heavens. I find this helps my body to know what to do. Even though I am not naturally a morning person, morning is the best time for me to meditate because it is when I am naturally most peaceful and when there are no demands on my time by anyone else. This morning for example, my body woke me at dawn. Even though I had been up late the night before, I had set the strong intention to rise at dawn to meditate and write. I didn't set my alarm, just my intention. And my body woke me, and I rose from bed easily, not feeling tired or disgruntled at getting out of bed.

What will not help you in creating a spiritual practice is to allow your emotions and resistance to stand in your way. Remember that you are like a baby learning to walk, and that having the same compassion for yourself as you would for a baby will help support you in learning a new skill. Guilt is the least helpful way to inspire yourself to do your daily practice. Piling shame on yourself only serves to make yourself feel bad about not keeping to your plan for spiritual practice, and in fact often prevents you from doing the practice as a "why bother" attitude creeps in. If you make yourself feel bad over failing, you will never succeed. The gentle approach allows you to recommit, to say, "Yes, I didn't do what I planned to, now I am going to try again." No one scolds a child when they fall down as they are learning to walk. Creating spiritual practice is almost as difficult as learning to walk for many of us, and requires daily effort and acceptance when we fail. So be kind to yourself, recommit to yourself. Let yourself know that it is okay if you fail, as long as you keep trying. Eventually, one day you will wake up and realize that you have been doing your spiritual practice successfully for days, and that you feel good and excited about doing it.

Fear is another common obstacle to spiritual practice. For many of us there is a fear that we won't do it right, or a fear of what we might connect to if we do the practice, or a fear of what we might become. When I first began meditating and creating ritual, I had fear that I would attract the attention of ghosts or other entities that would frighten and hurt me. In those days I had no connection to the loving energy that is available to all of us when we connect to Spirit. I had no concept of a loving power that only wants what is best for me. Discouragement was my frequent companion in those days, and I would pass through long periods of not doing my practice. But I remember that one week I began meditating daily because my life had become so unpleasant that I hoped the meditation would help. And suddenly I dropped into a zone of beauty and energy. I felt happier, more serene, and positive throughout my day, despite the fact that I had to get up before dawn to get time for my meditation. The fear and sadness I was feeling seemed to lose its power, and since that time I have moved steadily into joy, peace, ecstasy and freedom. This freedom is there for you too. You have only to surrender to it.

Attainable goals are best when learning meditation. Set yourself a task that you can quantify, like 5 minutes a day of meditation, in the morning. Once you have set this goal, report in to yourself, or to a friend who you have agreed to be accountable to. You can hang a piece of paper up in your meditation area and simply mark down when you do the meditation, just to keep track. Remember not to guilt or shame yourself when you fail, just to report the facts of how many minutes of meditation you have done each day. Set a timer if you like, so that you know exactly how long you are meditating. Focus on your breath and drop in. Allow yourself to enjoy the time rather than struggling against it. Follow each breath in and out and let all other thoughts vanish from your mind. In this state the mind begins to relax and unwind, and you will see the benefits throughout your day, in a more peaceful and centered attitude. I encourage you to notice the difference between days when you do your spiritual practice and days when you don't. Again, not from a place of guilt or shame, but simply to notice the benefits you gain when you do your practice. You may not notice the benefits right away, but in time they will come, and it is up to you to continue your practice until it begins to flow more easily.

Meditation, trance, and connecting to the non-ordinary world of power are practices that span many religions and spiritual systems of thought, because they have such power to bring us into the present. That presence is the goal of most spiritual paths. This first gateway is the foundation of sacred sexuality, because it supports us in being present to our bodies, to our emotions, and to our sexuality. It opens up a whole new world of possibilities for our healing, our growth, and our connection to Spirit. In each of the gateways that follows, this connection is where we start before moving into opening our hearts and souls to connection with the divine and with one another. Connecting to Spirit is where we begin, and where we end, even in our last transition beyond this life and into the next one.

• Chapter 2 •

Connecting to Spirit Solo

Earth-centered in its approach to spirituality, shamanism is a spiritual path that is practiced all around the world, throughout many different cultures, and with many different conceptions of God. What unites these practices is a shared concept about the spiritual world, an intuitive approach to healing the self and others. In shamanism, the journey to other worlds is a common theme, as well as cultivating the use of the breath for healing. These other worlds we travel to are the equivalent of our own subconscious, conscious, and superconscious minds. In shamanism they are called the lower, middle, and upper worlds. Each of these serves a function. Shamanism also uses a form of deep presence and awareness to heal others and the self, a deep looking within, and this is key to shamanic tantra. Our first goal in tantric connection with a shamanic approach is to cultivate a deep presence in the moment and a surrender to the will of Spirit. This surrender allows us to flow in our sexual experience, to let go of goals, and see the beauty in each moment of pleasure that we experience. It helps us to let go of judgment and shame. Creating an opening for Spirit to come in and heal us is really the point of this surrender. For me, what I call Spirit is the force behind the universe, and I see its presence in all of nature. As a shaman, I am guided in my practice by the flight of birds, the howl of the coyote, the running of the rabbit. I form connections to the natural world that are sacred, and that bring me to wisdom, knowledge, and healing.

Practice 1: Forming a Connection to Spirit

I invite you to explore your concept of Spirit as you begin this journey. Explore this question either in a series of meditations or through writing exercises. As shamanic tantra practitioners, we must first be willing to deeply contemplate the concept of a divine power. This is an exploration that you can do periodically to check in about your connection to the divine.

Sit quietly and think about these concepts, or get out a pen and paper and write about them:

What is Spirit for you? Is it masculine, feminine, or neither? Is it an old man with a gray beard? Blue many-armed Shiva? Aphrodite rising out of the ocean foam? I invite you to truly investigate within you not only what your picture of Spirit is, but your relationship to that picture. Without a positive relationship to the divine, creating a spiritual practice will be extremely difficult and lonely. I invite you to examine your past, to look for any wounds or judgments you have about connecting to a power that is greater than yourself. Many of us in Western culture were raised with the concept of a punishing, judgmental God that dispenses justice if we do wrong. Look within yourself and see if there is any part of you that can open to a spiritual power that loves you unconditionally.

Embracing Divinity

Within shamanism, many of us work with the concepts of Mother Earth and Father Sky, the first parents as well as animal guides or totems. For me, Mother Earth and Father Sky are the most loving parents who could ever exist, parents who have only my best interests at heart, and who love and hold me no matter what mistakes I have made or how many times I have turned away from their loving care. My animal guides and totems are powerful friends, who I can play and laugh with. I can ask them the "stupid" questions that I have about my spiritual life and not feel embarrassed. I can ask them for help and support when I am in need. Having this kind of support is so important for me, because part of life is that the humans around me cannot always meet my needs for support. But more importantly, going to Source for help and support makes it much more likely that my needs will be met.

Shamanic Meditation

Once you have created space you are ready to begin meditation. The breath is where we begin. Breathing brings an intense aliveness to our bodies. When we are breathing deeply we experience life as full, rich, and dynamic. When you are learning to meditate, breathe as if your life depended on it. Breathe into every cell and fiber of your being. Breathe into a deep awareness of your toes, your legs, your genitals, your belly, your back, your breasts, your throat, your head, your face and eyes. Every part of you can be awakened with the breath. The most basic form of meditation is to simply follow your breath, to focus only on the breath and nothing else. To go deeply within and feel the breath filling your lungs, moving your belly and chest out and in, feeling your mind become clearer as you breathe. Energy comes into you more and more as you do this practice, and there is a flow, a tingling that happens in your body, a streaming of energy in your cells. When you begin to feel this tingling or lightness in the body, you are truly in a deep meditative state. This state is completely within the body. In tantra we seldom pursue the trance state in which we leave our body behind. Instead, we pursue the trance state in which we go deeper and deeper into ourselves and into feeling each and every sensation in our bodies.

Practice 2: Following the Breath

Sit quietly in a comfortable posture and bring your awareness completely into yourself. Take a deep breath in through your nose, letting your belly fully expand. Exhale completely through your mouth, relaxing your body as you breathe out. If the breath is difficult, try adjusting your posture. Try lying down, or sitting in a chair that supports your back, legs, and feet. Create space within you for breathing. Try this practice for five minutes each day, and let this be your first meditation. Stay focused on the breath as much as you can, and if thoughts come into your mind, simply breathe them out the top of your head, or tell your mind thank you for the thought of ________, now I am going to go back to my breath. Keep clearing thoughts from the mind as often as you need to, and continue focusing on breathing. When you are finished with this daily practice, notice how you feel. You may feel a tingling in all or part of your body. Notice also throughout your day if you are tense or in pain; are you breathing? Try breathing at these moments throughout your day and see if breath eases the tension for you.

Once you are able to spend five minutes each day following the breath, you are ready to go deeper. Soften yourself into the arms of Earth Mother and learn to sink into her embrace by connecting to Her in visualization. Mother Earth is always holding us as we walk upon her, but we are not always able to feel her loving nurturing embrace. Consciously creating a cord to her from the base of our spine, we can pretend that we are trees rooting into her core, drawing up her juicy loving molten lava into our bodies when we need energizing sexual energy, or imagining cool water flowing up into us when we need refreshing. Sinking into her loving embrace and into this loving connection with her, we feel Her enfold us. We feel our connection to Her. Meditate on your connection to the planet, and how you are supported by the food you eat that grows from Her, how your bodily waste flows back into Her lands and oceans to create nutrients for plants and other creatures, beginning the cycle again. Feel your interconnectedness to all living things when you connect to Mother Earth, and you know for sure that you are never ever alone, that all of life is part of you, and you are part of all life.

Trees are powerful teachers of connection to the sacred, and we use this same imagery to learn to connect to the divine masculine. Kissed by Father Sky in every moment of our lives since we emerged from the womb, we learn next in our practice to consciously engage our connection to Him. He is the loving father, the balanced divine masculine energy that inspirits us with each breath. He is the stars in the sky that draw our gaze upward. Drawing his essence into us is enlivening, and we do this by simply imagining the other part of the sacred tree within us, imagining or feeling branches growing from the top of our heads up into the sky and the stars and the sun. We grow these branches tall, through the atmosphere of the earth and into space. Hooking into the star energies, we open the crown of our heads to divinely inspired thoughts and ideas. We feel this star stuff telling us how to proceed. I admit that I often get Spirit and Father Sky confused, and that I often think of them as the same thing, but I think in reality this is not the true nature of the thing. Spirit is that force that permeates everything, and Sky Father is a part of that larger force of Spirit. To connect fully with Sky Father, go out under the open sky and lie on your back and look at the clouds. Imagine that you can connect to these clouds and draw this vibrant and strong masculine presence into your body.

Once you have learned to connect to earth and sky, you are ready for the full Sacred Tree meditation. Balance between the masculine and feminine is the goal of this meditation, to be able to pull both these energies into yourself as you need them. Receiving the love of these parents heals the heart, and can cure relationship addiction and neediness. My partner and I made this the foundation of our tantric practice because I was stuck in tremendous difficulty in detaching emotionally and spiritually and physically from my tantric partner. Every time he would leave me to return to his life, I would be devastated for hours. I was stuck in an incredibly needy place, and had no practice for bringing myself back into a state of wholeness, no way to come out gently from my connection to him. We realized together that I needed a practice to consciously and lovingly detach from him and to come back into my own centered space. In the past two years this practice has been such a divine thing, to be able to shift my neediness and to let go of addiction to love and to relationship, simply through a few moments of devoted meditation. The feeling of peace and wholeness I had the first few times was like a miracle for me, and I was so grateful when I finally "got" this practice. It has become invaluable to me in learning to feel a sense of being whole and complete in myself.

Practice 3: Sacred Tree Meditation

To do the sacred tree meditation, sit in your sacred space and focus on your breath. Begin by following your breath as in the previous practice, relaxing your body and your mind. Once you have dropped into the breath, use a deep exhale to imagine that you are growing roots from the base of your spine and your perineum (the place between your yoni or lingam and your anus). With each exhale let these roots grow deeper, thicker, and stronger. Let them penetrate the floor you are sitting on, the soil beneath, the bedrock, and the molten rock beneath the bedrock. Let your roots wrap around the Earth's magnetic core and anchor you there. Breathe out into these roots to relax tension from your body. Breathe out anger, grief, sadness, frustration, anxiety, and any other negative emotions you'd like to let go of. Imagine that as you breathe out, these emotions flow out of your body, into the roots, and down into the Earth, where they become compost. Once you have taken several breaths to discharge your tension and negative emotion, begin to use your inhaled breath to breathe in the solidity and strength of the Earth into your body. This may feel like water or nutrients flowing up your roots, heat from the earth's core or simply a loving energy.

With your roots firmly in place, bring your awareness to the crown of your head, and imagine that branches are budding from the top of your head and growing up into the sky. With each exhale, let these branches grow tall and wide so that you become a mighty tree. Let them grow through the ceiling if you are indoors, then through the clouds and the Earth's atmosphere. Let them grow all the way up into the sun, and feel them hooking into the sun's warmth and radiance. Breathe out from your head and body distracting thoughts, creative blocks,

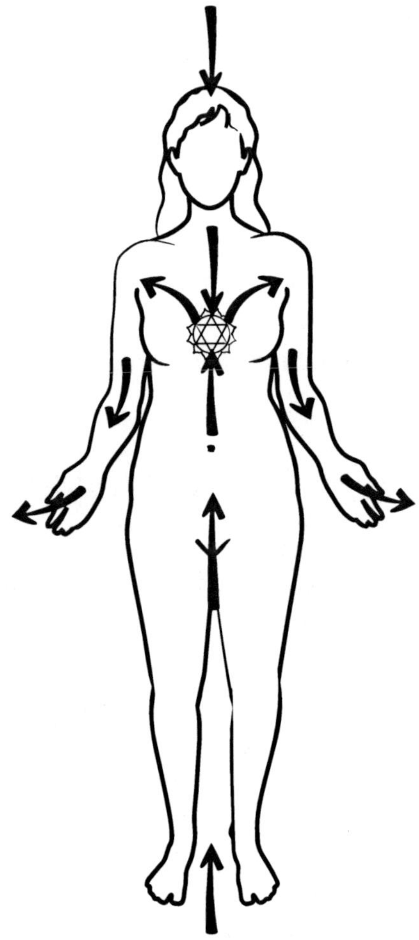

and sexual wounds. Let them just rise up out of you and float up into the sun to be burned as fuel for its radiance. Once you have taken several breaths out, begin to inhale the sun's warmth and radiance into your body, feeling it warm the top of your head and fill your whole body with warmth and energy. Feel your mind empty and sharpen. With your branches firmly in the sky and your roots anchored deeply in the earth, begin to breathe into your heart from both the earth and the sky at the same time. Breathe these energies and their support in through the top of your head and the base of your spine. Breathe them into your heart. Feel the centering there. When you breathe out, imagine these energies flowing out through your arms and hands. Take your time breathing this loving energy into your heart and out your hands. Notice if you feel any tingling or warmth in your hands and arms. Finally, place your hands on your heart so that you are breathing this love back into yourself, loving yourself, and notice how that feels. With each inhale bring love into your heart from the earth and sky and with each exhale, let this love flow out your hands and right back into your heart.

Do this meditation each day for at least 5 minutes when you are beginning your tantric practice. It is more important that you do the practice daily than that you do it for long periods of time. It is the daily act of reminding yourself of your center and of your connection to Spirit that is most important. If you can't see or feel the energy moving through you right away, just keep trying, and imagine that you can. You can try sitting with your back against a tree and let your awareness merge with the tree as it teaches you its gentle way of staying connected to all of life. Daily practice of this meditation can help to keep you centered, even in the midst of difficult times. These difficult times are when you especially want to do this practice, even though they are the hardest times to stay with it. The peace of mind that you will gain in these circumstances is well worth the work. And in time, this meditation can become ecstatic, moving sexual energy powerfully through the body, and creating an arousal that moves through all of you, merging you with Spirit and the bliss of that connection.

Prayer

When you are spending this quiet time in meditation, you may also wish to pray. Prayer is a communion that I go to when I need to tell everything that is on my mind and in my heart, when I need to let all my desires and hopes and dreams spill out of me. I have heard it said that while meditation is listening to God, prayer is talking to God. Both are important parts of your spiritual practice, but they require different states of mind. When I am in prayer, I am wholly devoted, heart open, expressing my love, my gratitude, my desires, my hopes, my fears. But most of all, in prayer I am not so much asking for things to be given to me as I am asking for guidance in living my life. I ask Spirit to show me what is the most loving thing I can do for myself. I love the feeling that comes to me when I ask this question, a rich satisfaction in my heart. I also love how cleansing it is, to simply let it all hang out with someone who cares so much for me, someone who cares more for me than anyone else. And sometimes I am indifferent, and I lapse into long periods of not talking to Spirit, often when I am angry. Other times I rail and rage at Spirit or at my guides for the hand I have been dealt. Lately my guides have been making some outrageous changes in my life, and I have been so angry about that! In particular they have been giving me relationships with men and then snatching them away, and all in an effort to teach me even more about my attachments and about my addiction to getting love from outside myself. I have been angry, despairing, and martyred. But lately I have moved into gratitude for what they have shown me, and acceptance that Spirit knows what is best for me. When I pray, I share all of this with them.

The place where I am most deeply moved to prayer and meditation is in nature. Whether in a garden, in the woods, or high on a remote mountain, I love to absorb the feeling of nature into my body. Walking in the sun, feeling the green leaves of trees around me, drinking in the stark beauty of the desert sky — these are all priceless gifts of nature. The natural world is full of love to give to each of us, a world of energy and freshness. Those who have a shamanic practice learn to observe the mysteries of nature at a deep level. This study includes watching the animals and plants that are their guides, and learning to breathe these creatures into their soul. A shaman learns lessons from the growth of trees, the dance of dolphins, the slither of the snake. When I observe the movement of the snake, I see the movement of the kundalini through my spine. When I watch the stillness of the blue heron, I drink in the patience I must learn as a healer. When I thrill to the leap of dolphins in the waves, I absorb uninhibited joy. Everything in nature is a teacher, just as everything in life is a teacher. The world is filled with metaphors and connections between nature and our own lives. Try your meditation outdoors, or in a place where you can connect deeply to the outdoors.

Animal Guides

Animal guides are an important part of our connection to nature, an unexplainable link to the divine that brings in certain qualities into our being. When you are beginning your shamanic tantra practice, it is important to identify your primary guide. To do this, go into meditation using the sacred tree meditation to center and connect to the shamanic world. Once you connect, ask the question, "Who is my animal guide?" Your answer will be the first image that comes into your mind. Once you have this guide, find a picture or small carving to place on your altar. Call on this guide daily in your meditation, allowing yourself to attune deeply to its energy.

Inspiring us on our journeys through the ordinary and shamanic worlds is the job of the spirit guide or totem spirit. They connect us lovingly to Spirit's will. Being closer to Source than we are, they guide us gently, sometimes even with tricks, letting us think we know what is happening, when perhaps something quite different is truly afoot. Recently I began a relationship with Coyote, an animal guide who is traditionally known as both trickster and healer. Out in the desert on a retreat, I found myself truly stuck in the middle of releasing some old guilt and shame and rage around my sexuality. Away from my camp and my tantric partner, breathing and doing yoga, working to release all the unpleasantness inside me, I didn't even realize how much I was stuck until I tried to release it with movement and found that I couldn't, it was just too big for me and I didn't know how. Every tool at my disposal was failing. I laid myself down into child's pose on my mat, surrendering and crying, asking for help. And suddenly I felt the distinct presence of a coyote. It was so real, I was convinced that if I looked up I would see a real coyote standing in front of me, sniffing my hands. But instead, I stayed in child's pose, in deep meditation, and I let Coyote help me, let the totem spirit that embodies all coyotes everywhere, the intelligent spirit of the animal take my pain. In that moment, I was finally able to shift. To connect to your own guides is as simple as asking for help in meditation, and help will come.

Journeys and Dreams

Another way that our guides can help us is through guiding us when we begin to travel the shamanic worlds in trance journey. Subconsciously we long for the trance journey, to travel into the world of our own shadow. The trance journey is like a waking, lucid dream, a place we can travel to at will by shifting our consciousness to a non-ordinary state. Your guide can help to lead you in and out of this state. You learn to get to this state by first practicing meditation. Eventually, you learn that you can go so deeply into meditation that you are beyond moving, and your awareness shifts from a place of lightness and freedom and mental clarity to a place of traveling into your innermost depths, a place that shamanism often labels the Lower World. In the lower world you travel into subterranean landscapes of caves of stalactites, places where there are rooms filled with jewels and flickering lights, peopled with your guides, who want to help you to heal yourself. When I am stuck with a particularly difficult problem in my life that meditation is not helping to clarify, I go on a guided journey of my own making, a trance journey. I begin by putting on a tape of drumming music. I lie down on the floor and cover myself with a blanket for warmth. I relax totally into the moment. I go into a beautiful natural place in my mind, perhaps deep in a forest at the entrance to a cave. I call on my animal guide to take me where I need to go. I communicate with any beings my guide leads me to. Sometimes I fall asleep doing this exercise, particularly if I attempt it at night. But even when I think I am sleeping, there seems to be healing that comes from the journey. The healing is a very deep non-rational sort, because it really comes from a non-rational place in the mind, a place that speaks to us in symbols and syllogisms, a place that really has no proper language. It is the same place that we go to in our dreams.

Messages flow to us in dreams, messages from our subconscious and from the deepest part of ourselves. Dreams open us to those messages that we may not want to hear, and through them flow the deepest wisdom of our inner self. Recently when I was feeling unloved by a man in my life, I dreamed that I had a dating relationship with the president of the United States, and I knew that my subconscious was telling me that I was worthy of the highest quality of person on earth, because to my child's mind, the mind that speaks in dreams, the president is still a symbol for truth and beauty, qualities that I want in relationship. Dreams have always guided me strongly, telling me when it was time to quit that horrid job, or end that horrid relationship, and recently they have been telling me of the good things to come. These are the messages. Open yourself to the dream life by preparing at bedtime to record your dreams. Make sure you allow enough sleep time to get into the dream state; dreams will not usually come if you are short on sleep. Keep a notebook next to the bed and a small flashlight for writing when you wake in the middle of the night. Your dreams will become a friend to you as you pay attention to them, a beacon in your life. All the wisdom that you really need is inside you.

Practice 4: Trance Journey to Find Your Guide

Go to your meditation space and put on some music that will allow you to go into a deep meditative state. If you have a recording of shamanic drumming, that is ideal, but other very soothing and repetitive music works well too. (Trance journeys are especially nice to listen to. We invite you to go to www.yabyummy.com/store and download a live audio recording of this trance journey.) Now lie down on the floor and make yourself comfortable. Put a pillow under your head and knees, and a blanket over you to create a sense of warmth and safety. Begin by following your breath, and then let your roots grow down to the earth, and your branches to the sky, as in the Sacred Tree Meditation.

Once you are firmly anchored in your connection to Spirit, start to imagine that you are standing next to a small stream. On the other side of the stream is a wall of high rock cliffs. Next to you is a forest that seems to go on forever, and you hear the songs of birds and the cries of an eagle off in the distance. The forest is filled with pine and juniper trees, and you drink in the rich smell of the trees as you stand and wait. You feel a sense of expectancy and excitement — you are here to meet your animal guide for the first time. You see an animal moving toward you now, emerging from the edge of the forest. This is your animal guide for this journey.

Your guide comes to you and greets you, and tells you to follow as they lead you into the forest. You notice a small footpath as you follow them toward the trees, and you enter the forest, feeling its aliveness all around you. Following your guide, you come to a clearing, a circular place in the trees with a soft floor of pine needles. Your guide tells you to sit down, and they sit across from you. Your guide begins to tell you about themselves, about what they symbolize for you, and you listen to them share. Ask questions about anything that you don't understand, and listen carefully to their answers. When your guide is done sharing, they offer you a gift, a symbol of their meaning to you in the world. You take the gift and thank them, putting the gift in your pocket.

Now it is time to return to the ordinary world, and your guide stands and starts to lead you back along the trail that leads to the stream. You travel with them, noticing once again the look and smell of the trees around you, and the songs of the birds. When you reach the stream, you thank your guide, and they remind you that you can call on them anytime, whether you are journeying in the otherworld, or wrestling with a challenge in the ordinary world. Now you say goodbye to your guide, and they return to the forest for now.

Allow yourself to come back into your body, wiggling your fingers and toes and breathing deeply. Take your time coming out of this deep trance, and roll to your side when you are ready rather than sitting up straight. Once you have returned to ordinary consciousness, see if you can remember the gift your guide gave you, and write this down, as well as any other information from your journey that you wish to remember. You may wish to obtain an object like the one that was gifted to you in the journey as a reminder of your connection to your guide. Or you may wish to obtain a drawing or photo of the animal that is your guide to use as a focal point in connecting to your guide in future meditations.

Chanting and Power Songs

One way to express the wisdom within you is to sing the melody of your own unique power song. A melody or chant that you create yourself has unlimited power, including the power to lift you up in a moment of despair, to bring love and abundance, and to center you. I learned in my early spiritual training to create chants. I found that it became easier for me with practice, and especially if I entered a meditative state first and thought of it as writing whimsical poetry. A few years ago, my chanting turned to singing. It seemed to happen gradually. I started to have the experience of waking up with short, simple words with melodies in my head, and I would write them down. If you are not musically inclined, then stick with chanting, for it is just as powerful. Any chant or song that you repeat over and over becomes a thing of power to manifest what is in your best and highest good.

A chant for love that I have used with my students is "Om, Shrim, Klim." This chant seems to help us drop into a state of feeling the love that Spirit has for us. "Om" is the sound of manifestation, of calling to you the things that you want. "Shrim" invokes Lakshmi, the Hindu goddess of love, beauty, and wealth. "Klim" invokes the Krishna, Hindu god of love. You may simply chant these sounds, or you may sing them to any melody you wish. The power of the chant is in the energy you give to it.

A very good example of the power of song is a chant I created a few years ago, out in the desert. A very long power song came to me, with a verse about each part of my life that was out of balance. I sang that song within a sacred circle that I drew on the desert sand with a stick, and drew pictures of my song on an agave stalk I found. That staff has become a beacon for me, a guide, because that song has become my centering song. In it is my ideal relationship (which has manifested), my ideal home, my ideal work (which has also come to pass), and so on. I have sung the song since then with my son on Bell Rock in Sedona while hiking, and he loves to hear it because he hears the power in it and how it weaves around me when I sing. I sing the song whenever I want to remind myself where my power lies and what it is that I want to make manifest in my life.

As your connection to Spirit becomes stronger, all of life becomes your power song, and you shape your life in alignment with Spirit's will. Allowing yourself to be whole and complete — and from that place, to reach for joy — prepares you to come into connection. You become ready to intertwine your song with that of your beloved, in the practice of connecting to Spirit with another.

◆ Chapter 3 ◆

Connecting to Spirit Together

Opening your heart to a spiritual connection with your partner sounds wonderful in theory, but how do you practice that? Flowing into connection becomes more effortless with repetition. By creating time together, you open to ease in joining your hearts and sexuality together. Red tantra, the practice of spiritual/sexual union with a partner, is so much more than just sex. In red tantra, you apply the spiritual practices you have learned in your solo, white tantra practice to the art of making love. In this context, the solo spiritual practices become partnered experiences that are fuller and richer, mixed with sexual pleasure, ecstasy, and the deepest love your heart has ever known. Married twice in my life and divorced both times, I thought I had experienced all the good and bad that love and sex and connection had to offer me. Practicing red tantra has taught me that I have only scratched the surface of knowing the deep connectedness of transcendent love, or of feeling ecstasy flow through me that evokes my connection to the Goddess. How this is possible I am not sure, but I experience it several times a week as I practice with my tantric partner. My practice with him is deeper and fuller, and the heart connection more powerful, the sex more ecstatic, than anything I had ever imagined was possible. Each week we spend four hours or more connecting to sex and spirit together.

Creating a Practice Together

I realize that finding this amount of time to share each week is hard, and that setting common goals in relationship can be challenging. It has been such a struggle for me to learn how to move in harmony and create a purposeful relationship, dedicated to growth, partnership, and healing, not to mention the thing we all seem to long for, love. I seem to struggle at each step of the process of setting shared goals, and often get into a power struggle with my partners. I want to be right, and I want to be in charge in relationship because it is safer for me that way than allowing the truth of the relationship to gently and effortlessly rise to the surface. With practice I am learning to come gently into discussions about shared goals. I am also learning to renegotiate these goals when my needs change. With these changes, my heart has become passionately engaged in the practice that we are working together. In my former relationships I always came to partnered commitments with a sense of dread that my needs would not be met, or my expectations would be disappointed. In this new framework of calmly discussing not only what I want, but how I feel about it, I find that I am much more strongly committed to any agreements I make, which in itself strengthens our work together. Sit with your partner, breathe deeply, center into the moment, and let yourself come to the discussion of your individual needs from a place that is both spiritual and connected to your desires and feelings.

When finding time to practice with your partner, patience and joyous agreement are the first steps. Because you are two different people who have busy lives and schedules, you will often have to try again and again to create the time to practice together. The best time of day for one of you may not be the best time for the other. Try to schedule time on your calendars when you can both be awake and alert. This may mean that you can only practice on the weekends because you are both awake only at lunch time. Many couples struggle with the difficulty of one person being alert in the morning and the other being alert only in the evening, and have compromised in this way. Do what it takes to create the time to connect.

The other difficulty is that you must both be committed to the practice. If only one of you is really interested in sacred sexual practice, then it is really better to stick with solo practice, and to work your solo practice while you are making love. No amount of wishing, nagging, and threatening will shift your partner into a place of wanting to do this practice if that desire is not already within them. Once you are both committed, however, then the fun begins! There is an infinite variety of experiences that you can have in this practice together, and the practice will deepen and enhance your relationship.

Engaging your deep presence in the moment when connecting with your partner is key to tantric practice. Opening yourself to your partner at the heart if you are a man, and at the yoni (Sanskrit for "vagina") if you are a woman, you become connected at a very deep level. This soulful resonance supports a kind of psychic surgery that heals difficult wounds and old habits. Creating a conscious energetic connection between your energy body and your partner's is the place where you begin to learn how to be completely present with each other and totally aware of how your physical and energetic bodies are interacting. The practice of connecting your roots and branches to your partner's brings you into a symbolic and energetic connection. You must agree with your partner to stay in a place of clear communication about emotions and boundaries when you come into this connection. Safety is essential. Without safety there can be no connection because your fear will armor you against true opening.

Practice 1: Partnered Sacred Tree Meditation

Find a comfortable position facing your partner, leaving space between you and not touching, for now. You can sit cross-legged on the bed or on pillows on the floor, in chairs, or even lying side-by-side on the bed. Close your eyes, and take three deep breaths. Now continue to follow your breath, in through your nose, and out through your mouth, as you imagine growing roots into the Earth and branches into the Sky (as you did in the Solo Sacred Tree Meditation).

Once you feel connected to earth and sky, begin to imagine that your roots are intertwining with your partner's roots, slowly growing together and interconnecting. Feel them wrapping around each other and joining you together. Notice if you feel a pull to connect with your partner, and for now just sit in the feeling of that pull. Now move your awareness to the top of your head, and imagine that your branches begin to grow into each other and interweave, until it is hard to tell where your branches leave off and your partner's branches begin. Notice again if you feel a pull to connect.

Now allow yourself to follow the pull that you feel, and come into physical contact with your partner. You may open your eyes as you come into connection, keeping awareness of the roots and branches that are connecting you, and how that feels. You may choose to simply come into sitting together with knees touching, or perhaps the woman may come into sitting in the man's lap. As you come into connection be aware of the degree of physical closeness that feels right to you, and only come in that amount, honoring your feelings and needs.

Once you are in contact, breathe together and enjoy the feeling of connecting your roots at your root chakra and your branches at the crown chakra. Let the man lead the breath while the lady follows. Imagine that the two of you are breathing in the warmth of the sun into your hearts and both sending that love down through your bodies to the earth. When you are ready to end the connection, slowly move away physically first, then slowly imagine that you are drawing your roots and branches into you and reconnecting powerfully to the Earth and the Sky. Often the goddess needs more time to slowly disconnect than the man so letting her lead this can be very nurturing. Thank your partner by putting your hands in prayer position and giving them a slight bow of the head.

Practice 2: Reconnecting to Self

This practice is great to do whenever you feel powerfully connected to someone else and want or need to come back into yourself and your own center so that you can be whole and complete within yourself. It can be especially useful in a monogamous relationship when you need to part ways and go about the business of your day. For polyamorous relationships (see definitions), it is a fabulous practice to do whenever you are struggling with jealousy or feelings of abandonment and loneliness. Finally, I recommend to my students that they do this practice at the end of any partnered exercise.

To do this practice of unwinding from your partner, first tune into the image of your roots and branches being intertwined with each other. This is something that naturally happens in the course of spending time with a partner. Notice also if your chakras (see Chapter 11) seem to be connected by energetic cords. Now begin the process of disentangling these cords, roots, and branches. Begin by imagining or feeling that your branches are slowly unwinding from each other, and that instead of connecting with your partner, all of your branches are once again powerfully connected to the Sun or the Stars in the sky. Then do the same with your roots, unweaving them slowly, and feeling them instead grow down into the earth again.

Now turn your attention to the cords that you have with your partner. Check each chakra, and any place that you find a connection that feels to you like a cord, gently remove it. I like to kiss my partner's cords and send them back to him, then reel in my own cords back into my chakras, integrating the beautiful energy that we have created together. Now come into your own physical and spiritual space, and breathe in love from Earth and Sky at the same time. Breathe this love into your heart, and then breathe it out into your arms and hands. Now place your hands on your own heart and send this love to yourself. Stay like this until you feel joyfully full of the love that Spirit has for you.

Reconnection to Self

Part of the practice of tantra is learning to connect and detach consciously, and with love. One benefit of this practice is a greater sense of wholeness and peace within yourself. It also allows us to come to each partnering fresh, letting go of the past, and of all the things that can get in the way of our spiritual practice with another. And finally, the practice of consciously reconnecting to ourselves after being in partnership gives you a chance to know who you truly are within, without the influence of others in your life. This process of unfolding to ourselves is a kind of wisdom, but wisdom has never really been my goal. Since I was a little girl, all I wanted was to live a joyful life, and indeed that is what many people, fragmented and wounded, long for. Even those who are happy always have room for more joy. Joy is a frequent result when we fully embrace our freedom.

One way that I have journeyed to this state is through learning to detach and attach consciously as part of my spiritual practice. Most of us allow energetic cords to form that connect us to other beings and objects at the chakras. Indeed, learning to detach from other people's emotions, and to do so with love, is essential for me in staying centered. This practice is so simple, and yet so powerful. As I do it, I find my center. I find strength, and eventually there is a joy and lightness that comes because I am truly free. I am no longer choosing to be in relationship because I must, because someone needs me, or because I need them. Instead, I am choosing to be in relationship because it feels good. When I come into a connection consciously, by connecting my roots and branches to another, I come into a place with my partner where I am fully present to him. This presence is a gift that begins to heal all sorts of old relationship patterns that do not serve me, as is the presence that comes when I learn to consciously disconnect.

Holding Space

Learning to hold space for your partner to share their emotions is probably one of the most essential skills to intimacy. To be able to be fully present when your partner is sharing their thoughts and emotions is invaluable in building trust. Trust is essential in opening and to reaching tantric states of intense bliss. The thing that keeps us from everyday bliss is a contraction of the heart and spirit. As soon as we begin to trust and open our vulnerability, magickal energies begin to connect us to one another and to the world. Unfortunately, many of us aren't taught to hold space for emotions. We are taught instead to pretend that emotions do not exist. But nothing opens us to deep sexual connection like knowing that we can share our feelings without judgment and be heard, or better yet, to feel safe in plunging into our emotional depths during the act of love. In the deeper states of tantric connection, it is common for women to cycle through a range of emotions, beginning often with pleasure, then cycling into grief and tears, then back into joy. If a man cannot hold space for the release of this pain, the woman can never move through into the place of ecstatic joy that comes after it. If a woman cannot hold space for a man to be powerful, sexual, and open and receptive in his heart, he will never be able to fully relax into a state of opening where he trusts her implicitly and knows that he can plunge into her depths without being lost there. The depths of woman can be terrifying for a man. He often feels overwhelmed, like he is being swallowed whole. Only when there is trust and vulnerability can the connection truly be made, the circuit that opens the couple to bliss. Practice this skill with each other. Take courses in communication (see Bibliography and Resources). Practice breathing and letting your partner express their emotions while you simply sit and listen without speaking. Practice acceptance of your partner as they are. This is the greatest gift you can give.

As you begin to create a spiritual practice together, you are entering one of the highest forms of partnership. Sharing a path allows you to co-create something that you both share a commitment to and passion for. This journey is enlivening and exhilarating for me, and seems to feed into every area of my connection. Not all relationships are ready or willing to embrace this path. In many situations, it may be best for you to work a solo practice while occasionally drawing your partner in. But if both of you are committed to sharing the passion of the tantric path, accelerated growth occurs through your shared spiritual intention. My partner and I share a deep calling and dedication to spiritual sexuality. Through this we came into partnership with each other, and both of us have been amazed at how quickly we have been burning through old relationship patterns that we had been stuck in for years. Along with this, we have also progressed phenomenally quickly in our sexual/spiritual lives. Our connection to Spirit has grown so strong that we are able to sense into each other even when we are not physically together. My personal connection to Spirit has grown so ecstatic that every meditation has become a sexual experience. Even as I write this book and allow the divine to flow through me, I feel the flow of that essence as a vibrant sexual aliveness and arousal. My world has come alive in incredibly rich hues, and my sexuality fully integrated into my life.

Moving Together

One way that I express my sexuality is through movement. Flowing together in the dance, we move as one. My partner leads and I follow. I drop deeply into my feminine, as he comes more and more strongly into his masculine, guiding me, moving me, showing me with his body what comes next, providing a frame within which my dance flows and creates and connects to him. Connecting, I become as open as the sky. The more we flow together, the more I trust. The more I feel my body, the more I harmonize in motion, the more I feel my spiritual and sexual energies move through me. Movement is a phenomenal practice for opening your body to sensuality and for learning to feel sexual ecstatic energy flow through you. This practice of totally present movement, where you are breathing together and deeply aware of each moment, each movement, each breath, brings you into a place where you begin to understand the goal of tantric lovemaking. Like partnered dance, sacred lovemaking is a practice of staying totally present and aware of your body and your partner's body while you move and breathe together. Movement offers us a way to experience this feeling of joined presence without the distraction of the lovemaking.

Perhaps dancing together does arouse us, but since we are not involved in any goal of making love or having an orgasm, we can allow ourselves to flow into the dance and into the moment. Women can learn to follow and flow, even if their partner is not moving the way they would like or want him to move. They can do the deep practice of acceptance and flow, just accepting how their partner is moving and moving with him, whether he is on or off the beat, whether he is flowing effortlessly or struggling. Men can learn to lead whether they are feeling confident or not, knowing that the woman is following and flowing without judgment or criticism. The man's practice is to learn to step up and take the lead, and to lead from a place of listening to the still quiet voice of Spirit, instead of the analytical and critical voice of the ego. His reward is knowing that whatever he does, it is perfectly right for this moment right here, right now.

Another movement practice is to learn to squeeze the PC muscle, the one you use to stop and start urination. When men squeeze these muscles it makes the penis rise and fall, like push-ups for the penis. When women squeeze these muscles, it squeezes the yoni, which feels wonderful to the lingam. Squeezing these muscles is wonderful for each of you when done solo, because it increases the flow of blood and sexual energy to the genitals. It also helps to increase awareness of this part of your body. When you learn to squeeze and release these muscles together, it creates a wonderful deep internal sensation of arousal without much movement or effort at all. You can also learn to use these muscles to help pull sexual energy into your body with your inhaled breath when you are in the sacred tree meditation.

Women can also learn to cultivate a pushing motion, one like that of pushing a baby out of the birth canal, but not with quite so much force. This pushing motion often leads to female ejaculation, a wonderful ecstatic side effect of learning yoni control. I urge both men and women to practice using their PC muscles every day to cultivate the movement of their sexual energy through the body. You can exercise these muscles anywhere, anytime, but it is often more pleasurable to work them with the breath, breathing in as you squeeze, and breathing out as you release the muscles (or push out with the yoni).

Stillness

Beyond movement in lovemaking, we come to a sweet ecstasy through the practice of making love in stillness. Learning to make love without thrusting and without much movement is a high art in sacred sex that allows you to focus on being present with each other, being present to the energies flowing through and between you, and being present to the sensuality of your bodies. When you are still with each other you are able to come fully present to the sensations you are feeling in the yoni and lingam, and in all of your body. The sensations that you feel when you are only breathing and pulsing your PC muscles are purely a result of the sexual energy moving through your body.

Tighter hold on the lingam results from working the PC muscles in the yoni. After a while of making love with a partner in this tantric way of stillness and squeezing the yoni muscles, my yoni begins to mold itself to the penis, fitting it like a glove, and the lingam begins to feel so soft on its surface that it is like velvet. This softness is sweet for the woman, and each pulse of the yoni or each slow stroke of the lingam becomes an exquisite pleasure, like a mini-orgasm in each stroke. You can practice also separating out the different muscles in the yoni as it holds the lingam in this exquisite embrace, experimenting with squeezing the low, middle, and high yoni. If you want to practice this on your own, use your finger in your yoni to sense into the movements that are actually happening. Then, when you are ready, try this delightful practice with your partner and have him see if he can tell which part of your yoni you are squeezing. Go on a journey of discovery with each other, learning the newness of this exquisite practice. Allow yourself to sink into bliss.

Through these practices of stillness and squeezing the PC muscles, you can slow down your lovemaking. Through this slowing down, you can learn to delay ejaculation and to make love whether the penis is soft or hard. Delaying ejaculation and choosing when to ejaculate are goals that many men have when they come to sacred sexual practice. To be in choice, a man must learn to breathe, to relax, and to work the PC muscle. Breathing moves the sexual energy through the entire body so that it does not accumulate in the penis, leading to ejaculation. Men can choose to orgasm without an ejaculation, allowing them to have multiple orgasms, and to continue making love for an extended time. In this practice, eventually the entire lovemaking begins to feel like one giant orgasm without beginning or end. Staying present and staying in the breath are important to continue to retain the semen in a highly aroused state. Retaining the semen also retains the man's chi, or life force, allowing him to feel more vital, virile, and strong. The more a man retains his semen, the more sexually charged he becomes, and because sexuality and spirituality are the same, he becomes spiritually charged as well from this practice, not to mention the increased energy he will experience in his daily life and his work. This is not to say that a man should always refrain from ejaculating, but that it can be a conscious choice whether or not to do so. Bringing the sacred tree meditation and the relaxed state that it creates into lovemaking allows a man to delay ejaculation by holding his sexual energy in a new way, by moving it throughout his body. In this meditative state you no longer have to divert your mind or pull back your sexual energy from the connection with your partner to delay. Instead, you come to a place where the desire to ejaculate is no longer overpowering, and you can flow into making love into whatever way Spirit leads you to.

Practice 3: Stillness

Come into energetic connection with your partner using the Partnered Sacred Tree Meditation. Now come into physical connection, and when you are ready, gently penetrate the yoni with the lingam. Be still with each other, and breathe together. If the lingam is not yet erect, as it often will not be in this practice, you can gently feed it into the yoni using the first two fingers of one hand (and a generous quantity of lubricant). Inserting a soft lingam into a yoni takes practice, so be gentle and patient while you are learning. Once you are connected and settled, breathe together without any thrusting between the lingam and yoni and simply feel the connection. You can add a slow rocking of the pelvis to the rhythm of your breath to help move the energy. Next add a squeezing of the PC muscles. The woman can try squeezing with her inhale and imagining that she is drawing the energy of the lingam into her yoni. The man can squeeze on his exhale, imagining that he is sending the energy of his lingam out into her yoni. Let the energy of this connection flow through your whole body. Feeling it as much in your head, hands, and heart as you do in your genitals. Stay with this practice for a while, and then flow into lovemaking if you like, taking breaks in making love to stop and be in this stillness several times. Notice as you get more aroused that it can feel really good to stop and breathe and feel the energies that the two of you are exchanging. Continue with the practice until you feel ready to end, trying to spend at least an hour making love and flowing in and out of this practice.

Practice 4: Ejaculation Mastery

Learning mastery of your ejaculation comes through two primary teachings: learning to relax as you become sexually aroused, and learning to move excess sexual energy from the lingam into your whole body and out to Spirit.

Begin your lovemaking with the Partnered Sacred Tree Meditation to get you really present in the moment and connected to your partner. Tell yourself that just for now, you will let go of any goals to climax or not climax during your lovemaking. Set your intention to stay fully present in the moment, and to let go of any worries about climaxing too soon. Now ask your partner to breathe with you, and to do a bit of massage on your body to help you relax. Breathe in the touch of your partner's hands and really allow yourself to breathe in the touch with each inhale, and to relax with each exhale. Once you are feeling more relaxed, ask your partner to use oil to gently massage your lingam. Your job is only to lie back, receive the touch, and keep breathing deeply. Pick some key words to let your partner know how close to ejaculation you are. Red for one more stroke and I will be past the point of no return and Yellow for getting pretty warm works well. As you get close to Yellow, imagine that with each inhale the sexual charge is flowing from your lingam into your whole body, your chest, your head, your arms and your legs. With each exhale really let go of any muscle tension you might be holding and imagine that the sexual energy is flowing out your body and back to Spirit through your roots and branches. Say Yellow if the charge still increases. When you say "Yellow," your partner's job is to hold their hands still on your lingam with a solid touch, while reminding you to breathe sexual energy up on the inhale and out on the exhale. If you get to Red then have your partner remove their hands from your lingam and hold your feet with their hands to help you release excess sexual energy and remind you to relax and breathe. Really push the energy through your body with your breath and with sound, letting yourself make any noise that wants to come out of your throat. This breathing the energy through your whole body gives you a larger container for your sexual energy. Notice if you can feel a tingling or warmth moving through your body as you breathe.

Continue breathing and staying present until your arousal level has dropped enough to start massaging the lingam again. If you are easily aroused, then let the sexual energy drop all the way to ground before starting again. Continue this practice through several cycles of arousal and getting close to ejaculation. If stimulation with your partner's hands does not get you close to an ejaculation, then move to stimulation with the mouth on the lingam and see if that brings you close to the edge. If this is still not pushing your edge, then move to intercourse, but stay in the Stillness Together practice as much as possible, using it every time you say "Yellow." Remember to keep breathing deeply and imagining that you are moving energy up to your belly, heart, and head with your inhale and out through your legs and feet as you exhale. If in the practice you move to an ejaculatory orgasm, try not to go into old habits. Stay fully present through the experience, moving the energy through your body right up to ejaculation, and notice if there is a difference from your normal experience of climax.

In addition to the sexual reasons you may have for learning tantra, it is helpful to have spiritual goals. Many men and women I work with have the goal of empowerment. They want to feel competent and radiantly alive as they walk through the world. My personal path to empowerment has come through first learning that everything I need lives within me. Independence and freedom are my touchstones, the foundation of my shamanic tantra practice, supporting my power as an individual. The more empowered I am as a person, the more I have to bring to a partnership, and the more energy there is to float into new and incredible places of connection with each of my lovers and friends. Freedom in partnership takes a strong commitment to owning my own emotional baggage, and a strong commitment to getting rid of it. We cling to people and to possessions in our culture to feel safe, but this clinging does nothing to support our spiritual growth, and in fact it impedes it. Almost always, the state of enlightenment is described as a sort of freedom, and this freedom does not come from a grabbing on to someone and insisting that everything must be done in sharing mode. No, freedom comes from letting go, from opening. Just as we must open to deep connection and intimacy, so we must also open to trusting enough to let go. We must trust that Spirit supports us, loves us, and wants us to be happy in our relationships. If we have this trust, there is no need for us to cling, to fear abandonment. And how much stronger we become when we feel confident enough to share our partner with the friends and family in our lives, to let go of jealousy about the time and attachments they give to others. Letting go of the fear of being replaced by another, knowing that this will only occur if it is the will of Spirit for us, and trusting Spirit deeply, allows us to find peace in freedom.

If we are truly free, then we are no longer attached to what other people do. Addiction to over-involvement in other people's lives is rampant in our society. We have this idea that it is our right to know every last detail of our partner's life, and to give our feedback about their every action. How freeing it is to realize that this level of interference with the life of another is not necessary or healthy. Healing codependency is essential to advancement on the tantric path, because it allows us to truly focus on our own spiritual energy development. When we are wound up in our needs from others and their demands on us, it is impossible to see clearly what is best for us. Addiction to people is more crippling and more baffling than addiction to alcohol or drugs. It is a habit for many, to spend much of their time in worry about other people, and this depletes our energy and is not healthy for us. Dropping into deep meditation each day helps, dropping in and asking for clarity about our habits of neediness and clinging and interfering. Listening closely to Spirit, we learn when it is appropriate for us to step in and help, and when it is to our detriment. Letting go of all this, we are able to at last unfold, as our own sensuality and openness increase, as we begin to run like the wind when we want, float like a cloud, flow like the ocean. As we learn to be one with nature, we see that nowhere is there a metaphor for neediness in the natural world. The creatures of nature are independent and self-supporting, although they may at times rely on one another for breeding and protection from predators. Humans are creatures of nature as well, and it is high time we allow ourselves to return to our natural state of letting our brothers and sisters make their own mistakes, and to only help when we are asked.

If we are truly free and independent, we learn that needs cannot always be met by our partner. Learning to seek support elsewhere is pivotal to your emotional health. Once you learn that you can create outstanding emotional support in other relationships, you are able to ease the pressure on your partner to carry your emotional burdens. Reaching out and putting yourself in the debt of your friends and, if you have them, other intimate partners, is a wonderful way to drop into trusting Spirit to support you. Knowing that Spirit will bring whatever support you need, whenever you need it, teaches that you need not depend on only one person for everything. In fact, I propose that the first place to go for support is to yourself. You can speak to your own inner child when you are upset, and provide the support you may not have received as a child. You can promise your inner child that you will take care of her. This can go a long way toward giving you the support that you need. The second place I urge you to go for support is to Spirit, to Mother Earth, and Father Sky. In this practice, I simply hook into my connection with them, and allow them to fill me with the support that I need. Even as I am writing this book, I continually ask them for support and for guidance. Once I have gone to myself and to spirit for my needs, then I begin to reach out for support to my partner, my women friends, my male friends, my other lovers, my spiritual teachers, and my spiritual family. Having a network of support has helped me to be happier and stronger in my daily life, to be able to let go more of things that are just not that important. And I can truly say that I feel much less needy than I was in the past, much more content in my own company.

All the practices I have given you in this chapter are only useful if you do them regularly and often. Just as I have learned that I must recommit to my spiritual practice on a weekly or sometimes even daily basis, I have also learned that I must recommit to my intimacy practice. This one is harder for me. I am the kind of person who is a little bit introverted, and would be very happy sitting alone on a mountaintop in meditation for a long time. But the truth is that I am not challenged enough by that path to grow from it. I am on the path of relationship and of right relationship to intimacy. This practice is not so much about a particular partner as it is about my way of relating, and getting clear about the obstacles I create to truly opening to others. For me there is heart armor laid down throughout my childhood and adult life, created by my fear reactions to abandonment and emotional abuse and limitation. I learned to protect myself in the only way I knew how at the time, but as an adult, this protection no longer serves me, and it gets in the way of the level of openness I want in a relationship. Recently I realized that one of my protections is to fail to remember difficult emotional conversations. When I finally reached a place of readiness to change this habit, I recommitted to being better at remembering, and started using the tool of typing these conversations into my computer as they took place. This may seem absurd, but it has changed completely the dynamic of my tantric partnership, my business partnership, and my parenting partnership. In business, it has allowed me to say exactly what I want, and then to fully hear what my partner wants, and from there to dialog about a solution. In my parenting partnership, it recently allowed me to negotiate a child support agreement without getting the lawyers involved, and I feel pleased with the final agreement. Intimacy is not forever unless we continually recommit to its practice. Intimacy is a state that is created by us when we allow ourselves to move through the hard places in ourselves, to be willing to have total awareness of our unhealthy behaviors, and to be ready to embrace positive changes. Once we get to this place, we become open to the possibility of a connection that gets better and deeper with time.

Using the practices in this chapter, you will learn to go deeper into connection with your partner, and begin your journey of finding the places within yourself that need healing. This leads to the next gateway of breathing love, a practice that embraces both the healing of heart wounds and a learning to truly experience bliss.

✦ The Second Gateway ✦

Breathing Love

• Chapter 4 •

Healing the Heart

Richness enfolds our emotional life when we open our hearts. The open heart is a metaphor for a feeling of love that we experience in our physical body. For me the open heart feels like a physical sensation of tingling in my chest and breasts. And sometimes an open heart can feel like horrible wrenching grief and sadness in my chest. The open heart is not always about joy, but it is always about authenticity, about a better way to be in the world, a way that cultivates peace, love, and flexibility. Why flexibility? What does that have to do with love? Well, if you think about it, there is an association of softness that comes with the open heart, and this softness, this pliability of the heart, is what allows love to flow between two people. We have talked about the spiritual connection that is the beginning of the tantric connection. In shamanic tantra, the spiritual connection flows primarily between the hearts and genitals of the lovers. When you create a circuit that connects the genitals to the heart, you create an opulent and sensual connection unlike anything you may have experienced before. The power of the heart connection is that you can create it intentionally. Osho, a great practitioner of tantra from India, said that the ultimate tantric should be able to make love to anyone. I feel the truth of this in my body when my heart opens wide. With my heart soft and able to receive another into my soul, I drop into a state of loving ecstasy where a sexual spiritual connection to anyone is possible. It is a state of love that no longer allows me to focus on the separation, the differences, between myself and another human being. It is a state of love that I hope to live in at all times someday. It is a state of love that allows me to be peaceful and joyous and accepting of others exactly as they are.

Surrendering to this love, and to the journey that begins when we decide to focus on love and sexuality in our lives, is the beginning of healing the heart. Without surrender, nothing is possible, because we continue to cling to our protections and our need for safety. Some of us even pad our bodies with extra pounds for protection, not wanting to be vulnerable to contact with others. Yet when we peel away the layers of body armor that we have laid down over our hearts, our genitals, and our bellies, we begin to discover a new sensitivity in ourselves. Not just an emotional sensitivity, but a new sensitivity of the body, a new aliveness. A feeling comes into us when we are touched, a new feeling, and every touch now becomes fresh and alive. The more we heal the body, the more we shift, until every touch can be an exquisite ecstasy, no matter who delivers it, where we experience it, or how it is intended. Shifting into the place of ecstatic bliss in our bodies is also a surrender, mostly to the idea that this level of pleasure is possible and desirable for us to have. Often, so much guilt and shame is a part of the armor that we must allow ourselves to be okay with the thought of pleasure stalking us. I used to wonder what this pleasure would be like, and when I dropped into it for the first time, I contracted in fear, and the bliss vanished. The second time I was less afraid, and ecstasy lived in me a while longer. Fear is always a contraction, an armoring against bliss. Tension in the muscles, fear in the mind, anger and bitterness in the heart, guilt and shame in the genitals, all of these must be released to embrace the way of the open heart and to shift our way of relating to a new level. All of these must be released to fully experience joy, freedom, and pleasure.

Releasing Fear

Fear is often caused by wounds from past relationships. Feeling anxiety, the manifestation of fear, is devastating to our present and future relationships. Sometimes for me, my anxiety is like watching a train wreck and being powerless to stop it. Sometimes I watch myself acting in ways that show my fear, and I watch the people in my life react to that, and I feel sad that this fear is still alive in me. Other times I find myself in a situation that used to provoke terror in me and I notice that the fear is gone. The healing of tantra is like that. Subtle, gentle, powerful, and sometimes sudden. It is so freeing to see long-standing habits fading away to yield to new ways of connecting that are based on love. One day recently I found myself stuck in sarcasm with one of my lovers, making hurtful remarks disguised as humor. I found that he was hurt by my words, and still I couldn't stop. Finally I took some time to sit in meditation and breathe into my heart to see why I was behaving in this way, and I realized that my cutting words were coming from fear, and not even from a fear related to anything in particular. With this awareness

I was able at least to intervene between thinking something cutting and saying it. I have been lucky to move through an awareness and healing of my fear, and it has taken me many years to do it. Your journey may differ, but the key to the healing is often some pivotal awareness or experience that comes to you. In this "Aha" moment you are ready for healing, and ready to embrace it fully. This regeneration changes your life, your relationships, your entire world, because without the old habits, you see everything through new eyes. To find your way to this shift, you must first raise your awareness of your present relationships and seek out patterns that remind you of past relationships. When you find yourself in a pattern you recognize, it is time to accept that you are acting from habit, and to let yourself feel the desire for change until that desire becomes overwhelming. Once that longing is anchored, then you are ready, because the passion for healing dominates your world. Allow Spirit to move through you, to have its way with your heart, and love you into an absence of fear.

As I have struggled to love and to let go of my fear, I have found that healthy sexuality is one of the best cures for depression, anxiety, and any stress-related ailment. Repressing or ignoring my sexuality and holding guilt and shame in my body had led me over the years to numbness, blocks in my energy flow, and sometimes eventually to illness. The guilt and shame I carried came partly from being told that I wasn't perfect enough, or pretty enough, or that I was too sexual. To avoid dealing with the unpleasant feelings I had about these things, I tried to segregate myself into little pieces, to not feel the feelings of hurt and loss of trust. I tried to check out from the world by throwing myself into reading novels, and into a life of enmeshment with a partner. I took my emotions and put them in a little box, labeled "Do Not Open!" but eventually the box was full and began to overflow. I reached a point where I could no longer be ashamed of myself as a sexual being, and where I was ready to release the guilt and shame I had carried for so long about who I was. To heal, I first had to empty the box, and put the pieces of my fragmented self back together so that I became a whole and integrated being once again. More than anything, the practice of shamanic tantra is about creating and maintaining that wholeness within myself, so that I can then bring that to relationship. I also learned to create safety for myself, so that I was able to stay present, and not hide from life by numbing myself to my feelings. This safety comes from the first gateway of Connecting to Spirit, knowing that I am always held by Spirit, that no harm can come to me when my roots are deeply in the Earth, my branches are in the sky, and I am listening to Spirit with my heart.

Wounds of the Heart

When we move into heart healing, we find that there are many wounds that show up in our lives as undesirable behaviors that keep us from connecting to ourselves and to others. Often the pain that we carry is so great that we cannot bear to be fully present in our daily lives and we find ways to numb ourselves. One way many of us choose to avoid feeling pain is through addiction. The addiction becomes a coping mechanism, something we cannot do without, something that seems to soothe us. But in truth we are slowly killing ourselves and denying ourselves the life of joy we are entitled to when we are trapped in addictive patterns. It is addiction whenever you indulge obsessively in anything to soothe yourself and avoid dealing with life. It's confusing, because a workaholic can work the same amount of hours as someone who is just really passionate about their work. An alcoholic can drink the same amount as someone who just enjoys the taste of fine wine. The difference is that the workaholic or the alcoholic will work or drink to avoid being present to life, whereas the hard worker or the vinophile are working or drinking because they love their work, their wine, and their life. They will still engage life fully and be available for emotional connection. There is a constellation of addictions, including addiction to work, food, love, sex, religion, drugs, and alcohol. This constellation of addiction gives us an idea of the difficulties we and our loved ones may face in our healing, and there are many very good recovery programs out there that can be of tremendous support together with the tantric healing path (see Bibliography and Resources).

Negativity, resentment, and anger are the worst killers of the tantric life. These wounds of the heart take us out of the present and into a world where we nurse our wounds from the past and imagine wounds in the future. This bitterness seeps in and poisons us, our relationships, and our ability to live full and joyful lives. Too often I have seen sex used as an antidote to bitterness, as a kind of addiction, and this way leads only to more hurt and frustration as the poison of anger drives away people from being in relationship. Look honestly at yourself and at your heart and ask if you are carrying resentment and anger in you. You must release these bitter seeds from your heart before you can fully connect to others or advance on the path of love. Bitterness is love's opposite. Anger is the enemy of the open heart. While anger is passionate, and releasing rage can be an important part of the path, it is critical to do so with full consciousness. When anger is unconscious, we take it out on our partners, who often stand in bewilderment at being blindsided with our sarcasm, criticism, and martyred attitudes. Breathing love is the spiritual antidote to anger, a companion to the tools of self-examination and awareness. Together, the spiritual and psychological practices of learning to love ourselves bring soothing and healing to our anger.

Another emotional wound of the heart that often needs healing is the wound of loss. So many of us carry the grief of loss from our childhood and our early adult lives and we do not know how to release it. I struggled long and hard with sadness until I began to realize that I had an addiction to it, that I was holding on to my grief because at some level I was feeding on it. I was creating passion for myself in my life by taking out my grief and sinking into it, adding a good dose of self pity for the heck of it. But pity and sadness do not lead us on the path to the joyful life, nor are they pleasant for those around us. There is a sort of perverse ecstasy in profound grief that takes hold of me on a very visceral and physical level. But habitual sadness leaves no room for authentic ecstasy that comes from within us. Gratitude has been my pathway out from this grief, to look at the good that came from the thing I am grieving for, and to see how I need not always sink into the pit of despair. Sometimes I can skim lightly through a loss, grieve it and move forward effortlessly. Sometimes I can remind myself that joy lives deep within me too. And lately I have had the most perverse and profound experiences of releasing grief only to find intense joy living behind my eyes. I have literally cried for hours only to drop into laughter and a deep peace and serenity. Like healing anger, healing grief requires both an inner awareness and resolve to let go, as well as a willingness to let Spirit take the grief for us. In the end we are powerless to heal it. But our guides and teachers know the perfect remedies, and we can learn to rely on them.

Wounds of the heart cannot be filled or fixed by another, and yet so many of us struggle with hoping that someone will save us, and drop into sadness when we feel alone and unloved. Despair is the hallmark of loneliness. We sit alone in our room, longing for someone, anyone, to fill the hole inside of us that aches for connection. We risk rejection over and over, we endure heartbreak, always searching for another to complete us. This search, this ache, has been idealized as romanticism. But the loneliness is really a state of mind. The longing for a partner will not lead to finding that perfect someone. Over and over I have seen that the perfect partner manifests when we feel whole and complete within ourselves. When I come to my womanly center, and see myself as perfect and beautiful, I no longer feel such a craving to be embraced by another. Ironically, this is when opportunities to connect and receive the masculine into my heart expand. Similarly for men, the more they seek a partner, the more desperate they become to connect, the less attractive they are to a woman. It is only when a man becomes fully committed to his purpose, path, and fire in life that he can easily connect with women he happens to find as he travels this path. These are the connections that will bring him a fullness and spiritual connection to his life. These connections are important, because loneliness is life-threatening, resulting in heart attacks, suicide, and any number of other dramatically unpleasant ends to this physical life. We humans are social creatures, and the heart, throbbing with the ache of loneliness, begins to affect the body. It is important for us to reach out and connect.

Abandonment in our early history makes it extremely difficult to connect, and exacerbates the ordinary human feeling of loneliness. Many of us with wounded hearts do not realize that this fear is driving us. When we are afraid of abandonment, almost anything can trigger an overreaction in our relationships, a cascade of emotion leading to hurt, anger, fear, and a desire to "counter-abandon" our partner, a kind of preemptive strike designed both to protect ourselves and to get even. It is important to heal our wounds of abandonment if we are to find freedom and peace in our relationships. If we have a hair-trigger, almost anything can be interpreted as abandonment. Going to the grocery store without saying goodbye, spending too much time on the computer, making love without looking into our eyes. Emotional abandonment does happen in relationship, but often we react to little things as though they were the original abandonment happening all over again. When this is the case, healing the core of the emotional body is called for, and this usually requires the help of a professional therapist or other healing support. Abandonment is a deep wound that does not heal easily. It is often at the core of codependency and addiction issues, and once healed, gives a new perspective on life. For me, there is a lightness, a trust that Spirit will never abandon me, and that if I trust where it leads me, I will no longer put myself in situations where I will feel abandoned. I will no longer be lonely, or angry, or frightened, because I always have my connection to Spirit and my love of myself to fall back on. This is a deeply centered place from which I can make much more healthy decisions about my life and allow much greater openness of heart.

Moving to Healing

Nurturing yourself is a key to the practice of breathing love, accepting who you are, honoring the divine spark that lives in you. We are each divine, we are each loving, caring, honoring human beings, and the more we learn to give ourselves what we need, the more whole and complete we begin to feel. When I care for myself with a hot bath every night, I feel decadent, and my body knows that it is loved. What nurturing can you do for yourself that feels loving and caring? Can you feed yourself a nutritious meal, or schedule some time to walk in nature? Or can you adorn and groom the body until it sparkles? Nurturing is all about focusing on the physical you, a thing that we often neglect. It is a fine art, this nurturing, and can include dressing to express the God/dess within you, or allowing yourself extra sleep so that your face will look more relaxed and lovely, and your body can feel more juicy and alive. Do the exercise of writing down the ways that you nurture yourself, and then feel into your body and see if it feels like you are doing enough. The body knows when it is cared for, and rewards us with increased sensitivity to touch and aliveness. This aliveness often takes the form of better health, less illness, and more physical stamina.

Once you have attended to your body, turn to the many healing modes that are available to you as you move through the journey of healing the heart. Counseling is often a first step, sitting with someone every week or two, working toward gaining awareness about your emotional patterns and learning to accept who you are and where you are on your journey. Once you have reached a place of awareness and acceptance, you can decide how to move forward with the business of healing your emotions. One option is shamanic healing, which is done by a shamanic practitioner and uses intuition and connection with spirit guides to determine what is needed. Another option is Reiki healing, energy healing that works on the chakras, with the precept that healing the energy centers of the body and opening the flow of energy will lead to healing of the emotional and physical bodies. And of course, shamanic tantra is a path of healing that specifically addresses the opening of the heart and its healing through connection to others. There are many other options out there, including homeopathy, acupuncture, and expressive arts therapy. I encourage you to explore and find what works for you, because no two healing journeys are the same, and what works for one person will not necessarily work for another. You must choose a combination of healing modes that you feel benefit you greatly, one where you see results, otherwise there is no use in wasting your time, money, and commitment. Once you find a healer you believe in, commit yourself wholeheartedly to the process, trust in Spirit, and let go. This is when miracles happen.

If you choose to walk the tantric path, healing of anger, fear, loneliness, and abandonment is one of the great gifts you can gain. Embraced in the safe and nurturing environment of the tantric healing sanctuary, you can let go completely of the wounds that need attention, trusting completely in the healer, and assisting the healer merely with your willingness to let Spirit move through you. When Spirit moves and you surrender, miracles happen. Aliveness never before experienced comes in and taps you on the shoulder. You open to a level of experience you did not even know existed, and the desire to let that ecstasy return begins to motivate your healing. Nothing motivates humans like pleasure, and this is the strength of the tantric path, that it lures us seductively through its sensuality, juiciness, and richness. Knowing what is possible, we want to drop in over and over again, and sometimes we may even be somewhat addictive in our pursuit of this drug of bliss. And yet the more bliss we experience, the safer and more healed we begin to feel. A practice that heals and enriches our lives is really not an addiction at all, but a spiritual devotion that we become passionate about. This devotion is a practice to which we wholly give ourselves over because we have embraced the safety it creates for us.

Tantric practice also provides social support, which is so important to us as humans. Support groups can be pivotal in our healing, because they bring us into an experience of each other, and begin to teach us the skills of communication, connection, and healthy boundary setting. The wisdom of Spirit speaks and moves through the mouths and bodies of the people we connect with in groups, and when we listen, we leave the group transformed. All human beings have needs for emotional and intellectual connection, and for support. Being a part of a group gives us more than one person to ask to get our needs met, making it more likely that it will happen. Groups in general show us that we can be lovable and that there are people out there willing to support us. There are many ways to find a group to connect with in your area, and I encourage you to make use of this aid in your healing and growth (see Bibliography and Resources).

Traveling toward a healed and healthy heart has brought so much bliss to my life. Soaring into a vast reservoir of energy I didn't know existed has become routine since I learned to let go of my tremendous neediness in relationships. Not that I am perfect, not that I don't slip into feeling needy now and then, but overall I have discovered a new freedom from worry about getting my needs met, and this has given me so much more time and attention to spend on the things in my life that matter to me. Now my relationships are no longer about me trying to extract my needs from my partner. Instead, connections with others have become explorations in the now. When I do slip and lose that flow, I re-center by focusing on myself, not on the relationship and how pissed off I am that it's not there for me at that precise moment. I find this new relationship model exhilarating and freeing, and I have discovered new levels of love within my heart that were previously untapped. In the past, I always confused love with pity and concern about another person, for me it was always about wanting to take care of someone or wanting someone to take care of me. Now love is a whole new experience, one of sharing common goals, sexual passion, and a spiritual practice. Love now means truly wanting what is best for the other person, and knowing that all I have to do is be their cheerleader. It's not my job to make their dreams come true, only to support their dreams with my whole heart. It also means asking for what I want, and not expecting my partner to meet all of my needs or to be perfect. Slowly I have learned to savor the joy of a partnership that is continually growing, loving, and authentic.

• Chapter 5 •

Breathing Love Solo

Cradling me in times of despair and in times of joy, Mother Earth supports me so deeply that no other support is really necessary. She imbues in my soul a safety that feeds me. Sobbing out my grief, I ask her to take my pain and give me love. She does. Venting and screaming my anger and rage, I ask her to take it. She does. Reveling in joy, I ask her to share in it. She does. Mother Earth is an incredible force for love and healing. When we connect to Her with our deep imaginary tree roots, we can breathe Her love in, grounding ourselves in the core of the planet, centering us in our bodies and our hearts. The love that flows from Mama Earth is unconditional. She doesn't care if you're sad because you made a mistake and loved the wrong person. She doesn't care if you were careless with your life and let a golden opportunity pass you by. She is the ultimate caring mother who holds you and rocks you and tells you everything will be okay. She loves you no matter what state you are in, or what you have done. When you learn to breathe her love into your heart, you receive a much more centered life, where the things that used to upset you no longer bother you quite as much, and eventually, not at all. You also learn to breathe in from Her deep reservoir of sexual energy, to increase your arousal when you want to, or to discharge excess sexual tension when you can't hold it. She is an infinite container of love and passion.

Containing me when I need to feel safe, Father Sky holds me in his arms tightly, so tight that I know everything will be okay and that nothing can harm me. I let go and trust him, feeling his power and strength flow into me. He comes to me when I am lonely, needing that male polarity for balance and passion. My connection to him frees my heart, opening me to greater passion and excitement about life. Breathing him in opens my fiery nature, and clears my mind so that I feel excitement each morning when I wake up, and joy as I move through my day. My connection to him, my breathing him in, has been the key to unlocking my heart.

Breathing the energies of Earth and Sky into your body is the basic practice of breathing love. Juiciness flows through you as you connect to the Earth and move Her liquid love up to the sky through imaginary branches that grow from the crown of your head. Breathing upward, you are like a tree reaching up to the sun, longing for warmth. Pulling the Earth energy through your entire body in this way awakens the divine feminine sexual force in your whole body, your shakti. As you draw the earth energy up into you and send it out to Father Sky, He receives it with warmth and joy. This breath from Earth to Sky lightens you, and brings the beauty of the kundalini into your face. It really is the world's best beauty drug, second only to sleep. Breathing this energy into your eyes and face awakens that sparkle that shows you are alive, awake, sexual, and receptive. Love moves through your whole body with this breath, magnetizing you so that you can pull anything to you, anything at all.

Strength comes into the body when you breathe from Sky to Earth. Breathing in through the branches in the crown of your head, you bring Father Sky into your body and send His radiance down into the arms of the grateful Earth through your roots. This brings men strongly into embodying their masculine, sharpening and electrifying their energy. In women, this breath awakens our luscious polarity with the masculine energy. Breathing the Sky Father like a lover through the body, women become again deeply part of their feminine power, and in some ways, this breath completes them spiritually. Men come into their strongest masculine essence with this breath, a place from which they can be strong in partnership, holding emotional space for a woman, and fully expressing their sexual power.

Loving Yourself

Embrace yourself, right now. Put your arms around yourself and give yourself a big hug. Feel that you deserve this love. You must focus on yourself if you want to cultivate a loving heart. Self-love is essential to loving from a place of emotional fullness. I have learned to cultivate this abundance of love through the practice of breathing love into my heart. When I do the practice of feeling love flow into me with every breath, I feel safe, held, and nurtured. I like feeling good, and this motivates me to keep doing the practice, to let love flow into me with each inhale, and fear flow out with each exhale. I also practice caring more deeply for myself, treating myself as I would a cherished lover. This means I buy myself flowers, chocolates, and gifts. I tell myself how wonderful I am. I pamper myself as I would want someone else to pamper me. And I also ask my friends and lovers to nurture me, when they can. I allow them to give me that support. Relationship, to be a true exchange of love, must be a place of giving and receiving. If we are focused only on giving, or only on receiving, there is imbalance, and we are unable to cultivate true loving. When the heart is open, joy and sharing flow freely back and forth. In this state a relationship becomes a healthy, shining transmitter of bliss. To reach this place, you must first focus only on you, on creating a free flow of love that emanates from your own connection to Spirit.

A part of learning to love yourself is gratitude. Living in gratitude creates a heart that is open and a joyful outlook on life. It trains us to focus on the good in ourselves and others, which expands the heart. Begin each day with the practice of gratitude. When you wake, list the things you are grateful for as you move through your morning routine. They may be small things, like gratitude for a roof over your head and food in your belly. Even being grateful for small things helps to heal the heart by shifting it into a place of openness. With this open heart, you can more easily love yourself and connect to the world. Allow yourself to breathe in all the love and magick the world has to offer.

Another important part of self-love is believing that you can heal. Trusting in your connection to Spirit to help you heal allows the possibility of miraculous growth and change. It helps to act toward yourself with the highest impeccability when you act as your own healer and listen carefully to Spirit's direction. Stay centered in what is in your best and highest good, and do only that, lovingly and kindly. Let it be okay if you fail, let it be okay if you succeed. Have no goals for how your healing happens. If you focus too long and too hard on the healing that you want and do not allow it to flow naturally, it will elude you. Let yourself flow into any healing that you do for yourself, and you will see that the healing is a journey that spirals to the center and back out again.

On this journey, also give yourself large doses of kindness. When you are compassionate with yourself, you will naturally be compassionate with others. This is the ultimate self-love, and it begins to change the heart in a subtle and gentle way. When you let go and offer yourself up, while holding the intention to open your heart as you breathe, your healings become more and more powerful. The techniques themselves are very simple. Your intention and your willingness are more important than any particular type of healing tool.

Aphrodite was not only the Greek goddess of love, but also the goddess of beauty. This is because the heart and beauty are inextricably intertwined. Invite beauty into your life as another way to breathe love into your heart. Notice the feeling that comes alive in your heart when you think about the beauty of a majestic sequoia tree or a purple and orange sunset. These things are so beautiful that they open the heart. In cultivating the open heart, you learn to cultivate beauty, not only in yourself, but in your surroundings. There is a special alchemy that happens in my heart when I look at a painting or sculpture that moves me, or listen to an outstanding poem. This alchemy transforms my soul in that instant into pure love and appreciation of the art. I suppose this is also why I believe that the creative energy is the same as the sexual and life force energy. I believe that beauty, the heart, and sexuality are inseparable. Surrendering to the way they twine together for me was an important step in creating the wholeness that I had always longed for. Creating beauty is sexy, and I feel sexy whenever I make myself beautiful. The aliveness that I feel within me when I see a really amazing movie or read an astounding book is the kundalini, the spiritual energy, the creative force that powers the universe and the world within it.

Using the Breath

Circular breath is powerful when you are working to heal the heart, and it is the foundation of the practice of breathing love. This breath does not pause between the inhale and the exhale. Full and deep breathing swirls the emotions through you and lets them flow freely. In circular breath you do not try to control the emotion, you just allow it to release from you. Venting like a volcano, you let the steam out, and feel the deep rivers of hot lava that long to flow to the surface. Or perhaps you flow like a river, powerful and focused, yet flowing around obstacles and wearing down resistance to the easiest flow of the water through the landscape. Use these visualizations of water or lava if they help you to release the emotions stuck in your body. Circular breath is the foundation of my practice of shamanic tantra, not only helping me to release and gain awareness of emotions, but also to promote the movement of sexual arousal through the body. Emotion and sexual arousal are closely bound together, and it is important to gain an awareness of both as you walk the solo path. Emotions locked tightly in the body create limitations on the ability to feel your sexual energy.

When the body is engorged with emotional crud and the heart is encircled with barbed wire and armor, it is time to purge the depths of your soul through the breath so that you can reconnect to your sexual self. Breathe deeply whenever you sense an emotion arising in you. The breath allows the emotion to flow through you and to release, to be felt, or to transform. We are human, and opening to the deep reservoir of emotion within us is a vital part of the human experience as well as the tantric experience. In tantra, we encourage the deep experience of all the emotions, both good and bad, and use the breath to release as well as to gain awareness of emotion held in the body. We want to learn to feel deep joy and to feel and release deep sadness, and so we learn to breathe in deeply through the nose and breathe out completely through the mouth. Notice that when you are not breathing, it becomes difficult to feel your emotions. Indeed, you may begin to feel tense or anxious when you are not breathing, and even have back pain or other discomfort in your body. Simply remembering to breathe restores the body and the emotional life to order. A simple breath takes you back into awareness and presence with yourself, and brings you back to your humanness.

Practice 1: Circular Breath

Breathing Love is the gateway within your soul that opens you to the experience of sacred sex. Circular breathing is easy to learn, and over time becomes a useful tool for dropping quickly into full body awareness. It can also be a tool for moving sexual energy to the heart, where you can transmute it to love.

Sit comfortably and take a deep breath in through the nose, letting your belly expand. Now exhale deeply and powerfully through your mouth, letting the belly contract and push the air out from your body. Continue to breathe in through your nose, and out through your mouth, making the inhales and exhales the same length, perhaps 5 counts each. Let there be no pause between your inhales and exhales, flowing immediately from one to the next, never holding the breath.

Do this practice for 5 minutes to begin with, and notice how you feel, Try doing it with eyes closed and open, and notice that with eyes closed you can sense more deeply into your body. Notice any emotions that come up for you as you breathe, and let them release from the body. Connect your roots to the Earth and branches into the sky as in the Sacred Tree Meditation to help you to release the emotions. Send them out on your exhale to be composted by the earth or burned up in the sun. Notice how different you feel after this practice, often I feel more grounded, peaceful, calm, and present. I find that journaling or sharing with a trusted friend about what came up for me during the meditation is a great way to ground the experience in me.

Opening to Bliss

Once you begin to heal and release from the heart, you are ready to cultivate joy in the space you've created. The heart can now become an overflowing cup of love, a container for positive emotions. Once you have let go of the pain stored in your heart, you can open to receive love from Spirit. This love can wash away all that has gone before to make room for all that is to come.

Practice 2: Breathing Love

Find a comfortable sitting position and begin the Circular Breath practice. Next put your roots in the earth and branches in the sky, as you do in the Sacred Tree Meditation.

Now begin to imagine that you are breathing love up from the Earth into your genitals, then into the belly, the stomach, and the heart. As your breath comes into the heart, imagine that the love you are breathing is cool, crystal clear water, and that it is swirling through your heart and washing it clean, then flowing back down your body and out your roots as you exhale. Continue with this breath for as long as your intuition tells you.

Next bring your awareness to your branches in the sky, and pull the radiant fire of the sun down into your head and let this gentle fire creep into your forehead, then your throat, then your heart. Feel it radiate and glow in the heart, waking it up, burning away and melting any armoring there, opening the heart to feel more love and more bliss. Continue breathing this fire of love in and out from your heart for as long as it feels good to you.

Now when you are ready, breathe in love from both earth and sky at the same time, filling your heart with it and letting your heart expand with each inhale to hold more and more love. When you exhale, imagine that this love energy is flowing down your arms and hands, and feel your palms and fingers come alive. Place your hands on your own heart, and send the love that is flowing from them into your heart, so that you are filling your heart with love both on your inhale and exhale. As you do this imagine that your heart continues to grow and get bigger. Notice that there is no limit to how much love your heart can hold.

Now gently come back into awareness and notice how you feel, and especially notice how your heart is feeling. Offer up your gratitude for any changes you feel.

In doing these practices of breathing in love and breathing out fear, I join myself to Spirit at the heart. The more I do the practice, the more open my heart becomes. The amount of love I feel flowing into me only depends upon my willingness to make the connection and receive the love. If I am armored at the heart, or in despair that I will never receive enough love, then very little comes through the connection in my practice, and I struggle. I must remind myself at these times, that Spirit loves me no matter what I do, or who I choose to be. Cultivating self-love through gratitude, beauty, faith, compassion, and breathing love creates a feeling of worthiness, and helps me to soften and open again. I'm not perfect, and my heart still flows in and out of openness. I have learned to be accepting and compassionate of wherever the connection is for me at any given time. When I am fully open, it is as if a beautiful green vine grows from my heart and connects to the unlimited source of love, so that I am never empty. Through this visualization and breath, I can receive love from Spirit at any time of day or night, in any situation. Once I started doing the breathing love practice daily, I began to notice that it was easier for me to connect with other people more fully, and to really be able to give and receive love deeply. I began to see that in many of my relationships, where I thought I was not being loved, that the truth was I couldn't receive the love my lovers and friends and family were trying to give me.

Once I began to really receive from the people around me, it created dramatic change in the way I connect my deep feelings of love to my intense passionate sexual nature. A channel seemed to open between my heart and yoni that blurred the boundaries between love and sex. I began to do this practice combined with self-pleasuring, to practice connecting my heart to my genitals. The amazing thing that followed from this was that my heart itself has become orgasmic. My breasts have become as orgasmic as my clitoris. This heart openness has given me a fuller and richer sense of my own sexuality, so that love flows through my entire body whether I am self-pleasuring or making love.

Practice 3: Awakening the Heart for Men

For many men, giving from the heart is easy and natural, but opening to receive love can be more difficult. Men often carry significant armoring in the heart that can be melted away over time with practices like this heart awakening ritual.

Begin by growing roots and branches as you did in the Sacred Tree Meditation. Start your circular breathing. Now imagine that you are breathing the liquid love of the Earth Mother into your lingam. Allow yourself to feel a flow of sexual arousal coming into you through your legs and feet and roots in the Earth. Stroke your lingam lightly, enjoying the arousal and imagine the Divine Feminine Earth Goddess is touching you with loving hands. Let go of any goals for orgasm or fantasy and stay in the moment of how your body is feeling. Now breathe this arousal and loving touch up into your belly, into your stomach, and into your heart. Let your heart become aroused and let it receive the loving and soothing touch of the Goddess. Feel what it is like to let her penetrate you in the heart, to open your heart and fully receive her. Squeeze your PC muscle (the one you use to stop yourself from peeing) to help pull the energy up on the inhale, then breathe it back down on the exhale. Continue as long as you like, noticing how your heart feels afterward.

Practice 4: Awakening the Breasts for Women

For most women, sexual arousal begins in the breasts. Awakening the breasts to feel love and sexual fire, and then to connect them to the yoni, is a powerful piece of the sexual healing journey.

Begin by growing roots and branches as you did in the Sacred Tree Meditation. Start the circular breath. Now imagine that you are breathing into your breasts from your branches, pulling down the warm loving sexual fire from the sun. Let this fire circulate through your heart as you did in the Breathing Love exercise, but now let it be exquisitely sexual. Imagine that the sun is your lover, and you are breathing his sexual passion into your breasts. Take your hands and use the fingertips to circle the breasts, and feel the tingling that awakens there. Imagine that your hands are the hands of your lover, the divine masculine sun, caressing and loving you. Let your body come alive, and keep breathing. Allow the tingling and aliveness in your breasts to move down through your belly and into your yoni and roots in the earth. As you breathe it down the body, feel the juiciness of the yoni come alive, then pull that juice back into the heart by inhaling, squeezing your PC muscle (the one you use to stop yourself from peeing) and feel the energy move back up. Continue this practice as long as you like, noticing the aliveness in your body.

When my heart is fully open, I feel loving and sexual at the same time. There is an openness and compassion that helps me expand my consciousness out all around me, not only to the universe of stars and planets above, but to the universe of people all around me. Others can feel this energy coming from me, drawing them in to my personal space for some inexplicable reason. An open heart makes us more receptive to love, more likely to find love and keep it flowing in our lives. Work to open your heart through practicing kindness and gratitude, as well as doing the practices in this chapter. Expanding his heart, the man discovers that an open heart is not to be feared, that his abilities as a lover expand, and that lovemaking becomes a powerful spiritual and emotional experience. Many men come to me in my private practice complaining of dissatisfying and empty sex lives. They instinctively know that there is something more to the whole thing, but they aren't quite sure what it is. This opening of the heart is part of the key to that puzzle. A woman's journey is almost the opposite of a man's. In healing her heart, the woman finds herself opening more sexually, and becoming more willing to connect deeply with men. As she opens, she draws men to her like a magnet, and her experience of connection with them becomes more joyful and ecstatic. To experience these things, to shift the heart, requires patience, surrender, dedication, and unconditional love.

• Chapter 6 •

Breathing Love Together

Insurmountable challenges sometimes get in the way of us being loving with our partner. Or at least they seem that way. In truth, no challenge is too great to overcome in relationship. It is instead a question of how loving and open the heart can be, and whether the relationship is serving the best and highest good of all concerned. Many people stay in marriages because they want to continue to provide a stable environment for their children, but a stable environment without love is not helpful to any of the people involved. So how do we create a sense of love that is so expansive that it seems unending? How do we recommit to being kind to each other and to creating love? And how does this create the emotional foundation for opening our hearts fully and completely to our partner? First we must acknowledge that there is no such thing as a perfect relationship or a perfect partner or even a perfect person! We must realize that we are not perfect ourselves, and that perfection is unattainable in bodily form. We are not here to be perfect! We are here to love and to experience our humanness in all its fullness. This includes our imperfections when we find ourselves in an argument with our partner. In this state, the most powerful thing we can do is to recommit to being kind. This is incredibly hard when we are angry, but of paramount importance if we want a loving relationship. Bitterness, anger, sarcasm, and ruthless silence do nothing to encourage the growth of a loving relationship. If we want love, we must embody it, and this is where the practice of first learning to breathe love solo is helpful. Taking some time out to do our own solo practice of breathing love, of getting in touch with the love that is available to us from Spirit, is a wonderful first step when we need to come into working through things in a relationship. And if we are able to work through things, we are able to open our hearts more because we build trust and belief in the love between us.

Holding a space of unconditional love in our hearts allows us to create safety for our partner, but how can we get to a place of doing that? The answer is in first giving that same acceptance to ourselves. There is no way to be in loving relationship if we cannot receive love. And the knack of learning to receive is in us. We all are capable of receiving love.

Yes, really. Yes you! We all can do it. I was so sure that I would never learn self-love after years of childhood and adult abuse and neglect. And yet as an adult I have learned to love myself so fully that a space of unconditional love for myself has begun to open. As that space opens within me, I am able to give that love to others, including my child and my partner. The practice of being kind is the first step to helping our partner feel safe. Once they feel the kindness we are cultivating in ourselves, they are able to open and to connect to us more fully. And we can take responsibility for our own openness by continuing daily to give unconditional love to ourselves. The more we practice opening the heart, being kind, keeping ourselves safe emotionally, the more we are able to give those same things to others, to let go and just open the heart wider and wider. This openness of heart creates a beautiful peace within us, and the truth is that we really do it for ourselves. This is why so many spiritual teachers advocate that we first learn to make ourselves happy, because happy people are kinder to others than anyone else in the world.

Healing Relationship

If happy people are more loving and more open, then it makes sense that blasting through past resentments in a relationship will lead to a more effortless and loving relationship with your partner, does it not? Clearing resentments is a difficult process for some of us, because we want to hang on to our anger forever and ever to protect ourselves. This anger and resentment poisons us and everything we touch. When I am angry it hurts not only myself, but if I express it inappropriately it also hurts my partner, my lover, my child, and my friends. I become like a wounded animal lashing out at anyone who tries to help me. In this place I try to remember that it is my responsibility to make myself feel better, not the other person's responsibility to grovel and apologize for whatever it is that I think caused my anger. Many times I discover, after taking a day to reflect and process my anger, that I wasn't really angry about the thing that I thought caused it, but in fact was angry about some other things that I wasn't even aware were upsetting me. When I feel very upset, it is almost always about a wounding from earlier in my life. So cultivating a deep awareness of your feelings, as we do in the 3rd gateway of Soul Gazing, becomes essential. But in the moment, for now, when you are feeling angry and resentful toward your partner, breathe love with them. This practice will open both of you, if you stay present with it, to a feeling of love. If you are really in the present moment, then those old resentments no longer exist. Those resentments live in the past. Becoming aware of what causes them, then releasing them by living fully in the present is the greatest gift you can give to yourself, to your relationship, and to the world.

Gratitude practice with your partner is another powerful way to let go of resentment and shift your connection with your partner into a more loving place. Let yourself put aside any tense or angry feelings of the moment and come into your heart. Search there for the things that you love about your partner, the things that bring you together, and speak about them with each other. Take turns, saying "I am grateful for _____." If you can't find it in your heart to be grateful for anything big, then pick something small, like "I am grateful that you put the cap on the toothpaste tube this morning." It may sound silly, but even being grateful for little things will help to open your hearts to each other.

When an argument is at an impasse, or when a conflict begins to spiral out of control and turn into a yelling match, it is time to retreat and take a deep breath. There is so much drama and insanity that often comes into relationships, and TV, movies, and novels in our culture have taught us that this is a normal and acceptable way to act. But is it really normal and acceptable to hurt someone you love because they are not seeing things the way you do? Or is this true insanity? When conflict in a relationship reaches a place of anguish or conflagration, then it is time to ask Spirit for help, and to know that through magickal coincidences, the conflict can resolve itself. At these times I connect to Spirit with the Sacred Tree Meditation and listen for guidance. This may sound like simplistic cop-out thinking, but I have seen it work over and over. I have even seen it work in my own divorce, where if I would just take a deep breath and a step back and ask Spirit to guide me, things would resolve effortlessly. In my current partnership I have seen it bring us to miraculous resolutions of many conflicts over things that had me in total mental anguish. Somehow our conflicts always resolve, no matter how painful. The trick is to take a step back, to take some space apart to breathe and let Spirit come in to work its magick, to perhaps shift perspective, and to juice us up with love. So often when we come back together, we can't even really remember why we were so upset with each other. Spirit works its magick on us over and over again because we are willing.

Another way to let go and come into a more open heart with your partner is the practice of breathing together. Sharing breath harmonizes you and your partner into a beautiful synchrony of total presence. Breathing consciously always brings us into presence with ourselves. It has such power to not only make us aware, but to sweep away anger and distrust, if we are willing to allow it. Sometimes it takes awhile. If you are new to the practice, if you and your partner have been building up old patterns and resentments for a long time, it may take awhile to clear. Regular practice together is the key. Practice when you are not upset with each other. The magick that is created when both partners are really committed to letting go of the past and recommitting to the present brings a power to the practice that is incomparable. The practice is simple to begin: You simply breathe together with your partner. The man leads, the lady follows. This may be hard for some couples who are used to doing everything cooperatively and as a team: To let one lead and tell the other to follow may seem somehow unfair or inequitable. And yet breathing together is like dancing. One person must lead, otherwise there is chaos and it all becomes a jumble. Letting the man lead allows him to begin to exercise the use of his inner divine masculine power, and letting the woman follow allows her to begin to experience what it is like to drop into the divine feminine state where she can relax and be guided by trust.

Practice 1: Circular Breathing Together

This practice is marvelous to use before you and your partner are about to talk about something difficult, or before you flow into making love.

Sit together or lie down together, facing each other. Come into connection using the Partnered Sacred Tree Meditation. Now, the man starts the deep circular breath, breathing powerfully so that the woman can hear his inhales and exhales. The woman joins him, breathing out and in with him.

Let yourselves drop into the simple harmony of breathing together. Feel the peace in not struggling. Do this practice for 5 minutes or more if you are both enjoying it. Afterward, use the Reconnecting to Self meditation to come out of the connection or flow into lovemaking. Notice how you feel.

Deeper Connection

Once we have mastered the art of breathing together, we are ready to try even deeper practices of connecting with the breath. Inspiration of our partner, breathing them in, is a powerful practice in receiving their energy into our selves. Similarly, breathing our breath out into their energy field intentionally allows us to give in a deep and powerful way that we may not have experienced before. We call this practice the Alternating Circular Breath. It is a practice where we change the partnered breath in unison to a breath where each partner breathes in as the other breathes out. This exchange back and forth creates a profound and awesome state of connection between partners, both by its intense focus on staying in the moment to pay attention to the breathing, and by the mystical energy that is exchanged between partners.

Practice 2: Alternating Circular Breath

My partner and I use this practice to help us learn to be more vulnerable with each other. Make sure your breath is fresh and pleasant for this exercise.

Sit facing each other and come into connection using the Partnered Sacred Tree Meditation. Now open your eyes and ears so that the woman can follow the man's breath. Men, start breathing the circular breath, making your inhales and exhales audible and powerful so the woman can hear them. Now bring your faces and lips close, so you are almost touching, and begin to breathe each other's breath. As the man inhales, the woman breathes out, allowing him to take her breath into his body. As the man breathes out, the woman inhales his essence and receives him into her body. Continue for at least 5 minutes if you can, longer if you like, each of you blowing your breath into the other and receiving the other's breath.

You can flow into lovemaking from this practice or choose to come out of connection when you are ready. Use the Reconnection to Self exercise to detach, and notice afterward how you feel.

Once you have spent some time with the simple practices of breathing together alternately, you are ready to come to the practice of the partnered heart circuit. In essence this circuit creates a melting and an opening in the heart and genitals that profoundly shifts the connection between you. This is a deep practice of a man opening his loving and vulnerable heart fully and completely to his partner. For the woman, it is the courage to send all the love she feels into the man. You may experience tears and sadness and clearing of many layers of difficulty between you as you connect your hearts in this way. Continued practice, combined with clear compassionate communication, is incredibly healing for relationships, and leads to a deep sexual arousal and connection. The circuit is different for men and women. Men breathe in at the heart, and out through the lingam. Women breathe the man in at the yoni and breathe out to him at the heart. This is a practice that helps to equalize the differences between men and women, the old differences that keep men locked in trying to get love only through the genitals and women locked in trying to get love only through the heart. In shamanic tantra we work to unite the heart and the genitals, to fix the split between sex and love by combining and mixing them, beginning with this practice. The woman melts and opens in her yoni, and allows herself to fully receive all the sexual charge the man wants to send to her. Conversely, the man melts and opens in his heart and learns to receive all the love that the woman has to give him.

Loving awareness of each other flows from the merging of the heart circuit, and taking this practice into lovemaking begins the process of mending that split between the heart and the genitals. When you practice in this way, you will begin to feel a flowing of energy between you that may feel like the coolness of water, or the tingling of an electrical current. Allow this tingling or coolness to flow through you, and focus on it. Bring it fully into your conscious awareness. These sensations are the feeling of energy moving through your body, and focusing on them usually has the effect of making them stronger, leading to a more and more powerful connection with your partner. Eventually, moving this energy between you will start to lead to all kinds of experiences in your lovemaking that will be new and exciting, or perhaps also strange and unfamiliar. Remember as you move into this practice that unfamiliar and strange is not necessarily bad. Sometimes our habitual ways of making love feel safer to us, and we have the desire to drop back into them whenever the new practices seem to be taking us somewhere we are not too comfortable with. Breathing love with sexual connection may start to open your heart more fully than you've experienced before, and that may be terrifying in how vulnerable it makes you feel. You may also feel more sexually charged than ever before. Remind yourselves that these new experiences are part of the tantric path, and that the more you open yourself to them and stay connected to Spirit, the more full and rich your life with each other will become.

Practice 3: Heart Circuit

The heart circuit is a powerful practice to do whether your clothing is on or off. Begin learning this practice with clothing on, to make it easier to concentrate on the energy circuit. Once you have mastered the basic practice, move on to challenge yourself with the ecstasy of the advanced practice.

Basic Practice

Sit facing each other and come into connection using the Partnered Sacred Tree Meditation. The best position for moving the energy in this practice is yabyum, the woman sitting in the man's lap. This position allows the genitals to come into contact even though your clothes are on. If you are not flexible enough for yabyum, you can try sitting on a chair or a couch together, or lying down facing each other with your pelvises in contact.

Now begin the Alternate Circular Breath together, the man leading. As the woman breathes in, she breathes sexual energy in from the man's lingam and pulls it into her yoni. She breathes this charge up from her yoni into her heart, turning it into love. Then she breathes out, sending all this love into the man's heart.

As the man breathes in, he opens his heart and pulls in her love. He breathes in, pulling this love down to his lingam and turning it into sexual energy. From his lingam, he breathes out powerfully into her yoni.

Really focus on the connection between you and your partner. Men, fully open at the heart when you breathe in, and strongly send your sexual charge out when you breathe out. Women, freely give your loving energy out your breasts on the exhale and strongly pull in all your man's sexual energy on the inhale. Continue for at least 5 minutes, or longer if you like. From this practice you can flow into lovemaking or Reconnect to Self to come out of the practice.

Advanced Practice

Taking the heart circuit into lovemaking presents more challenges. It becomes harder to stay present to breath and energy movement when you are sexually aroused. Pay attention as you do this practice, and bring yourself back into the breathing whenever you notice you are losing your concentration or ability to feel the energy move.

Come into connection the same way you did in the basic heart circuit practice, but now be nude with each other. Stay with the heart circuit breath, with each breath feeling the extra charge from your nude bodies. When you are ready, move into penetration using the Stillness Together practice. Remember that it doesn't matter whether the lingam is hard or soft for this practice. Now continue to practice the heart circuit with the lingam and yoni directly connected, and notice how the sexual arousal can pull you away from fully concentrating on your breath and on moving the energy between you. Stay focused by bringing yourself back into deep breathing every time you drop out of the practice. Notice what this practice does for your lovemaking. What is it like to open your hearts to give and receive love in such a conscious way? Men, how does it feel to receive in your heart and penetrate with your lingam? Women, what is it like to open in the yoni and connect that to your heart? Let yourself flow into lovemaking while still circuiting this energy. Remember to surrender to the flow, let go of goals for orgasm, and let yourself be ravished by ecstasy.

In all these practices, breath is the key. We contract the body when we stop allowing ourselves to breathe and emote fully in our daily lives. Unblocking emotional clogs is the real purpose of the breath, and breath

Yabyum Positions

is the foundation of every practice in shamanic tantra. The more we breathe, the clearer and more open we become. Circuiting sexual energy occurs naturally and easily when we breathe, and we begin to feel ourselves more alive and juicier in all the moments of our lives. Any breath practice we do without making love, can also be done while making love. Each solo practice is a preparation for moving energy while connected lovingly to another. Each breath or spiritual practice done partnered with our clothing on is preparation for a practice that is done with clothing off. And eventually there is no difference. The more we do these practices, the more that any spiritual energy moving through us begins to feel sexual. A simple hug with deep breathing becomes a spiritual and ecstatic experience. There is a place within tantra where our bodies begin to move energy so freely and strongly that we no longer need the stimulation of physical intercourse to have an orgasm. Energetic orgasms begin to be possible in everyday life, just from breathing in life and the world around us.

My experience of sex before walking this path was that of having the same experience multiple times. For me there was a routine and a pattern that I followed in lovemaking. When I learned to come into the powerful connection that breathing love and circuiting heart energy creates, my journey through sexual encounter became completely unpredictable, wild, ravishing and at the same time loving, heart opening, and more connected than anything I'd ever known.

Becoming Vulnerable

Paradoxically, as we move deeper into connection and into the merging of tantric work, it becomes more and more important to center ourselves and create an awareness of our part in the relationship. Cultivating an intense focus on the self and on the part that we play in creating any situation in the relationship leads to a great clarity and balance. You can use the breathing love practice to cultivate this clarity. The more we stay in this place of our heart's wisdom, the more our relationship becomes peaceful, free of drama and martyrdom, and the more our deep joy and quiet love can blossom. I used to think that real love meant great passionate fighting and tears to show that we truly loved each other, but I have learned that passion can take many forms. I have found that I prefer the passion of shared goals, spiritual practice, and ecstatic lovemaking to the passion of constant arguing, blaming, and "make-up" sex. Clarity for the part you play in any tension in the relationship allows you to first have compassion for your partner, and in sex to open your heart more and more to them. You begin to realize that any disagreements you have are often resulting from your own reactions and behavior. I have learned that there are many ways I can change my reactions and learn to let go of things that may just not be that important. This creates harmony in me, and I no longer blame my partner for my feelings. This is how I have come into the place of unconditional love.

With this clarity of self-awareness often comes awakening to barriers we use to keep us from fully connecting with our partner. Procrastination is one of the most insidious forms of resistance to opening the heart. It often is disguised as excessive busyness. A very full social and work schedule allows a couple no time to connect, and protects them from having to be quite so vulnerable. And yet this is resistance. We all make choices about how we spend our time and who we spend it with. Ask yourself the question, "What is really important to me?" And then begin to prioritize your life based on those answers. If you are working a tantric practice then the practice will be one of those priorities and you will find time to do it.

Another form of resistance is blaming the other for everything that is wrong in the relationship, and its sister, denial that anything you are doing is causing any difficulty in the relationship. So right now ask Spirit to help you humble yourself and let go of resistance. Let go of blame, anger, denial, procrastination, busyness, and any other blocks you have to opening your heart and doing this practice. If you are reading this book, then something is calling you to this path. I urge you to go within and take a look at what that something is, to be courageous enough to open your heart to something bigger than yourself. If this all feels too scary, especially the notion of opening your heart to another person, then begin by opening your heart to Spirit. Offer your heart up as a sacrifice, and let Spirit tell you where and when and how to live its opening. The passionate loving heart is its own reward. Once you have reached this point you will never want to return to your old life.

Making Love with Heart

Moving these practices into the physical sexual connection, and remaining in spiritual presence while being sexually aroused, is the heart of tantric sexual practice. In the fullness of a woman's breasts, and in our culture's obsession with them, lies a great secret: The seat of a woman's sexuality is in her breasts. In lovemaking, this means that most women prefer to have the breasts receive lots of loving attention. Try a half hour of massage and touch before moving to intercourse and see what happens. For women, this means that the practice of breathing love and opening the heart is the secret to the flowering of her sexuality and feminine essence. Women must learn to breathe into the breasts (Diana Richardson, *Tantric Orgasm for Women*). This practice is profound in the unlocking of the feminine sexual power, and in fact, the current of women's sexual energy often flows in the opposite direction to the man's, which, as taught in traditional tantra, flows up and out his head. For women, there is a strong current that flows down from the breasts and out the yoni, and when it is strong, it leads to multiple ejaculatory orgasms that flow though her like water. My partner senses into my yoni at these times and is overcome by myriad sensations he feels there, those of silky texture, juicy ejaculate flowing over his lingam, and of the yoni pushing out against him as she pushes out the ejaculate. These orgasms and this connection to my breasts have become for me the ultimate lovemaking experience, and clitoral orgasms are no longer the most powerful experience I have. Stimulation of my breasts alone can make me flow into an energetic orgasm that lasts for many minutes. This tells me that my breasts are not only for love, but also for sex, and this healing of the sex-love split has been very profound for me in accepting and loving my body.

Men come to more ecstatic lovemaking by awakening to the lingam as a part of their body that is not just for sex, but also for love. Learning to send loving energy out through the lingam begins with taking down the armor around the heart. When the heart opens, and a man allows himself to be vulnerable, his reward is a rush of sexual energy that shoots up from the lingam through his belly and chest, arms and hands, activating the heart as a sexual organ. Connecting the heart and lingam this way also allows the lingam to become loving. Connecting the lingam and heart creates wholeness and greater satisfaction in life and lovemaking.

Another liberating practice for me is reporting in to my lover about my reactions while we are making love. It has become a wonderful way to open up communication about which touches I like on my body, and where. It is very important to be compassionate when approaching this communication, and to simply and quietly resolve to yourself that you will not be rejecting or angry toward your partner, even if a touch they are giving to you is extremely uncomfortable. In the positive request cycle, you give feedback when your partner is doing something you like. You might say, "Yes, that feels nice, thank you. Would you please press a little harder with your fingers?" and when they do what you ask, say "mmmmm, yes, that's soooo wonderful, thank you." If your partner is doing something you really dislike, you can take a few breaths and relax to see if they shift to something you like better. If that doesn't happen, then you can say something compassionate like, "My body is really tensing up when you touch me with that much pressure, would you please touch me a little more lightly?" And then when they do what you ask, say "ohh yes, oh I love that, it feels so wonderful, thank you." You get the idea. Communication doesn't have to be difficult or confrontational. It can be playful and sensual during lovemaking, and it opens the heart to even greater possibility.

Playfulness is, in the end, the key. When our hearts are happy and open, free of resentment and fear and anger, we flow more naturally into a childlike state of wonder. This joyful presence is spiritual in itself, but connecting it to sex, or even creating it through sacred sex, has brought me a level of joy and healing in my life that I have never known before. Each day I seem to grow, gain more peace, and strengthen my connection to my spiritual/sexual self. My open heart is painful sometimes, because it feels the sadness in my life as keenly as the happiness. More often now, I feel that the joy and the sadness are balanced, and that with time my scale will tip toward an utter joy that will come to live within me most of the time. It is this that I wish for you.

✦ The Third Gateway ✦

Soul Gazing

• Chapter 7 •

Finding Awareness

The Third Gateway, Soul Gazing is about gaining awareness of our inner world. We have learned to connect and invite the divine in, and to become present though opening our hearts, and now it is time to dive deeper. The work of becoming aware is about exploring all the things in ourselves, and particularly in our shadow selves, that keep us from being fully alive and fully connected. The shadow is a part of the psyche that stores the pieces of ourselves that we want to hide, forget, or ignore. These parts may be negative or positive. Maybe we ignore our special gifts because we are afraid of success. Maybe we ignore our darkness because we want to be perfect. To come fully into awareness, we must do shadow work so that these buried parts of ourselves do not distract us from simple awareness of each moment.

Shadow work can be scary, because sometimes when we go within, what we find is a reservoir of emptiness and pain. We begin to avoid contacting this part of ourselves, doing anything to escape. We tell ourselves that the best thing for us is to stay positive by distracting ourselves. But this place of pain and darkness is part of us, and is not something we can avoid forever. If we allow ourselves to go deep, to feel these buried emotions, to ride out the waves of emptiness and pain, we will find unexpected riches there. I have lately become curious about my pain, ready to explore what lies in the depths of this emptiness for me. I have created space in my romantic life, to see what will fall into that emptiness. More and more, to heal from my addiction to men and to love, I have been spending time alone with myself. I spend my evenings riding the waves of my emotions to see what shore they will cast me upon. In doing this, I am beginning to contact my true nature. Although the feelings are sometimes painful, I find that I am somehow gaining an inner strength from facing them — not the strength of enduring, but the strength of knowing that I can let all of these feelings pass through me and I will still remain. The more I face these feelings, the more clarity I receive about my life direction, about what is best for me. The more I face these feelings, the more focused I am able to be in my life, no longer distracted by tickling edges of feelings not quite glimpsed. I know my feelings right now, at a very deep level. I dive into them and feel them, then I leap out of the ocean like a dolphin and feel the joy of flying through the air before I dive again. In this contact with my truest deepest self, Spirit speaks to me loudly. I hear its voice both waking and dreaming. Through this voice I know that I am well and truly loved, that all my feelings of loneliness and separation are really just an illusion.

There is joy sometimes, and there is also fear in this exploration. Frightening images from our past are often pushed down within us into a dark cavernous underground place. Eventually these images become crowded in upon themselves as the cave fills up with our repressed and unloved emotions and experiences. It brings tremendous peace to release these images and feelings from their hiding places, and also frees up oceans of energy that we may not even have realized we were using to hold all these things in. The shadow is the dark place within ourselves and all the dark things it contains. It is like a reverse image of us. As we become aware of the shadow, we are able to make friends with these unloved parts of ourselves and integrate them with our other parts, to accept that there are parts of us that we may not love or even like. Learning to love our bad points as well as our good brings a depth to us. We can be angry, for example, and no longer use energy to repress our anger when it comes up. When we are unconscious of anger, it can explode out of us without warning. But when we are aware, we see its buildup within us, and we learn healthy ways to release it before it turns into toxic waste that poisons both us and everyone around us. Learning to release scary emotions in a healthy way is part of the work of Soul Gazing.

From this going within, we develop a deep awareness, and a deep sense of who we truly are emerges. We move through life with what may look like foolish abandon to outside eyes, filled with sheer trust and joy in our connection to Spirit. We become focused. Men are focused on their purpose, women on their centers. Focusing on these things is helpful in finding your life path, the place where you have a deep sense of belonging, while at the same time feeling intensely alive. For women, learning to focus on magnetically pulling life into us allows us to become more loving and radiant, to open more fully to the experience of life, and to share connection with others. For men, focusing on the life purpose, time to make that a priority, to set goals, and to move toward those goals with power and purpose creates a deep satisfaction. When we are this alive in the moment, there is a peace and a rush of energy that comes into us. For me it feels like a tingling that flows through my entire body. For my partner, it is a rushing waterfall that rinses him clean. For you it may be lightning or some other force of nature that you feel wake up within you when you are fully here. Soul Gazing brings a full awareness of your entire body that feels good, like a cat stretching and lying in the sun. In the beginning, this sensation was unfamiliar, because I was so used to divorcing myself from my body. But as I have deepened in my practice, I have found that the body is essential in my meditations. Sacred sexual practice is a path to enlightenment through the body. On this path, coming into awareness of the body and your inner life is another gateway to a joyous and happy life.

Many of us still struggle daily to find this happiness, and we often find life to be a tempestuous experience. Over and over we are buffeted by the gale force winds of change, and we often feel devastated and drained when these winds blow through our lives. Practicing being fully aware and having gratitude for whatever life brings is one of the secrets to finding peace no matter what is happening in your life. Life will do what it does. Loved ones will be ill, or die, or move away. Friends will argue and abandon us. Lovers will leave, cars will crash, jobs will evaporate. But these are all just everyday occurrences in life. Once we get this perspective, this knowing that fate is not singling us out when bad things happen to us, we have the choice to embrace an attitude that all events are perfect. We have the chance to shift our view of life. When I stopped taking life personally, I became much more optimistic and much more serene on a daily basis. I am much less reactive to any major life stresses. Why should I take it on when someone cuts me off on the freeway? Why should I think it is about me when an employer decides to cut back? In my own life a few years ago, I was laid off and other things in my life immediately leapt into being, opportunities that have brought me more happiness and joy than I thought was possible. Staying open, and staying connected to our spiritual guidance allows most of life to take care of itself.

Awareness and Connection

Connection is so much easier in lovemaking when we stay awake to what our feelings are in the moment. Living in the moment, we cultivate a sense of wonder and exploration with our partners that feeds a juicy yumminess into our sexuality. When we are fully aware, we allow feelings to come up as we connect and make love, and we allow ourselves to feel and share those feelings with our partner. This sharing allows us to be fully there and fully experiencing, allowing ourselves to not know what to expect, to not know what comes next. In this place of wonder, we become like children, who are great teachers about presence. Watch a child in play or at work and you will see that they are totally in the moment and in their feelings. Children have no worry about saying how they feel. They give themselves fully to the experience of life, and they share that freely. They don't worry about whether someone will like them because they are crying. If we cultivate the ability to be like little children, to cry when we are sad or uncomfortable, to laugh when we are joyful, then we allow ourselves to experience the full range of human emotions, whatever they happen to be in the moment. For many of us, we have spent so long avoiding unpleasant emotions, that when we begin this practice of awareness it may seem like that is all we have. I promise you that after enough time passes of you allowing the sadness, anger, and grief to come up, joy, love, and ecstasy will also begin to come through. This is how we get to the ecstatic connection in making love.

Your own awareness and sharing of emotion is the greatest gift you can give to another person. Giving another your full emotional picture allows them to feel truly connected. This is also a tremendous gift to yourself, because this transparency of emotion makes your connections with others beautiful and wondrous, like seeing a rainbow on a rainy day. When we are unavailable to our partners emotionally, when we are divorced from the connection with them, harmony in the relationship becomes more and more difficult. A gray and insidious apathy creeps in, sapping the joy from life. Most of us would rather enjoy a relationship that energizes us and inspires us to greater and greater joy in life and to creating the things that are important to us. Try the simple practice of looking your partner in the eye when the two of you are speaking and you will be amazed at the connection this creates between the two of you. When your partner is talking, the simple act of looking at them without any goal, just looking, appreciating, and listening without interrupting begins the process of making you present to the relationship.

Connection and Fear

Connecting to yourself and to others with the eyes is the practice we often use in Soul Gazing to get in touch with our emotions. One emotion that often arises when we begin to connect deeply with the eyes is fear. You can learn to release fear by bringing deep awareness to the fact that you are fearful:

"I must not fear.
Fear is the mind-killer.
Fear is the little-death that brings total obliteration.
I will face my fear.
I will permit it to pass over me and through me.
And when it has gone past I will turn the inner eye to see its path.
Where the fear has gone there will be nothing.
Only I will remain."

Frank Herbert, *Dune*

The trick is to focus your emotional radar on feeling the fear itself, not on the thoughts in your mind that are creating the fear, or the other feelings that radiate out from the fear. When I am feeling afraid about something, I first take a deep breath to accept that I am feeling fearful. Then I ask myself what is causing the fear. Often my fear is about the unknown — the experience of totally not knowing what to expect. Then I shine a bright light on the fear and evaporate that fear with this light, just as a vampire is turned to dust by sunlight. When we shine the light of full awareness on our feelings, of being willing to feel them, breathe them, and understand them, they transform and release from our body. You can help this process along with movement and breath, using whatever form of movement you like, whether it is dance, yoga, tai chi, or some other movement. Staying present while moving is the key, cradling your inner child in safety as you acknowledge its fear and allowing those feelings to release from your body. Sing to yourself, tell yourself you will take care of everything. Just stay present as you would with a child who is crying, and rock them until they are soothed. Speak lovingly. Telling your inner child to stop crying usually only makes them cry harder, or forces them to hold in the fear and sadness until it explodes out of you.

Letting your inner child express themselves and keeping them safe will go a long way toward saying farewell to fear.

Emotional Armor

Peeling the onion is a metaphor for the progressive stages that healing moves through as you journey along the spiritual path. You remove a layer of armor that was protecting your inner child from the world and you from connection, only to discover another layer as time goes on. This is natural for most of us, and nothing to be dismayed about. Rather, it is a cause for celebration to know that you are ready to shed your skin again, like a snake, because it means you are growing. This is why the snake and the lizard are powerful symbols of transformation, because they shed their skins as they grow larger and more powerful.

Cultivating full awareness also helps you to know when you need help in healing the toxins stored in your soul. We cannot heal ourselves without the help of Spirit, and asking for help is important, but not possible unless we are fully aware of our emotional needs. Turning inward, peeling off layers of sadness and protection, has been so challenging for me. I will remove a layer of armor only to discover another deeper layer waiting under it. And yet I love this process, I love the way I feel when a layer is removed and I get a new sense of who I am in the world, a new openness in the heart, and lately, a new openness in my yoni. I am amazed at how far I have come, but also amazed at how the journey never really ends. I think that as long as I am embodied, this process will continue, that it is part of the human experience to be wounded and to gain enlightenment through healing from that wounding.

Emotional Needs

This practice of being fully aware of yourself can also start to unravel your needs in relationship. All of us have needs, and that is healthy. The desire for human connection, for example, is a healthy need. When we start to come into relationship, our needs often become confused, and bringing the focus back to ourselves is often helpful. Focusing in on our own needs first, and asking our partner which of those needs they can meet for us, brings us back into a strong and powerful relationship with ourselves. Our partners cannot always be everything to us, and there may even be times in the life of a partnership when our partners cannot support us in any way. It is up to us, in these situations, to get our needs met elsewhere, by taking care of ourselves, by connecting with our friends, and by connecting to Spirit. In this culture we have a tendency to become totally dependent on others to meet every need that we have. But it is best for our spiritual and emotional health if we first take care of the needs that we can on our own, with Spirit's help, and grow strong from this position of self-care. Once we have done this, then asking for connection and support from our partners and lovers comes next. This may sound like a trivial point, but it is important. We cannot come fully into connection if there is codependency or addiction living within that connection.

Numbing ourselves out and trying to fill the emptiness inside us with addictions to food, love, television, or other substances does not help us to meet our needs, and does not serve the person who wants to live the spiritually aware and awake life. In my experience, I cannot be aware of my feelings when I am under the influence of any substance, which means in that state I cannot share my emotional reality with my loved ones. When I am indulging in an addiction, I move into a world of fantasy, where I am no longer in touch with my true feelings and what is real. I struggle personally with relationship addiction, over and over going to a place where I want a relationship to fill an unhealthy need that I have in me, a need that comes from childhood. Whenever things start to get too stressful in my life, I want a relationship with a man to come along and fix it and help me not to feel the fear and anxiety. By being compassionate with myself and remembering to ask Spirit for help, I am learning to move beyond this place. Through my firm connection to Spirit, I have become more aware of my unhealthy patterns, and they have begun to heal. I have learned to sit in a place of longing for a man to complete me and to choose instead to focus on spending time with myself to tend to the emotions that are actually underneath that longing. Sometimes I ask a friend to support me as I move through these feelings. Abandoning life to give yourself over to any addiction is not healthy, and will stand in the way of your journey to discover a full connection to Spirit and to the people in your life. I am convinced that the only way to truly heal addiction is through the spiritual connection, because in many ways, addiction is a longing for Spirit to come into the body.

Addiction to the mind and the ego is another way that we often choose to avoid feeling. When we move into the analytical world of the mind, we escape temporarily from the feeling part of ourselves, and engage our capacity to go into a world of our own making. But this is not healthy either if it is engaged in habitually as an escape, because it still takes us out of connection with ourselves and with others. We are here on this Earth to experience it fully, not to dissociate from it. Living in a world of fantasy cannot take us to a place of growth. Our modern culture's obsession with TV, movies, and video and computer games, not to mention the Internet, lends normalcy to behavior that is really addictive. Watching TV or playing games on a computer or game box for too many hours a day can take you out of balance of what is healthy. If you begin to look at your behavior consciously, you may start to be aware that it is not the behavior you would like to have in your life. Hours in front of a computer or television, or overtime hours spent in a corporate workplace cutting yourself off from life are hours that could be spent in developing your spiritual life and healing yourself. This time spent will often bring you lasting joy that can't be found in a TV or computer or game. We learn to heal our need to numb out and avoid our feelings through Soul Gazing. There are several practices that allow us to gently and slowly enter the inner world of our shadow. One practice that shamans throughout time have used for deep emotional healing is the deep state of meditative awareness known as trance.

Healing through Trance

Trance is a state of being that takes us into an alternate reality where the ordinary rules of time and space and logic no longer apply. We can enter trance in a couple of ways, either going deeply into the sensuality of the body or leaving the body behind to go deeply into the secrets of the mind. The soul gazing gateway is focused on this deep going within, on opening the doorways within us that guard the passage to a freedom in ourselves that comes from acceptance of our physical body and acceptance of our mental and emotional selves. Through the practice of Soul Gazing you learn to become present to the mental and emotional self. Connecting to the mind and emotions deeply, you begin to see yourself more clearly, and to get a healthy sense of how to grow. If you call on the connection to Spirit that you created for yourself in the First Gateway, Connecting to Spirit, you can find strength to really look within yourself and become present to all the things that are getting in the way of your pursuit to lead a fully embodied life.

Through trance journey and dance work, we find full connection to our soul's center or purpose, which teaches us the exquisite awareness of ourselves needed for sacred sexual practice. We must understand our own magnificence and have compassion for all our failings as well. Only through awareness can we begin to heal, and only through healing can we come to full tantric connection. Anything in your emotional field that is unpleasant contracts you. If you are contracted you can never fully connect, because the connection and ultimately the merging that you will find in tantra comes from a full openness. You can only be open if you feel safe. So the work in soul gazing is to unlock the gates to our deep, dark, and denied selves. We open the gates to our underground vastness and go within to see what wants to be brought up into the light. Once we have done this work, we become freer and we begin to have a fuller connection to ourselves and to our partners.

Center and Purpose

Another piece of soul gazing practice for men is to explore their purpose. Unequivocally, there is a connection between a man's purpose and his penis. Almost any man who is not on his purpose and feeling lost and confused about that will become dysfunctional or uninterested in sex. This is because a man's purpose is vital to his ability to stay in the masculine polarity of connection and strength. A man without a purpose often feels emasculated without knowing why, and unfortunately he often blames his relationship for his lack of interest in sex. For men, Soul Gazing practices will give them an avenue to begin to discover their purpose, and if they already have a strong purpose, the practices will help them to refine and hone that purpose into a sharp sword of power. The sword Excalibur in tales of King Arthur symbolizes Arthur's dedication to his purpose of unifying the people and easing suffering through leadership. Upon Arthur's death, the sword returned to its resting place to await the next man who could grasp its great power and who wanted to align with that goal in his life. In his quest to be sexually whole, a man strives to find masculine polarity through finding his purpose. The more a man drops into his masculine power, the more certainty he has about what he wants to give to the world. When a man is certain and purposeful, he frees the women he connects with to be fully relaxed and receptive.

For women, the central Soul Gazing task is to unfold and open their center. This process is like allowing a flower bud to become a flower, magnificent in its beauty and fragrance. Dropping armor and boundaries and allowing a man to fully connect with us is the ultimate practice. When a man comes fully into our center, we experience a deep merging and connection, and the strength of his masculine power inspires us and wakes us up, bringing more and more of our shakti, or feminine power, to life. Men who are strongly on their path can serve as initiators for us, and if we are stuck and unable to find the fullness of our center, these men can be powerful allies in reminding us of who we are. I have become aware of my own center partly through my connections with men. Conversely, a woman can guide a man to his purpose by being open to receive and support the man whose purpose aligns with her center. A man's connection with a woman can bring him to clarity when he is lost, through finding that her receptive center and his purposeful energy seem to fit together.

The other piece for women in finding their power is to practice being still and going to the place within them where that power lives. Naturally connected to the Earth, and to Her rivers and oceans, women can begin simply by being in this connection as often as we can, through being in nature, gardening, walking on the beach, or sitting beneath a tree. When we go to these places of communion, and allow ourselves to go into a light trance state, we will begin to receive awareness about our own centers. We find wisdom within us about where our center lives in our bodies and in our lives.

My center is my spiritual path. Everything in my life radiates out from that. Every action I take is based on my desire for spiritual growth and connection to Spirit. Your center may be something else — creativity, emotional growth, a love of learning. When you find your center, you will know, because it is the place in you that everything radiates out from. It is the motivating force in your life. A woman's center is different from a man's purpose, because it's not something she must travel through the world in search of. She has only to look within. Look at your deepest longings, and they will lead you to your center.

In the practice of Soul Gazing and journeying through the caverns of our souls, we sometimes stumble across a ruby lying in the dust at our feet. If we pick it up and polish it, we may discover that it is a talent or bit of wisdom that we buried long ago to avoid something in our lives. Now is the time to bring this ruby out into life and to wear it proudly around our neck as a symbol of once again embracing that talent. In my own trance journey practice, these gems often merge with my body, symbolically becoming part of me again. Be on the lookout for these gems when you journey to the underworld of your own being. Perhaps you used to sing, but gave it up because your parents told you it was a waste of your time. Or perhaps you always wanted to be a painter, but got discouraged by trying to find time and money to create. Reclaiming these parts of yourself gives you a depth of soul that will support and strengthen you in life, and gives you many parts of yourself to embrace in times of difficulty. Wear these gems proudly and you fully embrace your richness and complexity, for all humans contain a world of thoughts and feelings and creation within themselves.

Journeying through your underworld caverns is the work of Soul Gazing. When you go through the Soul Gazing gateway, you travel deeply into your own shadow. On this journey you face your demons, and find the courage and strength to move through your life with awareness, feeling, and love.

• Chapter 8 •

Soul Gazing Solo

Snuggled into my temple space, I light four candles to mark my journey. East for the mind, South for sexuality/creativity, West for emotion/intuition, and North for the body. The candles mark a circle, and within their circumference I walk a spiral to the center, journeying to my deepest inner recesses as I walk the spiral pattern on the floor. The spiral I walk carries me to my own center, unlocking a gateway into my deepest soul self. Rabbit, my animal guide, leads me here, unafraid. This is his realm, and with him as my guide, I too, am not afraid. The darkness holds only safety for me, guides and teachers who want only to help and heal. Walking through underground caverns in this alternate reality, I discover symbols, like dream images, of wounds that are ready to heal, of emotions and patterns I am ready to let go of. The Soul Gazing Gateway was born of these journeys to myself. As I have traveled these paths within myself, I have received deep awareness of who I am, and have come to accept it. This acceptance of my deepest self allows me to heal, let go, and transform. I used to worry that I would never find all the things in me that needed healing, or that I was making things up when I traveled in these inner journeys. I have learned to let go of that worry and to accept that there are no accidents in the things that the mind imagines when I come into the trance state. Whenever I align with Spirit, whenever I allow that essence to fill me, I am always guided to images and experiences that speak deeply to me, and give me accurate guidance in how to move through the world. For the past few years, I have allowed this guidance to expand into my whole life, allowing Spirit to fill me as often as I am able to allow it. I have come to the understanding that my best decisions are based on the information I receive through this spiritual connection. As I follow this spiritual path to decision-making, more doorways of opportunity to explore the richness of life open for me. I have discovered such abundance within myself, and my life has begun to reflect this fullness. All I have ever wanted in my life was to find true happiness. I have begun to get glimpses of that joy, and I notice this blissful state is always connected with a willingness to also feel the emotions of grief, sadness, anger, and despair. We were created as humans to experience the full range of human emotion and to have a full range of human experiences. Soul gazing brings us to an awareness and acceptance of all these things within ourselves.

Looking in the Mirror

We begin with the mirror. I sit in front of the mirror and simply look at myself. I practice acceptance, I practice being totally okay with what I see there in front of me. I look at my face and my eyes and as I do so, I begin to have simple awareness of what my face looks like to others. In this practice, I am not trying to change anything that runs through my mind. I may have thoughts about myself that are not compassionate — I just notice them. I may have thoughts about myself that are egotistical — I just notice them. I may have thoughts of love for myself — I just notice. I just go on noticing and observing, and I do nothing else at this time. It is important to stay in awareness of my feelings, and I do this using the tools I already know, of staying connected to Spirit and of breathing deeply. These gateways help support me as I gaze. The connection to Spirit keeps me feeling safe. The breath keeps me present, and allows me to move any emotions through my body that threaten to become stuck. I breathe and I look. I gaze and I accept. I allow myself to feel. A simple exercise, but also very difficult. Most of us only look at ourselves in the mirror to shave or put on makeup or style our hair. Or perhaps we look in the mirror to find our flaws and fix them. But to look with simple acceptance of what is was new for me, and I found that when I began I could only do it for two or three minutes. More than that, and a wave of extreme discomfort would rise up in me and I would be forced to look away before my emotional self exploded. Be compassionate with yourself when you begin this exercise, and know that you may need to limit it at the beginning. Know also that with practice, not only does it become easier, but you become more deeply accepting of who you are.

Gazing into my own eyes in the mirror one day, I realized that there was a divine part of me living behind my eyes, the part of me that is the Goddess embodied. Feeling into this part of myself, which for me is sometimes Aphrodite, sometimes Kali, sometimes Inanna, I began to see that I embodied all Goddesses, not in the way of being proud and arrogant and all-powerful, but in the way of being beautiful and juicy and possessing mystery and openness. I began to see that I contained sexuality in me, and that my sexuality was waiting to come fully alive. This is one thing in myself that I had been hiding from for a long time. I didn't want to see my sexuality, because I was terrified of what would happen if others could also see it. Allowing myself to see this part of me helped me to accept it. In fact, as I learned to belly dance, I was forced to look at myself in the mirror for long periods of time, to perfect the movements of the dance. As I did this, my movements became more beautiful, and I began to see how I embodied the Goddess in my movement, in my body's form, in my face, my hair. I began to see all the beauty that was there within me, which was hard, because I had never considered myself to be beautiful or even pretty. I walked through life carrying so many negative thoughts about myself that I couldn't accept the possibility that I might be beautiful. With practice, I have become more aware and alive in my beauty and sexuality. I have learned to love my body, to adorn it, and to let the love within my heart radiate out. This is how we become truly spiritual beings having a bodily experience — we come into contact with our divinity, and we live that divinity in ourselves every day.

Once I was able to see the Goddess in me, my heart began to open, I began the practice of sending love to myself in the mirror, just as I always imagined the Goddess did. Only this was love from me, to me. Love that I knew was real, because I could feel it in me. I often practice saying "I love you" to my reflection. This can be hard at first, because so much negative self-talk can come up. When I love myself, my heart opens more than it does to love from any other source. I believe this comes from a deep trust in myself, a knowing that the love I give to myself can never be taken away. Struggling with abandonment fears since childhood, I have had so many experiences of love being removed from my life unexpectedly, by death, relocation, or just differing needs. This experience created a wound in me that as an adult was very hard to heal, because my sense of emotional safety was compromised. To feel safe, I try to cling to those I love, and that clinging becomes a suffocating neediness. To heal this deep longing for connection, which feels like a burning aching emptiness inside me, I spend time with myself, loving myself in any healthy way I can think of. I perhaps bathe myself in hot water, or paint my toes, or watch a movie that inspires me. I take myself out in nature, and I create a garden and a home that nurture me. Many of these are feminine ways to self-love. For men the path to self-love is slightly different. For men eating well, attending daily to personal hygiene, dressing to please yourself, and getting daily exercise are all ways to take care of yourself and bring yourself to health. So when you look into the mirror, hold love in your heart, and send that love to yourself. Let yourself feel it and breathe it in as you see the loving face in the mirror breathe it right back to you. You are the one person who will always be there for yourself.

Exploring the Shadow

Once you have worked with the mirror to remove labels, see your divinity, and love yourself, you are ready to explore the darker side of your own reflection. Sometimes the things that rise up in this practice are so powerful that I need the support of a professional healer, and when that happens I embrace the need and schedule the time for my healing, knowing that this is another way of getting healthy and healing the shadow within myself. The more of my shadow that I heal, the less I need to spend emotional energy holding it down and keeping it locked behind iron gates. This energy can then be used for so many other things in my life, and I find that I need less sleep and am more creative and loving. More importantly, I feel happy and joyous so much more of the time, and my connections in lovemaking become more ecstatic and profoundly deep.

Practice 1: Mirror Gazing

Gazing in the mirror is a challenging and growth-filled practice. There are several exercises to try. Notice which of these are challenging and which are nurturing for you. As you work this gateway, try to do 5 minutes of mirror work each day and journal about what comes up for you. You can stand or sit in front of a large mirror, or procure a hand mirror that you reserve especially for your practice.

Connect to Spirit with the Sacred Tree Meditation while engaging the Circular Breath before beginning each exercise.

A. Acceptance

Look at your face in the mirror as if you are seeing it for the first time. Instead of picking out all the flaws, gaze at your face gently. Look at yourself as if you were an object in nature, and drink in your beauty. Accept yourself for who you are.

B. Unnaming

This is a practice adapted from the book ***Witch Crafting*** by Phyllis Curott (Broadway, 2002). Do the practice of removing all labels from your face. You no longer have names for your eyebrows or nose or mouth. Look at yourself with a sense of wonder, as if you are a little child, and say to yourself "there is a beautiful curving moist thing" that may describe your lips. Go deeply into looking at your own eyes, and look as if you have never seen eyes before. Imagine you are an artist, taking in each detail so that you can recreate it on canvas. Removing labels from yourself opens you to new possibilities of joy and freedom, and new ideas about who you are.

C. Sending Love

Look at your reflection and practice repeating "I Love You" to your reflection in the mirror. As you say this to yourself, let yourself receive the love. Notice what comes up for you as you do this practice. This is a powerful way to learn to love yourself.

D. Shadow Gazing

Now as you gaze in the mirror, let all that is deep within you come to the surface. Let all the unacceptable thoughts, feelings, and images just roll to the surface of your eyes and face. Stop holding back anything that wants to surface now in you. Keep your connection to Spirit as you do this, letting it keep you safe so you can truly spiral into your darkest center, and know that as you do this, you are shining a powerful light of awareness into it. Shine that light, open the gate, and let everything flow to the surface where it can be seen, accepted, healed, released, or whatever is appropriate. Allow yourself some resting time after doing this exercise, and plan to do some act of healthy self-love afterward, such as time with your journal or a hot bath or shower to fully process the emotions. Often doing this exercise for 5 minutes will stimulate days of deep contemplation for me. I allow that contemplation to weave in with my normal life, going about my life with the awareness that this is alive in me. Journaling about it or talking about it with a trusted friend is often a real support.

E. Gazing for Guidance

Once you have explored your deepest, darkest feelings about yourself, and cleared out the painful and dark emotions you have been holding within, you may wish to try using the mirror to get in touch with your intuition. Clearing out negative emotions creates space for messages from Spirit to come into your awareness. Following this guidance can help you to make decisions that truly serve you and help you to grow.

This time, when you look into the mirror, allow Spirit to guide you to whatever messages it has to share with you. Gaze at your eyes, and let them be the windows to a deep place of wisdom within you that knows all things. Let your mind open as you go deep inside yourself to an inner sanctuary. Let your eyes defocus so that the image in the mirror begins to shift in front of you, and any images that Spirit wishes to send you for guidance begin to flow in. You may see a shift in the image of your face to an animal or another human face. You may hear a voice in your head speaking to you, you may see images of life, of events and places yet to come, or of times past. Just allow yourself to receive the vision of whatever is coming through, and receive it with gratitude. When you bring this practice to a close, be sure to consciously reconnect to your roots and branches and to come fully back into ordinary reality through moving and breathing, and perhaps also through eating. You may wish to write down your experience soon after doing this practice, to anchor the images in your awareness. This is one of the deepest practices of soul gazing, to gaze in the mirror for guidance about your life. This is a practice similar to gazing into a crystal ball, a type of divination, but it is also a practice that connects you to your own reservoir of inner wisdom.

F. Seeing the Divine

Look within the mirror to see that you are the God or Goddess incarnate in flesh. Call the divine into you and see yourself transform in the mirror. See the magnificence in yourself. See as you look in the mirror, that somehow the awe-inspiring beauty of the Goddess is moving through you, and see that beauty manifest in the mirror, know that you are the Goddess right here in this mirror, right now.

Soul Retrieval

Trance journey is another deep practice of Soul Gazing that works without the mirror and travels into the shadow. One type of trance journey, called soul retrieval, has been done by shamans throughout time to heal the wounded soul. Deep in the shamanic underworld lie pieces of human souls fragmented by the pressures of lives without any room or understanding for a healthy expression of our true selves. Our sexuality is often the first to go. Forced by parents and society to split ourselves apart, often at an early age, we ache for the pieces of our sexuality to be mended with the rest of us, but have no skills or knowledge of how to call them home to ourselves. Learning to journey shamanically to the underworld allows us to explore with our guides the places where the soul fragments live, and to restore those fragments to ourselves. We empower ourselves as our own shaman by recovering these puzzle pieces and fitting them back together to make ourselves whole and strong. This journey is taken with the help of the animal guide you received in the Trance Journey to Find your Guide in Chapter 2. The journey uses shamanic drumming music in the background or some other repetitive soothing music to quiet the mind and take you to a deep place of mental quiet. The role of your guide is simply to keep you safe and lead you to a place where the lost fragments of yourself are located. Your guide will help you by showing you some process for recovering these parts of yourself, and for incorporating them back into your body. It is good to rest and take good care of yourself after a soul retrieval, as it can bring up a lot of emotions to your awareness. Soul retrieval is a gentle but powerful healing practice.

Practice 2: Soul Retrieval

This journey is geared toward helping to retrieve the parts of you that may have been lost through sexual shaming or guilt.

Put on some drumming or other repetitive and calming music. Lie down on the floor and make yourself comfortable with pillows and blankets. Put your roots in the Earth and your branches in the sky, and begin to breathe deeply. For many it is best to be guided on this type of journey. We invite you to go to www.sixgateways.com to download our audio recording of this trance journey.

Follow your breath into your innermost self, and let your awareness flow down into your genitals. Imagine yourself becoming very small, small enough to look at your own genitals and to see them as an amazing landscape. Call your animal guide to come and be with you as you go on this journey, and ask them to lead you to any parts of yourself that need integration. Your guide enters your yoni or lingam and beckons you to follow. You step into your own inner landscape and see that it is like a great tunnel leading to a cavern within you. You follow your guide through this landscape, noticing the amazing features of you as you journey, letting your guide lead you to a place within where lost parts of you live.

Ask these parts of you to tell you why they fragmented, and then ask if they are ready to reintegrate. Ask your guide for help in showing you how to take these parts back into yourself. Take a few moments to experience this integration and notice how it feels. Now let your guide lead you out of this landscape, and thank them for their help. Allow your awareness to expand back into your entire body and come fully awake and aware and present. Take your time returning to ordinary consciousness, and be sure to rest, eat, and care for yourself after what may have been an intense experience. I find that recording the experience in a journal further helps me to reintegrate these lost soul parts.

Moving with the Shadow

Now that we have talked about a number of practices that involve a deep stillness, it is time to look at some practices that involve moving the body. Once we have learned to cultivate a deep inner awareness, combining that with movement becomes extremely powerful for our healing. Focusing deeply on moving my body in completely unfamiliar ways while looking into the mirror, belly dance was my first experience of deep concentration in the body that yielded powerful emotional releases. I had worked enough with chakras (see the Fourth Gateway: Waking the Dragon) in my spiritual training to know that the new movements I was practicing were somehow opening and unblocking these energy centers in my body, but the key to what was happening was the deep concentration on my body. In particular, I remember trying to learn to slide my ribs side to side over my hips. It was so hard! I had never before moved my body in this way, and it felt extremely odd. And yet as I persisted, deep tension in my belly began to release, and laughter began to pour out of me. At the time, I needed that laughter more than anything for my healing. This deep movement of the belly dance became my lifeline to joy and sanity, and I began to rise early every morning just so I could practice. I still continue this practice in the mornings when I can, even though I am a night owl who really dislikes mornings and wants to sleep in. I rise, I meditate, and I dance. When I do this I open the gates to my emotions, good and bad, and they pour out of me as I rest in my connection to Spirit.

Gazing into the mirror as I move, I see my reflection telling me that I am a work of art, an embodiment of the Goddess, an image of grace. I didn't always feel this way! In the beginning I would look in the mirror and see every fault of my body, of my movement, and I hated it! I hated looking at myself because I didn't love myself. So for a time I stopped looking in the mirror and I just focused on dancing and being in my body, developing a love for myself out of the sheer joy of movement. Gradually I began to shift. Every once in a while I would work in the mirror to prepare for a performance and I would occasionally catch a glimpse of myself when I felt loving about what I saw. This was phenomenal! All of a sudden I began to see myself differently. Sometimes I really saw myself as a beautiful Goddess. I invite you to gaze at your full reflection with love while you dance or move. Put on some music that inspires you and gaze into your own eyes as you feel into your body. Watch yourself move when you are fully present versus when you are thinking about a million different things, and notice the difference. There is a difference. When you bring yourself into a meditative connection with Spirit, breathe love into your heart, and then gaze at yourself in the mirror. Notice the shift that comes in the ways that you see yourself.

This shift of perception in how we see ourselves opens us up to true healing guided by Spirit. Another way to play with shifting perception through movement is a practice called Shadow Dancing. This practice lets you open to a fascination with the purity of your movement. You come into contact with the symbolic representation of your shadow self, that part of you that can only be seen when a light is shining on it. In this practice, allow yourself to go even deeper into what is buried in you. Dance and move as you give yourself over to experiencing your depths. To set up for this, use a photographer's lamp and a wall. Put yourself between the light and the wall so that you can see your shadow dancing on the wall. Now dance with it, like Peter Pan. Remember how important it is to have your shadow. Remember how sad Peter was when he lost his shadow, and rejoice in the richness that the shadow brings to your being. Know that any and all of the buried feelings and qualities of your character that are contained in the shadow can be brought up for feeling and transmuting just by this dance you are doing with yourself. You may or may not have conscious awareness of what it is that is shifting or healing in you, but that is really okay in my experience. It is the intention of having the healing take place that creates the change in you. As you dance unafraid, the shadow will come forth for a rebirth into the light.

Patterning Your Life

In my search for rebirth, I travel to places in nature that speak to me. Sitting in the desert, I find my home. I go again into my inner depths. I listen to the sound of Raven's wings as they beat the air above me. I feel the sun begin to warm the air. I sit on a large boulder that casts a shadow just large enough to hold me and my assortment of animal totem rocks. In the desert, I realize, shadow means coolness and life, a nurturing and healing place. Arrayed around me in a circle, my totem rocks symbolically define my center. Each totem is a part of me. The rocks symbolize the animals that are my spiritual guides. To go to my center, I first connect to Mother Earth. Connecting my roots to her is a lifeline, especially when I am lonely or needy and am tempted to grab on to someone to help fill my needs. A woman who is truly on her center stays there and does not waver in the face of anything. Like the Buddha, she sits, and the world comes to her. In this beautiful place, she pulls in everything she needs. When I let myself be pulled off this center by the daily demands of life, I feel tired, drained, and irritable, not to mention needy and lonely. But as soon as I remember to breathe into my connection with the Earth, I come back to my center and to what is most important to me. From this place I create miracles, and only the things that are in my best and highest good come into my life. Soul Gazing work helps us to find this center within us, and to stay there. My center is to be in my home space and to express my truest spiritual nature through creating and healing, to share my love with the world through my spiritual work. When I am off my center, I give away time I would have spent being spiritual and creative, I get distracted by other people from doing the things that matter to me. When I am in balance, I pay attention to my inner priorities, and I balance time with lovers and friends with time for being in touch with myself. Knowing where my center lies helps me to stay in a place of happiness and passion about my life. On my center, I feel whole, loving, and accepting of myself and others. On my center, I come easily into the place of full integration of my sexual and loving self with my mind, emotions, and body.

Practice 3: Finding Center (for Women)

Knowing where your center is helps whenever you are feeling overwhelmed, or trying to make a life decision. Do this practice to get clarity about what center is for you.

Take some markers or crayons and paper and have them ready nearby. Now go into the Sacred Tree Meditation and begin the Circular Breath. Let your awareness flow into what gives you pleasure in life. As you start to get a sense of what this is for you, grab your paper and art supplies and start writing or drawing these things. Let your mind go, and let it flow. Notice if there is a pattern, a center that connects all of these things for you. Some centers women often find that connect the pleasures in their lives are art, beauty, spirituality, family, nature, or love. Notice what your own center is, and go back into meditation, seeing if you can feel that within your body. Make a list of ways that you can honor your center and stay closer to it.

For men, the journey is not about center, but rather about purpose. The divine masculine energy tends to crave experience, movement, and doing and being out in the world. This is what feeds the spiritually evolved man. A man on his purpose is like the hawk. As the hawk flies through the air, his eye is fixed on the ground below, single-minded in its search for nourishment in the form of a rat, mouse, or rabbit. As the hawk is fixed on this single task, so the man who seeks his masculine power is intently focused on his purpose and on the path toward that purpose. To connect with this purpose the practice is twofold: First to connect to Father Sky, second to follow that connection's guidance to the path that calls him. My tantric partner likes to suggest to men that they write their own eulogy as a way of really tapping into what it is they want to accomplish in their lifetime. This is a powerful and profound practice that often leads to a lot of awareness about what is or is not working in a man's life path.

Practice 4: Finding Your Purpose (for Men)

This exercise helps men to get a stronger sense of their purpose and path in life.

To do this, get out a piece of paper and pen, or just your computer. Begin by dropping into the Sacred Tree Meditation and then engaging the Circular Breath.

Think about your life and your desire to know your purpose, that thing that Spirit has called you to do. Think of three strong and powerful words that describe this purpose, then set a timer and write like mad for 5 minutes. Use these three words in your writing. When the time is up, stop yourself and read what you have written. Somewhere in this writing will be keys to unlock the secret of your purpose in life. When you find this path, and follow it, you will find more satisfaction and more joy in your life, than on any other path you could take. Once you have done the mirror and trance work of facing your darkness, it will be much easier to see into what this purpose is. It should also be easier to find within yourself the willingness to let Spirit lead you there.

On your center or purpose, life becomes clear and decisions become easy. Finding this center or purpose is the ultimate reward of the Soul Gazing practices. These practices are probably the most challenging of all the gateways, because they access so much within us that can be painful and difficult. For many years, before coming to these practices, I lived with a large reservoir of fear and anger inside me. This reservoir affected everything I did, and warped my reactions to life and to the people in it. I was an unhappy person, with no ability to let go of that unhappiness. I went to therapy, and found that to be a wonderful support as I began to open these doors, but it was not enough to heal my wounds. I needed the connection to Spirit to truly change my way of being in the world, and to see that I could choose to be happy, to let go of my burdens, and to heal my wounds. In this journey, I became discouraged many times, and there were many times that I doubted that I would ever find any kind of peace. Today I still struggle, but it is a different kind of struggle, more clearly one within myself. I used to think that life was the thing that was making me unhappy, but I have come to see that I am the only one who decides whether or not I am happy or unhappy, that other people have no power over my emotions — that is my realm alone. I can choose whether or not to accept other people's ideas about me. I can choose whether or not to be upset by other people's actions. I can choose how I respond to the inevitable changes that life brings. I can be happy if I choose, and I can allow myself to feel my feelings. I can find a deep happiness that comes from truly living in my emotions, befriending them, but remembering that there is more to life than just the emotional world. I can sink into the pleasure of my body, the fire of creating, the enlivenment of the mind. We all have choices about how we engage the world and how we relate to ourselves. Moving through the depths of me, I emerge whole, and healed, and deeply myself.

• Chapter 9 •

Soul Gazing Together

Loving me with his eyes, my partner holds me in his gaze and we breathe together. In me I feel the rise and swell of ocean tides, of primeval forests and of a primal growl/purr of the cougar that lives within me. I center into my power and my femininity as he gently looks into me and my soul begins to open. At first I jump into the joy of it, of being fully seen, of being so loved that a man will gaze at my face with awe and arousal. But the longer we gaze at each other, the more I unlock the gates within me, the closer I get to the place of fear, where the denied and rejected part of myself lives. I begin to feel my ugly and unacceptable inner shadow self becoming visible to my lover, and it isn't a part I want to reveal. What is sexy about this? My inner voice screams in fear and wants to run, to hide, to trance out, to fill the mind with thoughts, to do anything but stay present to this ugly stepsister inside who is dirty and bitter and haggard and pregnant with rage and grief. And still I hold his gaze. I let him look into me, I let him see the fear, and I begin to cry. He still holds my gaze as I emote, as I feel all of my feelings, not just the blissful ones. I stay with it, breathing, knowing that acceptance of this part of me will let me be free, and will teach me to open even more to love, to sex, to joy, and to bliss. He holds me as I sob, as I scream, as I growl, as I try to run. He brings me back over and over to myself.

On a bed topped with starry lights hung over a red silky fabric canopy, I lie with my partner. With him inside me, but not moving at all, I breathe into my yoni and feel the passion and purpose of his lingam surge into me. I exhale and feel all my love and radiance for him flow out through my heart and my hands, wherever they are touching him. We stay with our breathing and then pause to drink water, staying connected at the lingam and yoni. As we breathe and pulse our PC muscles, the energy begins to move and I snap into gazing at him. I see the love and rapture in his eyes, and I open my own gaze to let him flow into me. I feel the bliss of this connection, of this practice, and my heart sings with joy.

True love is not about wishing for something in our partnership that is not already there. You can never create love in this way. True love is a full unconditional acceptance of the truth of the relationship that you are in, and still loving, still holding that person dear. Dropping out of denial is the first step. To stop telling yourself you have the perfect relationship because that is what you wish for. To stop telling yourself that you have all the love you need when you don't, to stop seeing the potential in your partner or in the relationship instead of the reality of what is there. True love, accepting our partner for who they are, begins with gratitude for what is present in the relationship. Look carefully and you will find the things that mean so much to you, that keep you in the relationship. Come into the beauty of what the relationship is, the full truth, the full depth of who your partner is. Let yourself see them clearly. You may even wish to make a list of the things you are grateful for about your partner and the things you accept about your partner. And then notice what you don't accept. Notice how it is an obstacle to going deeper, to loving fully. A woman cannot open to her partner if she is always disappointed in him. A man cannot dive fully into his partner's ocean of love if he is always hoping she will be different. Dropping into full love and trust of each other, letting go of the obstacles of denial and expectation will bring you into a much deeper and more loving connection, or it will show you that the relationship is no longer in your best and highest good.

Practice 1: Non-acceptance and Gratitude

Take out a pen and paper. Use the Sacred Tree Meditation and the Circular Breath to bring yourself into connection with Spirit.

Now start writing a list of the 10 things you have the most trouble accepting about your partner. These might be character traits, behaviors, or even needs they don't meet for you. Focus on the 10 things that trouble you the most. Once you have your list, take a deep breath and feel all the feelings you have about this list. Really feel, and then imagine what it would be like to accept these things without wanting to fix or change them. Often these are things that we don't like in ourselves, so learning to accept these things can be a self-love exercise as well.

Now take up the pen again and make a list of 20 things you are grateful for about your partner. Notice whether it is easy or difficult, and notice if you can feel an opening in your heart as you think of the things you are grateful for. When your list is complete, breathe it into your heart, and notice if it helps to accept your partner further. Realize how much you have to thank them for.

Connecting with Awareness

As in solo practice, staying aware of your fear is a critical part of deepening your connection with your partner. Gazing into each other's eyes and seeing what arrives in your awareness is the beginning. When you are ready, you may move into partnered practice, making love with very little movement while holding the gaze with each other, staying in gentleness in the lovemaking at first, men holding a gentle and strong presence for women to open. If your partner doesn't practice with you, you can still do the practice of looking into his eyes and at his face as you are making love, to stay connected. If the man can stay present for the woman's fear to be unveiled, it will make it easier for her to observe it and trust that she can be safe. This can be hard — hard for the man to keep his eyes open, and hard for the woman to trust enough to let her feelings flow. For most women, there are layers and layers of fear, whether from past abuse or from old attitudes of guilt and shame. Magically, the more trust a woman is able to put in her partner, the more these layers of fear can dissolve. Men also move through fear, but more often around sexual performance. A woman can hold space for this by continuing to receive the man no matter where his arousal state flows, allowing him to remain in union with her whether he is erect or not, whether he is aroused or not, whether he ejaculates or not. Releasing all demands on the man to pleasure her allows him to find his path in the union and to be more present for her.

Practice 2: Eye Gazing

Eye gazing connects us to a much fuller awareness of the emotions we have for our partner, and creates connection through vulnerability. Here are some practices to try with each other. Notice if these are challenging, and give yourselves breaks by just closing the eyes if you need to. Try exercises A-C for 3-5 minutes to begin, allowing more time for exercise D.

A. Simple Eye Gazing

Connect to each other using the Partnered Sacred Tree Meditation and begin Partnered Circular Breath. Now breathe together and gaze at each other with total acceptance. Look at your partner's eyes as if they were flowers, and notice the beauty in each part of them. Women, soften your eyes and receive the energy of your partner's gaze. Men, softly penetrate the woman's eyes with your energy, connecting deeply to her soul. Notice how you feel while doing this practice.

B. Body Gazing

Connect to each other using the Partnered Sacred Tree Meditation and begin Partnered Circular Breath. Now try gazing at each other's bodies with the same acceptance as you did in practice A. You may do this exercise with clothing on or off. Notice how you feel. Is it easy or hard to receive your partner's gaze on your whole body? Is it easy or hard to look at them with total acceptance?

C. Holding Space

From this practice of simply gazing in the eyes and at the body, we move to a practice of allowing emotion to flow between us. In relationship women need to release emotion to stay in their feminine, and the masculine can assist them by "holding space" for this release. This exercise can be challenging so wait until you are both feeling emotionally strong before doing it. Sitting together, touching or not, while eye gazing, the woman breathes into her belly, feels into her emotions and allows these emotions to rise up into her eyes. The woman then shares these emotions with words, using "I" statements and focusing on how she feels. The man reciprocates by listening, by touching compassionately, perhaps even by hugging the woman to help her release her emotions. His role is not to fix anything he hears, just to listen. He sends all the charge she gives him down into the Earth through his roots, letting the emotions pass through him and not holding on to any of them. When we add eye contact to this practice, we get to learn about staying present when our partners are off center. We learn a new way to support them by becoming a firm foundation. A woman can learn to do this same practice in the face of a man's anger or grief, staying calm and present as he releases or speaks about his feelings. This is a way to give love to our partner that asks nothing of us other than our simple listening ear and receptive eyes. Holding our partner with our eyes and loving them, we feel our connection in whatever space we are in. And we support each other by being simply loving.

D. Eye Gazing in Lovemaking

Now combine Simple Eye Gazing with the Heart Circuit and with Stillness Together in lovemaking to add another layer of connection that is powerful and

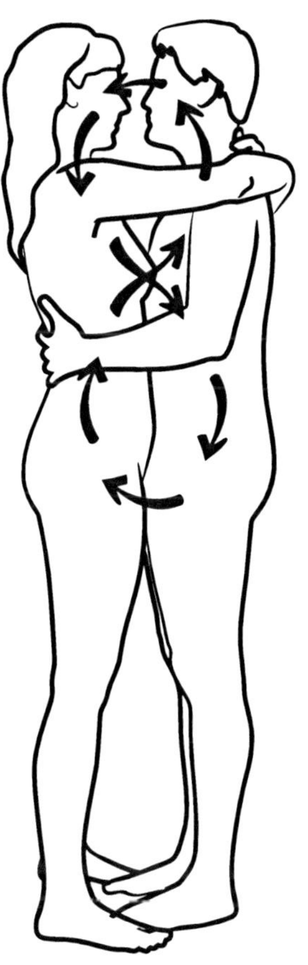

present. Connect at the heart, breathing each other in, and use your breath to imagine you are moving energy from lingam to yoni and from woman's heart to man's heart, to establish energy flow from the heart to the genitals. Now add the gaze to bring the soul into full and powerful focus. Adding the eyes brings a stronger connection and awareness of your partner. With this connection and awareness, notice what lies underneath your connection. Holding the eye gaze while breathing through the heart is a difficult task, and in the beginning we allow ourselves to close our eyes if we need to. Women can imagine that they are receiving their man energetically through both their eyes and yoni on the inhale and pulling this all to the heart and sending it out from their heart on the exhale. Men can imagine that they are sending their loving sexual power out both their lingam and eyes on the exhale and pulling love in from the heart on the inhale. See if you can hold your gaze through orgasm, and notice the powerful emotion that washes through you. Through this practice we begin to heal the split between the masculine and the feminine, the split that comes from a man's natural focus on his lingam and sexual connection, and a woman's natural focus on her heart and on loving communication.

Acceptance and Unconditional Love

Because the role of the man in our culture is so often to seek out and pursue the woman, his wounds often revolve around acceptance and being received. The greatest gift a woman can give a man is to fully receive him, both in her emotions and in her yoni. Receiving him in everyday life, accepting what his purpose in life is without judgment, accepting how much money he makes, how he dresses, how he creates, these are all essential when you come into soul gazing. A beautiful practice is for the woman to tell the man that she accepts him as he tells her everything that he wants acceptance about in their relationship and in his life. Even more powerful is for the woman to practice receiving the man in lovemaking, no matter what he is doing, to allow him to guide and orchestrate the lovemaking connection as if it were a dance, to let herself flow and accept and joyfully receive whatever it is that he initiates. If this isn't possible, then to compassionately and kindly ask for something different is the next best thing, to ask without judgment about where the man is leading her. To say, "I would love this, would you be willing to do that with me?" And if he says yes, to say thank you warmly and sincerely. Notice that in this situation, the woman does not comment on what he was doing when she made the request. It is vital that there be no judgment when the request is made.

Another marvelous tool for making requests and talking about feelings in a relationship is Nonviolent Communication (NVC) (see Bibliography and Resources). This tool focuses on defusing intensely emotional discussions by creating and sharing a strong awareness of the needs underlying our emotions of upset and anger when they arise. When we communicate our needs, the result is phenomenal, especially if our partner is able to reflect back to us what they heard us say. We feel heard, and we get in touch with what the need is that is causing our distress. Then we learn to ask our partner for something to help us meet that need. It is a hard process to dive this deep into your emotions, and I know for me in the beginning I struggled to name my emotions in every discussion with my partner, because I was so out of touch with myself that I couldn't name more than two or three basic emotions that existed in me. And yet through careful communication with my partners, I discovered that there was a whole range of positive and negative emotions within me. This was really big news for me. I had no idea that I had that many choices of what to say about my feelings. I was amazed at the clarity that came into being as I shared my deepest needs and what I needed as support.

Compassionate communication is of paramount importance as you start to dive into sharing difficult feelings. It is so important to be clear when you communicate, to share your own feelings and to not blame or judge the other person no matter how strongly you might think they are responsible for your feelings. Another person cannot make you feel anything — you are in charge of creating your reactions to what other people do. We can see the truth of this by realizing that no two people react in exactly the same way to a given situation.

Becoming more compassionate, accepting, and loving leads us to embody the divine masculine and feminine energy in our daily lives. Part of embodying the divine in partnership is learning unconditional love. The gratitude and eye gazing exercises in this chapter pave the way for this. Unconditional love is a practice of radical acceptance of another human being, of loving them no matter what they do. Through the years I have struggled with one of my lovers in particular, wanting him to change certain behaviors, wanting to accept him the way he is, feeling extremely stuck in wanting and hoping for a shift. This is a beautiful chance for me to grow, to learn to love him no matter what he chooses to do. This is an opportunity for me to practice keeping my heart open. The open heart is the basis of sacred sexuality, and it is not a selective open heart, it is a love that encompasses all of our beloved. So with this lover of mine I struggle to learn to love him no matter what he does, no matter who he chooses to be. I bring the challenging parts of who he is into my heart. I breathe love into it and I ask Spirit to help me to accept and love him anyway. I ask Spirit to guide him to his own healing. I have so much gratitude for this lesson, because I know that as I learn to accept him and to allow him to be who he is, I am giving myself the priceless gift of a loving heart, and I am giving him total acceptance. The more we judge another person, the more we nag and criticize them, the more they feel badly about themselves. When we can totally accept another, they can take that acceptance into themselves and turn it into support for growing into their full potential. And this is how unconditional love heals.

Practice 3: Secret Telling

This is an exercise for men to practice sharing, and women to practice acceptance. It is written for men to share their secrets with women, but it is useful to try having the women share secrets too.

Begin by doing the Partnered Sacred Tree Meditation and then do the Partnered Circular Breath for a few moments.

Now sit with your partner and communicate with her. Whisper in her ear and tell her your secrets. Begin with something easy — you really did have time to fix the doorknob but didn't want to, you feel afraid that you aren't good enough at your job, you worry about money. But then move into the deeper side of all those things you have been hiding — you look at other women, you want sex more often than you ask her for it, you have a secret fantasy...let it all hang out and let her listen and accept that yes, this is who you are. Men, focus on yourself. Use "I" statements and keep the secrets about you. Do not say, "I secretly wish that you would lose 10 pounds." Instead you might say, "Sometimes I am not as attracted to you as I was when we first met and this scares me." She will sit with you and listen. Ladies, this is your chance to show how much you love your man. Listen to him, just listen. No fixing, no judging, not even any commenting. Listen and listen and then listen more. The more you listen, the more your man will share with you, because the more you listen without judging, the safer he feels.

Acceptance is something that we all crave, to belong, to be loved. When a woman sits with a man and allows him to communicate everything that is clouding his soul, she becomes a goddess of kindness and mercy, and she teaches him to give that mercy to himself.

Making Love with Spirit

Fully in the moment with one of my lovers, I dropped in so deeply in our first connection that each time he touched me, my entire body dropped into waves of ecstatic kundalini energy. I felt so fully seen, so loved, and so cherished that I dropped into full surrender to the moment. I felt like a priestess being worshipped by one of her followers in reverent awe. Holding my eyes with his, he penetrated me with his gaze, and sent so much love through that look that I reeled back in joyful surprise and opened, wanting more. More and more love began to penetrate me in waves, and I began to feel all of my body open to his, allowing anything and everything that he wanted. I became a vessel for his love, an ocean of pleasure, a sea of desire. The waves whipped higher and higher in my inner sea, until my desire surged through me so strongly that I thought I would burst. Carrying me into the bedroom, he finally entered me, and my yoni opened wide to receive him, then grasped him tight, milking the love and presence from his lingam, surging love into his heart, which seemed to open wide. Becoming more and more aroused, my nails scratched his back, and he roared out loud, penetrating me even more deeply. My inner gates opened to him, my cervix blooming, the inner lotus ready to receive all that he was, feeling nothing but oceans of love and desire. In this connection I learned the power of full openness, that there was a place in my body that is accessible when there are no old obstacles in the way of a connection between two people who have intention to honor and be present with each other. In this openness, I become the Goddess making love with the God, and my personal identity seems to melt away. I merged with Spirit completely. Over and over again, I have experienced this merging when I am willing to open.

In a tiny tent in the desert, candles flicker and the heater hisses propane into the flame that warms our naked bodies. My braids hang down the sides of my face as I lean over my lover from a straddle position. I feel naked, and sensual and powerful, and I begin to feel the energy of the land enter into my body. More than that, I feel the presence of the Goddess rise up into me, the Goddess of the people who once lived and loved and died on this land. I feel this in me and embody it, open to it, fully call in the presence of the Goddess as I make love, and looking down at my partner, I see his eyes widen in astonishment, and he says to me, "Your face is the face of an Indian princess, a goddess!" I am shocked that he sees what is alive in me, what I haven't spoken of or hinted at, only felt within me, and I feel Her rush into me even more, as She rides him, enjoying the sensuality of my body, as I enjoy the energy of Her presence in me. This is the sacred rite of the Goddess or God in lovemaking, to call this energy into you so that there is no separation between the God or Goddess and you.

In shamanic tantra, the woman receives the man and magnetizes her power to pull him in. Before she learns to do this in her yoni, she first learns to do it with her eyes. To start with, she softens her eyes as she and her lover look at each other. For many women, this practice is difficult, bringing up fear around being so vulnerable to his passion and purpose. I often feel a fear of being lanced by a sharpness that I feel in the masculine, and have had to learn to trust and drop into the receptive state, knowing that the man will not cut me with his eyes. This sense of safety we have talked about before, but it is the heart of tantra for women, to feel safe, to feel loved, to feel connected. If a man uses his penetrating gaze to try to get some response from a woman, to try to penetrate her with his energy before she is ready, his efforts will only lead to her withdrawing and shutting down. The man must learn to approach the woman gently at first, and to gradually allow his gaze to become more intense as she is able to open to him. A woman, on the other hand, must be willing to trust the man, to know that he will not hurt her, that his intention is clean. Of course this first means that we only practice eye gazing and tantra with men who we know are trustworthy, and who have a commitment to embody the balanced masculine for us.

Practice 4: Making Love to the Divine

In this exercise, you practice seeing the divine in your partner.

Begin by doing the Partnered Sacred Tree Meditation and then begin the Partnered Circular Breath Gaze at your partner, while making love or otherwise, and see the God or Goddess in them. Imagine, if need be, that you can see the essence of the god or goddess moving into them through their head or pelvis. Also allow yourself to feel the divine enter you. Open your eyes to all the things about your partner that are amazing and magickal. Keep your eyes engaged as much as possible, resting them and breathing in your own divine essence when you need to take a break. Remember to end this practice with Reconnecting to Self.

If you open to this way of seeing your partner, you can begin to mystically heal conflict in relationship. When I do this practice, I see all that is best and most wonderful in my partner, and I send forth all that is best in me. I become the Goddess for him and allow him to become the God for me.

As we learn to be fully present, as we get to know our inner demons and decide to let some of them go, as we discover the magick of gazing into our partner's eyes, we begin to realize there is so much more to discover with our partner. Be gentle with yourself, and slowly devote yourself to this dropping in, to making each time of making love like the first time, as if you have never touched each other or been together before. Cultivate a sense of deep connection with each other, and be willing to be deeply present to what is between you, whether or not it is pleasant. Allowing this authenticity and vulnerability with others, we grow, and we come to know ourselves more deeply. We come to know the depths of our soul, both good and bad, and from this we open to change, which is, after all, the most inevitable part of life. As we learn to be in relationship in a new way, in a moment-to-moment connection, many of the old rules and restrictions drop away. There can be so much fear as this begins to happen, and we won't do it perfectly at first. It is the steady and resolute practice that brings us to an expanded place in relationship, a commitment to change, to surrender, and to flow with the will of Spirit for each relationship that we are a part of. Learning that clinging to structure and rules for relationship comes mostly from fear, we invent a new way to relate, a way that moves through the heart and the genitals, integrating all of who we are, as we move closer to ecstatic union with Spirit.

✦ The Fourth Gateway ✦

Waking the Dragon

• Chapter 10 •

Opening the Body

Blindfolded, I try to focus on my breathing as loud, pounding music fills my ears. I move and try not to bump into the myriad bodies that I know are around me. With my blindfold on, I put on an intention to come deeply into my body. The music seems to go on forever, and I move through waves of fear, pain, nausea, and weakness. I have been told to keep moving, even if I only sway and breathe to the music, so I keep on moving. I move through numbness, I move through ignorance, I move through fear, I even move through feeling ridiculous. I keep dancing. I dance even though I have been ill and my body and lungs are weak. I dance with trust that Spirit will guide me. I feel the black jaguar spirit merge with mine, the totem of my sexuality, and we dance to stalk the prey of a passionate life together. We purr, growl, stretch, and flex our claws. I keep moving, and the music keeps pounding. I worry I will bump into the person next to me, or that I will do too much and faint and be trampled. I put my trust in the facilitators and I keep moving. I hear a rattle come through the space near me, and my body feels it clearing the air around me. I keep moving. Finally the music comes to an end, and I lie down on the floor and I fly. I leave my body, which has been thoroughly worked, and I cruise into a land of pure Spirit, where my guides welcome me.

Before I began to dance, I had a sense that there was a problem in my body, that I needed more exercise, more movement. I knew that I was often tense and had panic attacks. I had begun therapy, but still didn't have much awareness of myself or what was alive in my body. And then dance awakened me. My panic and anxiety lessened. Moving in my belly dance class and practicing at home, I became aware of my chakras as physical entities in my body. I felt the dance movement work them and begin to release things I had held in my body for a very long time. I went out on a date with someone new and felt all my chakras come alive and stay activated just from one kiss. I was clearly on to something, so I continued to study the dance, becoming passionate about it. I wanted to learn, and I wanted my body to get better at moving. But little did I know how much the dance would wake up the parts of me that were numb. There were parts of my body that had little to no awareness living in them. Through the dance, my body slowly began to awaken.

The chakras I have been speaking of are energy centers in the body that are recognized by many spiritual cultures around the world. They have been most notably and specifically defined by the Hindu religion, which identifies seven major chakras. Each chakra is associated with a color and an archetype for me (see Table of the Chakras, p. 138). Each of these places in the body stores emotion about different parts of our life. For example, the throat chakra is connected to how we express ourselves, both through communication and in our creative endeavors. Waking up each chakra lets the body come alive fully and be vibrant and balanced. Awareness of the chakras also lets us know what areas of our life may need work. Trouble with our stomach, for example, might relate to feelings of powerlessness or inadequacy, since the stomach chakra is the energetic seat of empowerment in the body.

When we repress our emotions, when we choose not express ourselves, we instead store these feelings in the body. As we store emotion in this way, we tend to keep it in the part of the body that is associated with the upset. So sexual shame, guilt, and trauma are often stored in the genitals, and very often this storage results in a numbness or lack of feeling in the lingam and yoni and in the lower abdomen. Trauma around our sense of our identity and power in the world becomes a fear of being ourselves, and is often stored in the stomach. I call this numbness or tightness armor, because it is there to protect us. The problem is that once we no longer need protection, the armor isn't that easy to remove. Dance movement and breath are powerful tools for taking off armor, and for arousing full sensation in the body. Once the body becomes fully open, sexual energy naturally begins to flow through the entire body. Having done the work of learning to Connect to Spirit to feel safe, Breathing Love to become present, and Soul Gazing to face our inner demons, we become ready to make changes in our body awareness, to fully embrace the beauty of life.

I had an extreme example of what can result from repressing emotion when I was a young woman. I thought that I had an incurable disease. I was nauseous all the time and had no appetite. I dropped mass until I weighed only 95 pounds, at which point I went to the doctor to see if she could figure out what was wrong with me. I remember that we

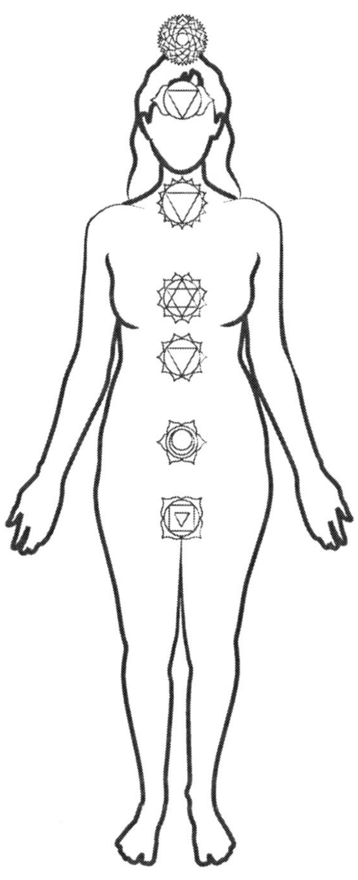

did a number of blood tests and an exam, and in the end she came back to me and asked if my life was stressful. I told her that everything was fine. To this day I get a good laugh from how unaware I was, and how I had no experience of a body without fear and anxiety deeply rooted in it. This is a great example of how, when these emotions are locked in the body long enough, we begin to sink into an array of physical and mental ailments. I wish I could tell you that I learned to let go of my fear overnight, but the truth is that I went through a slow and gradual healing process. My process of healing has been most profoundly accelerated by dance movement and yoga, because these practices help me to release emotions from my body.

Releasing emotion is important, because the body cannot come fully alive when it is covered with the armor of emotions long past. When old resentments and wounds are in the way of our feelings in the present, we

Table of the Chakras

Each chakra can be associated with colors, archetypes, oils, and elements. Many of the correspondences in this table are taken from Anodea Judith's "Wheels of Life" (Llewellyn, 1999); others are from my own experience and practice.

Chakra	Color	Stone	Element
Root	Red	Garnet	Earth
Belly	Orange	Carnelian	Water
Stomach	Yellow	Citrine	Fire
Heart	Green	Adventurine	Air
Throat	Blue	Turquoise	Sound
Third Eye	Violet	Amethyst	Light
Crown	White	Clear Quartz	Ether

cannot experience what is right in front of us. Holding on to these old feelings is easy, because they are stored in our body's memory. We have made a long-standing habit of keeping them. Letting go of old feelings is harder, and takes a gentle and compassionate approach to healing. Beginning with massage is one way to soften in the body so that we can remove armor and more fully connect to ourselves and our partners. Think of it this way: If you are wearing a suit of metal armor, you cannot feel the touch of your lover's hand on your skin, because there is something

Chakra	Quality	Archetype	Deity
Root	Vitality	Earth Mother	Changing Woman
Belly	Desire	Lover	Sedna
Stomach	Power	Hero, Father Sky	Great Star Man
Heart	Love	Healer	Coyote
Throat	Communication	Artist, Oracle	Grandmother Spider
Third Eye	Vision	Seer	Bright Star Woman
Crown	Connection	Sacred Fool, Sage	Raven

in the way. It is like this with old emotions. Old baggage creates a layer of calcification over our muscles and prevents us from fully experiencing things. It is the work of shamanic tantra to develop full awareness of the body, to feel into where the body is blocked, and then to release those blocks by moving and breathing and emoting and connecting.

Dancing is a passion for some, a chore for others, but it is the act of moving your body that is essential. For women I recommend and teach belly dance because it keeps us at our center and moves through all of the seven chakras to awaken and stimulate them. For men, the equivalent practice seems to be tai chi, qigong or some other martial art form that emphasizes presence and breath in the action of the body. Developing deep body awareness, shedding old beliefs about how we look or our ability to move in ways that are graceful and magickal, is all key to finding a positive body image.

In the mornings now I rise to meditate, and on most of those days I move before meditating. I love the way this anchors me in my body for the day and helps me to let go of any emotional residue not dissipated by sleep. As we journey on any spiritual path, we strive for clarity, and clarity is only possible if we remove all the excess thoughts and feelings that get in our way, like dirt on a window. As we clean the window of our inner selves, we can see in and out of our dwelling place. Each day I move at least for a few minutes, and I have learned to breathe with the movement to create a beautiful meditative state within me. For me, sacred sexuality is anchored in the body, even though it embraces the emotional, mental, and sexual/creative parts of who we are. By moving my body, I seem to create cleaner and cleaner windows in my soul, and the clarity increases. I also find that my health is improved, that my immune system is stronger, I need less sleep, and I am full of energy and aliveness.

Moving my body in belly dance has opened me, and I have seen the women in my classes find an openness too, a joy in the dance that is passionate and sacred for them. I began with simple movements, and I continue to use these simple movements in my daily practice, even when learning complex choreography and challenging dance steps. As I learned the belly dance, I discovered that each chakra had a movement that would awaken it if I moved with total presence and stayed in my breath. As I moved through the chakras with this method, I found that old emotions began to release from my body. I became more free, more open, and full of life force. I bean to feel better about myself, and surprisingly, I began to feel more sexual. It took me a while to make this final connection between sexuality and movement, because I wasn't ready to embrace that part of myself. I was afraid that allowing myself as a woman to dance in a way that was sexual and sensual would confuse the public, who would associate my dance with stripping or exotic dance. All of this worry came from my own sexual shame and guilt. Finally I realized that belly dance is a movement form that is inherently sensual. I cannot remove the sexuality from this movement any more than I can remove the flow from water. The two are one. So as I moved away from my shame and guilt and began to experiment more freely, I found a gold mine of sensual and sexual experience present in the dance. And slowly I began to realize that teaching this dance really should encompass the art of sacred sex. I saw that the dance itself was a solo tantric practice of moving the sexual energy up and down the spine.

To cultivate awareness of the body, we focus in. We learn to breathe in ways that bring us into mindfulness of our muscles and bones and internal organs. We learn to stay in the mindfulness for extended periods of time, first in our solo practice, and then with a partner. If you never give a second thought to your body, if you do not care deeply for it, it will eventually fail you, like a car that is thousands of miles past its needed maintenance. The body must be cared for not only in eating well and exercising, but also in nurturing through touch. We really underestimate how important touch is in this culture, hugging timidly, handshaking only briefly. Many of us miss out on the beauty of prolonged hugs, and how good they can feel. Cultivate awareness of how it feels when someone touches you, of how your clothing feels against your skin, of how it feels to move. Live in a deep awareness of your body, whatever it is doing. If you are making love, pay attention. If you are washing the dishes, feel the soapy water on your hands. If you are wearing a fur coat, feel the luxurious softness on your skin. When you hug your lover, really take a moment to feel their body pressing up against you, and just notice what is present in that contact.

Tools for Opening

Lying on the massage table on my belly, I hear soft music playing and smell incense burning. My lover massages my back, my shoulders, and my arms. As he massages my hand I feel an immense sense of relief, and I begin to cry great big gasping sobs. Something stored in my body magickally releases, and I feel lighter. Dropping into this timeless space of nurturing with him again and again, I feel transformed and gifted with a profound awareness of how wounded my body really is. Before receiving massage, I didn't realize how wonderful it would feel. Being touched lovingly and sweetly, receiving someone's full attention and touch, taught me to fully inhabit my body, which became a huge gift as I was learning to belly dance at the same time. Together, dance and massage have taught me about the sensuality and pleasure that is available to the body.

The other phenomenal tool for awakening my body has been yoga. I found there were some parts of my body that were still resisting full awareness in my belly dance practice and I felt stuck, but I couldn't seem to make myself add yoga class to my already busy schedule. That all changed when I became pregnant and began to deal with debilitating nausea, anxiety, and depression. Spirit gave me a push by sending me a yoga tape for pregnancy through a friend. That tape became my lifeline to a happier life. I began to work with the tape almost every morning, and I found that it helped with all of my symptoms. The effects of doing the tape lasted for a few hours. Where belly dance seems to grind up the chunks of dark black emotion that are stored in my body, yoga seems to gently and lovingly smooth out the energy of the whole body and bring me into a sweet place of open serenity. Sitting in this tranquility, I open, and I feel the divine flow into me. My body feels good, and I am in a deep contentment. Yoga is not about getting yourself into the most twisted position possible, rather it is about finding the edge of your ability to stretch or to balance, and learning to surrender to the emotions and bodily sensations that arise as you breathe and center.

Chakras and Kundalini

Nwyvre (literally "Dragon Fire") is a Druidic word for the sexual/creative/spiritual energy that runs through the body, also known as kundalini, or chi. To safely awaken the fire of the dragon, we begin to cultivate deep body awareness through movement, breath, and meditative practice. There are many warnings in older textbooks about the dangers of awakening the kundalini if a student is not properly prepared, tales of mysterious illnesses and madness. In my experience, the kundalini only has these effects when it is forced through the chakras before they are ready to open. The safest and quickest way of waking it up is to do a gentle daily spiritual practice that includes breath and movement. You may also find that a really good way to awaken nwyvre is through self-pleasuring with deep full breath, strong body awareness, and intention to move energy through the body. Whatever you do, let it be a gradual and gentle process, without forcing or goals. Come to your practice each time with openness and awareness that the energy may not move where you want it to, but knowing that if you are fully aware and connected to Spirit, it will move in some perfect direction.

Fully open and balanced chakras also create a much better sexual experience because each chakra is a place where we are able to give and receive sexual energy. We can experience ecstatic releases of energy that feel like orgasms in any of the chakras, and each chakra has a different feeling to it in this ecstatic state...a stomach chakra orgasm exploding from the solar plexus feels much different from a clitoral orgasm or a belly chakra (g-spot or prostate) orgasm. Orgasms in the third eye bring us to an intense spiritual state of mental clarity and wisdom, while orgasms in the g-spot seem to fill up my cup of desire and release any negative emotions of fear or need I have been holding onto. As part of lovemaking, with ourselves or with our partners, we can massage the chakras to bring awareness and energy to them. We can also kiss, lick, scratch, or tickle each chakra. We can blow on them with our breath. The more the chakras open, and the more we allow our sexual energy to flow through them, the more we are likely to have the ecstatic experience of the energy moving up and down the spine with an orgasm, or our merging with our partner and with all of creation, which is one experience available to us as we journey along the tantric path.

Once we begin to have awareness of our own bodies, we can check in to see how our chakras are operating in our relationships. Usually a relationship has parts where it works well, and parts where it is more challenging. For example, if you struggle with your communication, then there may be some problems in the throat chakra for one or both of you, and some healing that could be done there. One way to approach this healing would be with Reiki. Another would be learning nonviolent communication (NVC) (see Bibliography and Resources) and practicing it with each other to see if the throat chakra connection can be shifted. Or perhaps in your relationship you struggle with wanting to be right all the time and have your partner do things your way. This indicates trouble in the stomach chakra, and you could approach healing here also through Reiki, or through learning to let go of feeling powerful by dominating others. This looking at chakras to improve your relationship is an approach that requires tiny steps to shift the situation. Gaining an awareness of where you are not connecting is the first and most important step. For me, just having awareness of where the disconnect is helps me to let go of attaching a lot of significance to the challenges that are arising in the relationship. And the motivation for me is just this: to experience a full connection of all my chakras lining up with my partner's so that we can connect. This is truly tantric bliss and ecstasy.

Journeying through the chakras is the Fourth Gateway to Sacred

Sexuality, and opens wide the door to our body and a deep awareness of what it can do. This is possible because the first three gateways have opened us up to feeling our safety in spiritual connection, our presence in each breath, and our inner world of emotion. We begin chakra work with the solo practice so that we can first awaken our own body before working to connect with the sacred body of another.

• Chapter 11 •

Waking the Dragon Solo

Healing and awakening the chakras has been a slow and gentle process for me, up until the past few years. I spent many years sitting on my meditation pillow, waiting for instant healing and enlightenment to strike. I went to yoga class, read spiritual literature, chanted, did ritual, danced, and received healing work. All this prepared me for meeting a powerful shaman, whose work with me blasted through years of sexual shame and guilt. Suddenly I was catapulted onto the path of being a woman in her full power. The dragon power within me came alive, as if my body were remembering its true identity and purpose. Sexual power and vitality began to run through me constantly, becoming part of my being. It was a reintegration for me, an awakening to the rightness of uniting my sexual, creative, and spiritual selves. I was becoming the dragon power I was named for — fiery, powerful, and wise. As I began to work with the sexual energy inside me, I discovered a deep body wisdom and knowing about how to awaken the sexual fire in others. Setting a strong intention for myself to heal and surrendering to this healing was what made my powerful shift possible. This intention and surrender is critical on the tantric path, as we learn to sharpen and focus our minds into the ability to master the energies within us and to flow with divine energies that we awaken in our bodies.

To awaken the dragon fire for sexual healing, we begin with meditation, breath work, and movement. Combining heart-centered healing with intentional and ecstatic movement, we come into a place of rapture. In this blissfully present state we clear the chakras of their blockages. Once you dedicate yourself to these tools, the more sexual practice of moving energy while self-pleasuring becomes easy. Because the body has learned to move energy in meditation, breath, and movement meditation, it is able to do the same when you add sexual arousal to your practice. You learn to stay present in the face of sexual desire. So often, as soon as we get aroused, we lose our connection to Spirit because we fall back into old habits. When working the sexual modality, we learn to make a clear intention to work it as a spiritual practice, to breathe, and to center, and stay on that center as we pleasure ourselves, letting go of old habits of striving for orgasm. We learn to let Spirit lead us to whatever experience we need.

There are many simple practices to get you started on your way to awakening sexual energy. You can begin clearing negative energies from each chakra with a cleansing ritual to start your daily practice. Not only do these rituals clear your energy body, they alert your subconscious that you are shifting into sacred space, and make it easier for you to settle in to a deeply present state. Each day we take on energies from the world around us. One ritual to remove those energies that are not a part of us is bathing the aura with sacred smoke. This helps prepare the energy body for circuiting sexual energy. You can buy sage for smudging and an abalone shell to burn it in at your local metaphysical shop or on the Internet. Place the dried sage in the abalone shell and light it, then blow out the flame so it smokes. Pass it over your body, lingering anyplace where you intuitively sense something that needs to be dissipated. You can also smudge each chakra individually, pausing to really make sure that all the extra energies have been cleared. Smudge your entire living space if you want to clean up the energy field around you. If you are allergic to or dislike smoke, you can use a small bowl of water with a few pinches of salt to clear, anointing each chakra with the mixture.

Another soothing and delightful way to clear your energy field is to slip into the tub for a soak. Amplifying the healing and cleansing effects of this is sea salt, which also helps to clear the aura. If there is a particular chakra that you want to stimulate or soothe, put 5-7 drops of that essential oil in your tub (see the Table in Chapter 10). You can also add the essential oil to your favorite unscented oil or lotion to get a yummy after-bath concoction. Generally you need about 20 drops of essential oil for a 100 ml container of lotion or oil. I keep a selection of oils near my bathtub, and when I am in need of some soothing and cleansing, I take this bath and emerge feeling extremely refreshed and renewed, like the old legends of Goddesses bathing in their sacred pools.

Practice 1: Chakra Meditation

This meditation is a great daily check-in exercise to see where your sexual energy is flowing freely and where it might be blocked and want some extra attention.

Go into meditation using the Sacred Tree Meditation to connect to Spirit.

Begin the Circular Breath.

Now take your awareness to your root chakra, located in the perineum (the space between your yoni or lingam and the anus). Breathe into this part of your body by using your practice of moving energy with the breath. Notice if you can feel this part of your body. Now imagine that you can see a whirling disk of red light there, and notice if this light is too bright or too dark. Use your power of visualization to adjust the intensity of the light.

- Breathe your energy into your belly chakra just below your navel and tune into and adjust its whirling orange light.
- Breathe your energy into your stomach chakra, just below the ribs, at the solar plexus, and adjust its yellow light.
- Breathe your energy into your heart chakra, in the center of your chest, and adjust its green light.
- Breathe your energy into your throat chakra, in the hollow of your throat, and adjust its blue light.
- Breathe your energy into your third eye, in the center of your forehead, and adjust its violet light.
- Breathe your energy into your crown chakra, in the top of your head, and adjust its white light.

Notice how you feel when this meditation is complete, in particular if your sexual energy is moving more freely.

Journeying into worlds where symbology reminds us of the things that move through our lives is a powerful shamanic healing experience. Profound healing occurs when we let go of knowing how it will happen in any rational design. Putting our trust in our guides and in our intuition, we move into a world where the irrational is real and where anything can happen. You can use meditation time to look at each chakra to see what is needed for healing and happiness. With each chakra, let yourself notice the color, the texture, any symbolic objects, and any lessons your guides give you to learn. You may also choose to work with only one chakra per meditation session, especially if you are aware of deep healing that is needed in that area. Spiral into yourself with this practice and allow the healing journey to begin.

Another deep healing technique for the chakras is to bring breath to each chakra center as part of your meditation or movement work. In this work you imagine that each chakra has lungs, and let it expand and contract as you breathe. You feel into each chakra deeply and notice any physical tightness or other sensations like tingling or heat. Notice also whether the muscles are tight or loose in this area. This is a process not only of clearing the chakras, but of bringing awareness of the body connected to each one, so that when you come into partner practice you will be able to fully open and connect these energetic points in your body.

Practice 2: Dragon Breath

This exercise combines chakra visualization with breath, using powerful circular breathing to open up the chakras and allow energy to move freely through them. Never force this breath. If you notice a block that is not moving, just accept that as reality for now, and keep doing this exercise to move the energy each day, perhaps adding the Chakra Movement practice.

Begin with the Sacred Tree Meditation to help you connect to Spirit, and the Circular Breath to bring you into the present moment. Now imagine that you have lungs in your root chakra, and breathe into it, see your root chakra grow and expand as you inhale. Exhale powerfully from your root, imagining it releasing and relaxing and clearing out blocks. Remember to be gentle and not force the release. Continue to breathe in and out from the root as long as it feels right, 6 complete breaths is a good place to start. Now on the next inhale breathe up from your roots through your root chakra and into the belly chakra, and then breathe out back down and out through your roots. Imagine that you are breathing nurturing loving energy up into your belly chakra and allow this energy to clear out any blocks on the exhale sending them to compost through your roots. Continue this process, moving up through each chakra in succession. When you reach the crown chakra, you will be breathing up from your roots all the way up to your crown, and back down. This breath helps to open the central channel for the dragon fire, or kundalini, to move up and down the spine. Stay with each chakra until you feel complete. If you are unsure, then practice 6 full breath cycles for each chakra.

Come out of this practice gently, taking your time and noticing how you feel Notice what you feel both in your body and in your mind.

Moving the body feeds the soul and opens a whole new world of healing that many of us may never have explored. Learning to connect movement to spirituality unlocks new levels of relaxation and peace in the body. Learning to stay present and aware as we move helps us stay present and aware as we move through all of life. What if you could learn to come into a way of moving that would bring you totally present to yourself and to each muscle and sinew that you are moving? This is what chakra movement does. Once you learn to breathe into the chakras, you add a layer of movement over the breath to deepen your awareness of the energy centers in your body. Through this practice you discover an entirely new and different world that is waiting within you.

Patting your head and rubbing your tummy is hard at the same time, but not impossible to do, and once you get the hang of it you feel quite a sense of accomplishment. It is the same with breathing and moving at the same time. At first it just feels like too much to concentrate on all at once. But the practice becomes beautiful and powerful as you get the hang of it, and you go deeper and deeper into presence. There is a place of presence where you become exquisitely aware of your body in the movement, where each inhale is connected to a contracted muscle, and each exhale is connected to a relaxed muscle. Eventually you find a place where you do not move your body at all unless you are breathing. I first learned this practice as a dancer learning to perfect my performance on stage. I learned that the more energy and presence I brought to my performance, the more entranced my audience was with my performance, and the more connected I felt to my dance. This presence and deep body awareness is something that all the great dancers know how to create in their bodies, and it leads to a deep sensuality. Mikhail Baryshnikov is a powerful example of this presence. He can fill an entire auditorium with his presence in the dance, even when he is only dancing to his own heartbeat. This being in the moment is something that dancers and tantrics both know, that movement defines the moment.

Practice 3: Chakra Movement

This is a powerful practice, and one that I often do as a daily meditation to get my sexual energy moving through my body.

Begin by connecting your roots and branches to the earth and sky, as in the Sacred Tree Meditation, but this time standing instead of sitting. Begin the Circular Breath, and keep the breath flowing with each movement. Do each movement in succession, beginning with the root chakra.

1. Root Chakra — Rock the pelvis forward as you inhale, squeezing your PC

muscle (the one you use to stop the flow of urine) and your buttocks. Rock the pelvis back as you exhale, relaxing your PC and buttocks. Keep the movement and breath flowing for 10 repetitions (or more).

2. Belly Chakra — Move your hips in a circle as if you were spinning a hula hoop around your waist. Exhale as your hips move to the back of the circle, and inhale as they move to the front. Keep the breath and movement flowing together for 10 circles (or more).

3. Stomach Chakra — Now glide your ribs in a circle just like you did with your hips, feeling the muscles in your upper stomach contract at the back of the circle as you exhale, and relax at the front of the circle as you inhale. Do this for 10 circles (or more).

4. Heart Chakra — Take your arms out to the sides and stretch them back behind you, squeezing your shoulder blades together and inhaling and expanding the chest. Now bring your arms forward in front of you and contract your chest, exhaling strongly. Repeat at least 10 times and keep the breath flowing.

5. Throat Chakra — Move your chin forward and back in a birdlike motion. Exhale as your chin moves back, and feel the squeeze in your throat muscles. Exhale as you go forward and feel the release. Repeat at least 10 times and keep the breath flowing.

6. Third Eye — Roll your head around, dropping the chin at the front as you exhale, trying to touch your ear to your shoulder at the sides, and lifting the chin and inhaling as the circle goes to the back. Notice how this movement opens awareness in the center of your forehead. Make at least 10 circles, being gentle with your neck and keeping the breath flowing.

7. Crown — Gently spin yourself, breathing in through the top of your head and exhaling down through your entire body into your feet. If it is hard to spin 10 times all in one direction, try spinning 3 times in one direction, stop, and change direction. Notice how your crown feels when you spin. Keep the breath flowing.

Ground after this exercise by jumping up and then landing with a forceful exhale. Sit in meditation for a few moments to close, and notice how your body feels. Once you get the hang of these movements, try using them to consciously move sexual energy through the body.

Deeper Chakra Practices

Once you have developed a strong awareness of the chakras and worked a bit at moving energy through them, you can start to move sex-

ual energy through the body in an even more conscious way. You have practiced a bit circuiting energy up and down the body, as well as breathing into each of the chakras.

You have learned that you can bring the sexual energy all the way up and send it all the way back down any time you want, to open your energy channels and to feel sexual energy in your whole body. This is a prelude to partnered sacred sex, where you learn to move sexual energy not only through your own body, but to circuit energy with your partner. Once you have laid this foundation, you are ready to move into the practice of self-pleasuring rituals. These rituals allow you to tune into your sexual energy in a whole new way. They allow you to practice moving sexual energy while aroused, without worry or distraction from your partner. They teach you a way of being that you can later bring into your sexual connection.

Practice 4: Self-Pleasuring Rituals for Women and Men

Ritual for Women

This self-pleasuring ritual is designed to let you explore moving sexual energy through your whole body by combining breathing and meditation with sexual arousal. It is a deepening of the Breast Awakening exercise in Chapter 5.

Create a beautiful and sacred environment for yourself. You may wish to bathe, light candles, and burn incense. Place a few of your sacred objects on the bed, to remind you that this is sacred time with yourself. Also have some oil, lube, and lotion on hand for massaging your body and your yoni.

Connect your roots to the earth and branches to the sky. Begin the circular breath. Next lightly circle your hands on your breasts to awaken your shakti. Notice how this begins to awaken your yoni, and continue to breathe and imagine you are moving energy down to your yoni from your breasts and back up. As you are ready, begin to touch and massage the outer lips of your yoni, taking your time to drink in all the sensations. When you are ready, move into massaging the insides of your yoni, using either your hands or a sex toy.

Now as you become more aroused, stay focused on your breathing, and start to imagine moving your sexual arousal all the way up to the top of your head as you inhale and squeeze your PC muscle. Then flow your energy all the way back down to your root and yoni as you exhale and relax the PC. Let the energy flow where it will. Notice that this is powerful with or without an orgasm.

Ritual for Men

Like the women's ritual this exercise is designed to teach you to move sexual arousal through your whole body. It will also help with ejaculatory mastery as you learn to drop into a meditative aroused state and let go of the need to climax.

Have some oil or lube on hand for arousing the lingam, and create sacred space for yourself by smudging or lighting candles, if that appeals to you.

Connect to Spirit with your roots and branches, as in the Sacred Tree Meditation and then begin the Circular Breath. Now begin to stroke your lingam with a slow and gentle touch. As you become aroused, begin to breathe that arousal up from your lingam into your belly, then up to the stomach, then the heart, throat, third eye, and crown. When you inhale, squeeze your PC muscle. Imagine that your inhale pulls sexual energy all the way up to the top of your head. Now when you exhale, imagine sending the arousal out through your penis and down through your legs and feet. Continue breathing and imagining in this way as you gently massage and stroke your lingam.

Do your best to stay out of fantasy, present only to what is alive in your body. Let go of the need for orgasm, and bring yourself up to the edge of ejaculation and then back down to less arousal at least three times. At this point, you may wish to climax. When we get into an expanded sexual state, ejaculation may be more challenging. Try not to go into old patterns to force an ejaculation, simply stay in the moment without any goals. Stay present to the feeling of your touch and continue to breathe the energy through your whole body. Let the ejaculation happen naturally. As you begin to ejaculate imagine shooting your energy out the top of your head.

Notice if you feel tingling or shivering in your body during this practice, or heat. These are all signs of the sexual energy moving through you. Over time you may find you are able to do more cycles of arousal and that you are having orgasms during some of these cycles without ejaculating. After a while you might try this practice without ejaculation and notice how different you feel afterward. Men give up a lot of sexual energy when they ejaculate and choosing when you want to give up this energy is a powerful part of the practice.

As we are ready to go deeper into our chakras and our sexual energy we can do work with the archetypes for each of the chakras, through calling them into our meditation or movement or self-pleasuring time.

We call them in and invite them to move energy with us, or we call them into our bodies and ask for their assistance in our healing. Sitting with the Healer archetype in my heart, for example, can be a powerful opening. I allow my heart to expand in my mind's eye until it is large enough to hold a divine healing energy. I feel joy that this support is there with me. I let this energy flow through me from my roots and let it flow back into the Earth as it desires. Learning to let go of control, to surrender to how these divine energies move through me, to trust that they have only love for me and that I am safe has become an important part of my practice. Allowing the Goddess or God to flow into my body's field requires an act of faith and trust, but the benefits of connection and ecstasy are their own reward.

You can also do a deep nurturing practice with your chakras by doing energy healing on your own body. To do this practice, you simply rest your hands on the part of the body you want to heal, while staying connected to Spirit and breathing. In this practice, you let yourself feel deeply and notice how the energies are flowing in each chakra. Notice if you can feel healing energy flowing from your hands. There is really no difference between healing energy and sexual energy in the body. By doing the practices in this chapter and learning to move sexual energy, you are also learning to move healing energy. You may feel tingling or heat in the parts of your body that you are giving healing to. Just allow yourself to receive the healing, even though it is coming from your own hands. I myself have had some very powerful healings this way, especially at times when I have been lying in bed feeling ill. Sending loving healing energy with your hands is phenomenal to do on your own body, because you can reach each chakra without much effort. If you do this practice when you are ill, it can often shift you into a deep sleep that allows the body to heal while it rests.

Working with color is another playful and effective way to support the healing of the chakras. We amplify a chakra's vibration when we wear the color associated with it or surround ourselves with that color. I wear yellow if I am having a day when I don't feel empowered, orange when I am struggling with my emotions, purple when I want to feel spiritual, red if I need more vitality. Often a shift in my chakra balance is reflected by a choice of color in my environment. Many years ago everything in my house was green and purple, heart and third eye chakra colors, because

I needed more love and spirituality in my life. Today I surround myself with red, orange, and yellow to awaken the root, sexual, and power chakras. I have acquired a "Rainbow" wardrobe of clothing and jewelry over the years, so that on any given morning I can find something to wear that represents the chakra I want to send focused love and care to. Eventually perhaps I will wear white, the color that contains all of the colors in the rainbow, and which speaks to me of hope, healing, and beauty.

The journey to awaken my body through attention to my chakras has been challenging, rewarding, healing, and enlivening. It has opened me to a whole new world of experience that lives within me. Whether moving deeply in a meditative state, or pleasuring myself and breathing the energies through me, at their heart these practices are about feeling good in my body. On the sacred sexual path, we do not shy away from the difficulty of removing our armor and releasing our hard emotions, but we also embrace fully our pleasure and joy in life. As spiritual beings having a human experience, we allow ourselves to have that experience. On the sacred sexual path, the body is spiritual. Sex is spiritual. Joy is spiritual. Tantric shamans seek enlightenment through the body, through connection to nature, through connections to others, through experiencing all that is. And on this path, we come to realize that everything is sacred, most especially our bodies, no matter what shape or size or color we are. We become ready, after treading the path of awakening our own dragon fire, to combine our fire with that of another.

• Chapter 12 •

Waking the Dragon Together

Making love, I open, and I feel a new ease beginning in me, an ecstasy born of a day of pampering, relaxing, and being with my beloved. As my lover and I come together for the third time, I begin to feel the kundalini pulse up my spine and out my chakras, exploding like little orgasms at each center of energy. The pleasure of it grows until I am swept away and I lose all sense of space and time. There is nothing else in the world except this moment and this lovemaking and this ravishment by fiery joy. I tell myself to open, open, open, and we come more and more into connection. I feel my lover fall deeper into my energy, and I breathe him in, take him in, allow his energy to flood my body and my soul. Suddenly there is an explosion in my stomach that feels like an orgasm, a blasting through of tension that has been stuck there for days, and I fall back breathless. He doesn't stop, he stays merged in my energy, swimming in me like a dolphin, diving in and out of my inner ocean until I am so ecstatic that every bit of me reaches a place of ecstasy where a river of light travels up my spine and explodes in my head. I ejaculate and also climax in my yoni, my g-spot, my sacred center. I pull the orgasm from him and he dives in completely, not holding back, screaming in joy and freedom and pleasure.

Waking the chakras together is the next level of ecstasy for lovers who have learned how to connect, be present, and share emotion together. If you learn not only to have an awareness of your own chakra centers, but to also merge with those of your lover, you can reach new heights of ecstasy together. The first step is to learn to become aware of your partner's chakras, sensing into them with your touch. You take turns with this, with one person being the sensor and the other lying quietly on a bed or other comfortable surface, then changing places. This is a practice where you learn to really feel in, and let the first impression in your hands or your mind tell you the state of the chakras. You can also sense into skin texture and temperature at each chakra, as this often tells you if a chakra is under- or over-stimulated. Heat in any part of the body usually indicates a lot of energy focused there, as it is in healing a wound. With the chakras, heat usually indicates the strong presence of the sexual. Anywhere on the body that is extremely cold is probably less open and not running as much sexual energy. In this exercise, you need not do or say anything, just notice the state of the chakras.

Practice 1: Partnered Chakra Meditation

This exercise teaches you a heightened awareness of your energy centers as you begin to connect with another person.

Connect to each other using the Partnered Sacred Tree Meditation and begin the Partnered Circular Breath.

The man begins by placing his hand on the woman's crown chakra, letting it rest there without moving. Staying with the breath, he notices how her crown chakra feels, without commenting out loud. The woman breathes and notices what it is like to have his touch there. Keep your hand still for at least one minute.

Repeat this exercise for the Third Eye, Throat, Heart, Stomach, Belly, and Root chakras.

Now switch roles, and let the woman sense in by placing her hand on the man's chakras.

At the end of the exercise you may wish to share about your experience with "I" statements, saying, for example, "I felt a lot of tingling in my hand when I touched your crown chakra" or "I felt warmth in my belly when you put your hand there."

Remember to do the Reconnecting to Self exercise in Chapter 4 when you are finished.

Chakras and Relationships

Sensing into your partner's chakras allows you to start a dialog with them about these connections as they relate to your relationship. Each chakra has a relationship area associated with it: Root is money and finances, Belly is sexuality, Stomach is power and how it is held, Heart is love and compassion for each other, Throat is communication, third eye is shared dreams, and crown is shared spirituality. Having an awareness of where these relationship areas are located in your body and how you are connecting there gives you the ability to work at healing your relationship through spiritual practice. Be sure that any communicating you do about this uses "I" statements. So for example you would say "I don't feel a strong connection to you at my stomach chakra, and I have noticed that I have been having some struggles with feeling disempowered in the relationship. I'm wondering if you have noticed anything about this part of our connection?" This can then open a dialog about your needs in the relationship, and from there you can learn to ask for what you need, and perhaps come to some agreements. However, needs aren't always in alignment, and it may be that talking clarifies that for you and allows you to create a plan for getting your needs met in some other way.

When you talk about these issues, be sure to ask your partner first if they are in an emotional space to be able to hear. It's also important to allow yourself to boundary with your partner if you are not able to talk with them. You can simply say, "I'm not able to talk with you about that right now," and ask perhaps to schedule a time to talk later. Respect for each other's emotional states and boundaries is important when having challenging conversations. Learning how to talk with each other compassionately is also a key to actually moving through challenges and letting go of old relationship patterns (see Bibliography and Resources).

Preparing to sit down for a talk with my partner, I was nervous because I knew there was a lot of tension between us around the topic we were going to discuss, and I also knew that there was a good chance we would come to one of those places in relationship where you realize that your paths are diverging. But being in fear, I am not on my center, and it certainly does not serve the relationship or the discussion to have me in that place. So I felt into my connection to Spirit at Earth and Sky, and I breathed. I asked for my will to align with the will of Spirit for me, and I brought out the sage. Lighting the bundle of white sage, watching it smoke in its abalone shell, moving it over my body at each chakra, I felt a powerful shift, a relaxing and letting go into a peaceful state where I could think clearly again. Just as you can smudge yourself with sage individually, smudging yourself and your partner with sage is a way of coming into the practice together. Now, as we both connected to each other consciously, we were able to stay connected to Spirit, stay present, and keep our emotional awareness open as we each shared about our challenges with the relationship. After an hour of staying connected, of breathing deeply to stay present, and of using breath to release excess emotion, I felt a shift deep in my power center. My belly relaxed, and instead of tension, I felt a glorious freedom. I knew in that moment that everything would be okay, that we had come through this challenge together.

Moving energy between the chakras is another powerful practice for dropping in and clearing old patterns in relationship, especially if both partners are in willingness to shift. In this practice you learn to sense in and move energy at each chakra, similar to the way you learned to move energy between you in the heart. You learn to experience the unique feeling of these energies in each chakra, opening yourself up eventually to experiencing an orgasm through connection at any chakra in the body. In this practice you move energy back and forth at each chakra, learning to give and receive energy at each part of your body.

Connecting the chakras is also fun to do in various sexual positions, adding an awareness of the energy body to your lovemaking, which will bring you even more fully into your connection with each other, and into the present moment, as well as allowing you to heal the chakras so that they become fully alive and connected to one another, creating a wholeness in your energy body.

Practice 2: Connecting Chakra Energies

This exercise teaches you how to circulate energy at each chakra, a practice that helps you learn awareness of the energy connections between you, and to experience the bliss that comes from connecting your sexual energies in other places besides your hearts and genitals.

Connect to Spirit together using the Partnered Sacred Tree Meditation. Start the Partnered Circular Breath. Come into connection with knees touching. Begin by placing your hands on each other's heads, connecting with the crown chakra. Continue to breathe together. Now imagine that you are sending energy to each other at the crown and receiving energy from each other at the crown. Keep breathing and notice how this feels. Keep your hands still for at least one minute.

Now move your hands to each other's foreheads, and feel into the third eye. If your partner's hand needs physical support, use your free hand to help support it. Stay here for at least a minute and notice what you feel. Continue on through the throat, heart, stomach, belly, and root chakras. Remember to keep breathing and to send and receive energy at each chakra.

When you are finished, share with each other about your experience using "I" statements. Remember to do the Reconnecting to Self exercise when you are finished, to help you come back to your own center.

Another way to connect and work through relationship healing is to move together. Dancing with my partner, we play with connecting each chakra together in dance. We begin with the root chakra and pounding drum music, connecting our pelvises as if they are glued together, me following each movement of his, letting him trace the dance for me as I melt into endless gyrations and patterns of my hips moving through the air. I squeeze my root (PC muscles) and I feel a surge of sexual energy flow into me and up into our bodies where they are connecting. The music changes to a flowing, romantic, watery sequence, and now our bellies are magnetically attached, and still I follow as he leads me in the connection and in the dance. We continue up through all of the chakras, getting creative at the throat and the head, laughing like little kids, playing, moving to the music, feeling our connection. For me, nothing brings my connection to my body and my chakras alive like dance. In moving and breathing, I open my body more fully to the channeling of the energies through me. If you can dance with your partner, you will increase the amount of sexual energy available to you because this is inherently what moving the body does. As in partnered yoga poses, you connect your energies to create circuits, but dance brings in an element of surprise, of the unknown, of playful being in the moment that is unique to it as a practice. I once met a very wise woman who said to me, "move your body every day." Moving the body feeds the soul.

Practice 3: Moving the Chakras Together

In this practice you begin to learn the art of moving together. You also get to be a little bit silly and play and laugh together. In this exercise the man leads the movement and the woman follows. Together you get a bodily experience of how you are connecting with each other at each of your chakra centers.

Choose some music that is fun and easy for the two of you to dance to. While standing, connect to each other using the Partnered Sacred Tree Meditation and begin the Partnered Circular Breath. Now start the music and stay with the breath, but also give yourself permission to play! Start with dancing the root chakra, keeping your pelvises together as if they were glued. Now let the man lead the movements for the next couple of minutes. Let yourselves laugh and experiment, and enjoy this practice. Keep breathing and notice what it's like to have the root chakras together as you dance. How does it feel? Can you imagine energy flowing between you?

Now glue your lower bellies together and dance the second chakra for a few minutes, staying connected, breathing, and playful. Continue up through all the chakras, getting creative and playful where you need to.

When you are finished, cuddle and share using "I" statements. Remember to Reconnect to Self when you are done.

Making Love with the Chakras

In the shower, he soaps my naked body to remove the sticky reside of whipped cream, strawberries, and chocolate from our love play. Once I am clean, he comes into connection with me, pinning my body against the wall of the shower, looking into my eyes and breathing with me. I am helpless to follow my own breath, and am drawn into his breath, his eyes, and his energy. As we breathe I feel the hardness of his lingam against my leg, and I shudder with Kriyas, little orgasms moving up and down my spine, clearing out the stagnant energies that have collected there over the last few days of my illness. I feel alive! Powerful! And the energies begin to move back and forth between us, as each chakra lines up and adds its energy to the connection. When you breathe your kundalini up and down your spine and feel into these connections, the amount of sexual energy you are moving increases. Connecting at the chakras gives us places where the energies move back and forth between our bodies and increases our pleasure in lovemaking. We can work these chakra connections consciously, or we can just allow them to share energy naturally to begin, waiting until we are deeper into the practice to focus on particular chakras.

Moving chakra energy in lovemaking is not only ecstatic, but healing. Making love with my partner, I draw him into a sitting position with me. He grumbles, and I can feel the weight of all our disagreements, and of our needs that are in different places. I draw him into breathing with me, circuiting energy between the genitals and the heart. As I give all the openness I have into opening my heart, into giving to him, as I receive all that he has to give into my yoni, the heart circuit opens between us and his eyes and mine become moist, feeling into the love that we have shared over many lifetimes. I feel the circuit and the breath begin to clear the black, sticky residue of disappointment from our connection, and I feel my yoni begin to sing with joy as my heart opens in compassion for the things he wants from me that I cannot give. I feel myself let go of all the things I want from him that he is not able to give me and just drop into the joy of unconditional love. I feel into my belly and stomach and I see we are blocked there too in our connection. Gently I begin to open myself to him, to see where and how the connections will form, and to see if energy is able to move between us. I feel the belly unlock first, flaming into sexual desire that rocks my body with shivers. I lean in and breathe even more strongly. But at the stomach I am stuck, feeling the door of my power firmly shut. I come away with an awareness that for now, we are not able to meet as equals in that part of our lives, and I accept it. I ask Spirit to help us heal this part of our relationship and I let go of the outcome, knowing it will heal in its own time.

The yabyum position is powerful for lovemaking, but can be challenging at first because it requires a lot of flexibility in the body. I never used to be much of a fan of yabyum position in lovemaking because I found it uncomfortable and hard to stay upright in. Then I began to work with my healing partner, and we found that staying in yabyum for the breath and energy practices was very valuable for us because it kept us connected to each other and focused. Somehow it seemed to connect our energies well. Then one night in making love, we flowed into yabyum quite naturally and it was amazing. The connection between us was stronger than in other sexual position, and I felt my yoni come more alive and the sexual energy move much more strongly both between our chakras and up my central spinal channel. We continued on until we both climaxed in this position. The climax was so strong that it moved both of us to return to this position over and over. There are lots of ways to make yabyum more comfortable, as you can see in the illustration. You can put a pillow under you to make sitting more comfortable, or you can even try using a chair. Yoga practice will help to increase your flexibility, which has general benefit in lovemaking because it allows you to flow into more sexual positions and thus to be more creative, present, and in the moment in your lovemaking. You can also balance with your hands behind you, or put the man so his back is up against a wall for support. When the spine is straight, the energy does indeed move more strongly.

Although learning to move sexual energy through your body is a beautiful solo tantra practice all on its own, bringing it into lovemaking opens the door to transcendent experiences where you open to an even fuller communion with your partner and with Spirit. When we breathe strongly for a long period of time it alters our consciousness and creates a space for Spirit to flow in. To me, it feels like an openness in the top of my head and in my entire body. It is the ultimate feeling of wholeness, where I become one with the Goddess, and at one with her, I am also whole and complete, sharing the experience of lovemaking with my partner. So when you make love, breathe fully. Move the PC muscle so that your nwyvre, your dragon fire, can flow through your entire body. Circuit the energy up and down your body. This you can do whether or not your partner practices tantra with you, and you will still open to amazing experiences within yourself. If you are breathing with a partner who breathes with you, then the gateways to connection between the two of you open wider.

Practice 4: Transmuting Sexual Energy

Now that you have learned to move sexual energy up and down the body using the exercise in Chapter 12, and to connect your chakras in this chapter, you are ready to work with moving sexual energy to the third eye in lovemaking. Moving sexual energy to the third eye allows you to use sexual energy for your spiritual growth, and for manifestation of the things you want most in your life. In this practice you learn to move energy between yourself and your partner at the root, heart, and third eye chakras, bringing a blissful ecstasy to your connection.

Sit together to begin and connect with the Partnered Sacred Tree Meditation. Begin the Alternate Circular Breath together.

Now come into yabyum and place the lingam on, but not in, the yoni. Keep breathing, and begin to move energy between the two of you. The woman breathes in the man's sexual energy through her eyes and yoni, and pulls it into her heart. She mixes this sexual energy with love energy and sends it back into the man's heart as she exhales.

The man breathes in her love at his heart, and then breathes it up to his eyes and down to his lingam, mingling it with his sexual energy and then penetrating the woman's eyes and yoni with that energy. The woman breathes that loving sexual energy into both her eyes and into her yoni, receiving his love and sexual power on the inhale. She pulls that energy into her heart and then sends it out as pure love on the exhale. Stay in the alternate breath and in the circuit. As the two of you become aroused, place the lingam in the yoni gently using the Stillness Together practice. Continue now with moving the energy between you, but also pulse the PC muscles. The woman squeezes these muscles on her inhale, pulling energy in. The man squeezes the PC muscles on his exhale, sending energy out. Flow into gentle movement of the lingam in the yoni, staying present to the breath and the energy movement. You may change positions if you like, as long as you are able to stay in the moment and in awareness of the energy moving. Notice any emotions that start to flow in you with this practice and let that happen. Continue making love with awareness, presence, and connection. See if you can stay in this energy connection all the way through orgasm, and notice what that feels like. Enjoy the feeling of bringing your sexual and loving energies into the third eye.

After you are complete in this practice, give yourselves plenty of time to transition and share with each other about your experience. When you are finished, you need not reconnect to self if you are sleeping together all night, but can save that for the morning when it is time to transition back to ordinary life. Otherwise, do the Reconnection to Self exercise when you are ready to part ways. Notice all the energy you are able to keep from this practice.

Tantric Orgasm

Now that you have learned to bring the connection of your chakras in lovemaking, you are ready to take this practice into a new experience of orgasm. Sink into the joy of connecting these previously unexplored parts of the body while you are intensely aroused or even about to climax. Feel the connection to each other. Women, your task is to open at each chakra, to fall into an openness where you are willing to let your man penetrate you in any part of your body with his energy — in the eyes, the throat, the stomach, the belly, and of course the yoni. Full and complete openness is always your goal, and as you take all this energy into you, let it gather in your breasts and shoot out into your man, like milk flowing into a baby's sucking mouth. For men, it is the opposite — to let yourself go in connecting to your woman. To let yourself fall into her, to penetrate her, to move your energy into her inner ocean without fear of drowning, knowing that she will give back to you as much or more through her heart. And to let yourself receive her heart energy into yourself, not to be afraid of feeling.

Transmuting the energy of the orgasm during lovemaking is for men the ultimate practice of sacred sexuality in the body. It is, for most men, the draw to this practice, to attain mastery over their bodies and their minds. The self-pleasuring ritual in Chapter 11 is preparation for this. By focusing the mind on the breath and on the feelings and sensations in your body, you can learn to delay orgasm, not as in the past by tensing the muscles in the belly, but instead by opening the stomach to move the sexual energy up to your heart and head. Eventually, this practice leads to full body orgasms, and to multiple orgasms without an ejaculation.

Women are wired differently than men, and it probably comes as no surprise to learn that for them the sexual circuit moves in the opposite direction when they are learning to expand their orgasm. As in the Awakening the Breasts practice in Chapter 5, women transmute love energy into sexual energy. In my experience, learning this transmutation leads to longer, stronger orgasms and to female ejaculation.

The partnered practice of Waking the Dragon is the first of three gateways that begin to engage the whole body in partnered sacred sexual practice. In my life, this practice has brought dramatic shifts in how I connect to my partners, and to how I feel about my relationships. After a year of relating to my partner in this very spiritual and sexual way, I intuitively sensed that there were spiritual practices that could help us move through conflicts with each other. Suddenly, my relationships became more fulfilling, and I felt more satisfied in my connections. The healing is not without pain and challenge, and allowing the dragon fire to burn through old blocks in the relationship can sometimes create a need for emotional space to process on my own before I am ready to come back into the connection. I have seen that this healing is dramatic, and creates lasting change. Slowly I feel myself moving to the pure core of relationship, where rules and structure are no longer important, and all that matters is the will of Spirit, the connection between us, trust, and unconditional love. For me, these are the foundations of a truly tantric relationship.

The Fifth Gateway

Weaving the Elements

Chapter 13
Balancing Your Life

Surrounded by flickering candles and powerful women, I move to the music that weaves through the room. Stamping our feet, we begin with feeling the heartbeat of Mother Earth in the beat of the drum music. Swaying together, we sink into our watery feminine depths and explore our darkest and deepest emotions. We move through water into fire, and suddenly we are blazing fiery lights, too bright to gaze upon for long, dancing our joy, our sex, our anger, our creative radiance. We spill ourselves into the void and into the world, waking up our bodies, our yonis, our hearts, and ourselves. Deeply in the dance, we rise into air, becoming light, soaring above everyday worries, flying on wings of Spirit above everything that can possibly pull us down.

The Elements are powerful metaphors that describe the balance of our lives, through their connection to the parts of life that make up the wholeness of who we are as human beings. Earth symbolizes our physical self, Water our emotional life, Fire the creative/sexual/spiritual energy, and Air the mental realm. Combined, the elements create Spirit, the indefinable "who" in "who am I?" A balanced life leads to wholeness, and finding ways to balance the elemental energies in my life has been essential to leading me down the path to bliss. If I am out of balance in any one area of my life, I feel it as a kind of knowing that something is not right. Balance, on the other hand, feels delicious, powerful and alive, making each day joyful and satisfying. When I feel out of balance I check in with myself to see what I have been neglecting. Perhaps I am not spending enough time in nature, or getting enough exercise. Perhaps I haven't been eating well or taking care of my body's need for touch and maintenance. Perhaps I haven't been allowing myself to feel my emotions fully, getting too caught up in busyness to stop and breathe into what I am feeling in the moment. Or perhaps I am not getting enough time with other people, or time alone to create. Or maybe I need more sex, more humor, more play. Sometimes I feel overwhelmed by trying to balance all of this, and that feeling tells me I need to stop doing and come into a place of quiet, to sense into myself and see what I need to feel whole and joyful about life again. For life is meant to be enjoyed! We are not here to suffer, we are here to learn and to grow. Suffering isn't necessary, even when we have inevitable pain in our lives. If, instead of wallowing in our pain, we feel it and then prescribe some balancing activity from the menu of the elements, we can move toward a life that includes both pain and ecstasy, a sense of complete sovereignty in ourselves. As we cultivate the spiritual life, we find more ways to be in connection with Spirit and all that is. In the practice of Weaving the Elements, we create a life tapestry with the help of Spirit and our spiritual guides and teachers. We connect ourselves to nature through powerful allies and through our meditations. We begin to feel a wholeness that is permeated with joy and love for ourselves and one another. Through this balance, we come more fully into connection with ourselves and our partners, learning to dance the harmony of the universe, to experience a full range of life, and to catapult ourselves into the adventure of this human experience.

The element of Earth is the foundation of all other elements. It is the place we begin. Earth speaks to me of the body first, my physical safety, health, and abundance. Earth is the world of nature that came before man walked upon this world: the rocks, the mountains, and the dirt. It is the flowers, plants, and trees that grow with abundance and determination. Earth brings me a sense of safety, and I often go out into the oak woods to find a boulder to sit on, to bring me back to a sense of solidity in myself, a sense of being safe in the world and in my body. I crave this element, perhaps because for me, safety in the world has been my major wounding and healing. The forests and gardens and hills near where I live have become places of refuge for me, where I feel strongly my connection to Spirit, and know that all is right with the world. My guide to the world of Earth, to all its beauty, as well as some of its subterranean majesty, has been Rabbit. He was the first animal totem to appear in my life, coming to me first in physical form, as a beloved pet, then later beginning to appear in my dreams and meditations. Animal guides are like this, for me. I often dream about them first, or make a connection to them in the flesh and become aware that they are an important teacher and helper for me. Rabbit was instrumental in teaching me how to feel safe in the world, taking me to underground rabbit warrens in my journeys, and lending me a place of safety with His family under the Earth when I had no safety in my own world. This place of safety and others live in my imagination, but they are very real. They are a part of

Table of Elemental Correspondences

Element	Direction	Life	Totems	Colors
Earth	North	Physical	Wolves, Rabbits	Brown, Green, Black
Air	East	Mental	Birds	Pink, Yellow
Fire	South	Sexual, Creative, Spiritual	Cats, Snakes, Lizards	Red, Orange
Water	West	Emotional	Water Animals, Dolphins, Whales, Otters	Blue, Turquoise
Spirit	Center	All	Ravens, White Animals	White

a non-ordinary reality that seems to be where most of my spiritual life takes place. Learning from Rabbit, I became able, in this other reality, to root myself into the Earth's underground places, to travel below her surface into vast caverns full of wisdom, and to find a deep sense of rest and safety. In the flesh, Rabbit taught me about gentleness, softness, and how these qualities do not mean being passive. Indeed, when Rabbit has graced my home in the form of a beloved pet, he has always taught me that like him, I can be gentle, I can hide and keep myself safe from predators, and I can defend myself when necessary.

Stamina, vitality, and endurance are some of the rewards of balancing the Earth element within yourself through attention to the physical body. When you rise up in the morning feeling awake and alive, when your body feels good, when you are able to move through your day without fatigue, when you sleep well at night, these are all signs that your physical body is in balance. When you move through your life feeling safe and abundant in the world, these are signs that the Earth element is in balance within your spiritual self. When I am in doubt about my physical body, I check in to see what is most needed to bring me into balance. I may choose rest, nutrition, exercise, or perhaps some spiritual practice around safety and abundance. Recently I fell off the exercise wagon, or rather, over the past 6 months had been going through a slow decline. All of a sudden I realized that I wasn't doing my normal morning workout much at all, and I began to notice parts of my body changing, and my energy dropping, as a result. For me it is hard to stay motivated, too, because I don't fight with my weight like many people do, so not exercising doesn't mean that I gain weight. But I notice that I don't feel good when I don't exercise, and that I start to feel depressed and lethargic. So slowly I have been getting back to it, starting by adding an hour of exercise to my schedule three times a week. For me, once I have gotten through the first few weeks of a routine, it becomes easier, and I wake up in the morning looking forward to it. It is like this for me with anything I am trying to balance in my life, first I have the desire to balance it, then I accept that I haven't been doing it, and next I decide upon a course of action. Putting this action into practice takes awhile. When I am balancing the Earth element within me, this slow pace of change is natural, as the Earth element itself is slow-moving and restful, and at the same time vibrant and alive. When I feel all these things in myself, I know that the Earth element is fully expressed in me, and that I can turn my attention to balancing other parts of my life.

Air

The element of Air is associated with the world of the mind, and with our ability to think, not to mention the air of nature itself, the winds, the clouds, and all the creatures that fly. My journey through the Air element has been the most difficult part of my elemental balance. For each of us, there are elemental energies that feel natural and energies that feel somewhat foreign. For me, Air has a strange and alien quality, and I find it hard to embrace that part of who I am. I tend to be somewhat serious and intense, staying in the world of my emotions and my physical body most of the time, with increasing integration of my sexual/creative/spiritual life. But Air, the mental realm, is not a place that I tend to live in. I don't memorize facts just for the knowing, I don't enjoy endless hours in mental pursuits. When I write, it comes from my emotional and creative selves more than from a place of thinking and planning. Most of the time, the connection to Air within me is elusive.

The second animal guide I was given on my spiritual journey was the golden eagle, a bird native to the Southern California lands I have lived on for the last many years. In the dream where I first met my guide, she was caught, tangled in a web clinging to a wall, and unable to get loose or to fly away. As I watched her beat her wings and scream in the dream, I knew she was speaking to me about my own life, about how I was caught in a net of my own making, and how I needed to cut away the tangles and let myself soar. I wrote a song for her after that dream, and would often sing about her soaring. In meditation I would imagine taking the form of an eagle and soaring high above the world, getting a fresh perspective. When I finally came to a place of willingness to begin cutting the web that tangled me, to extract myself from all the limitations that were keeping me from being fully myself, a Native American friend gifted me with an Eagle pendant to wear, "for clear vision" he said, "and to help you soar above all this."

For me, air has two associations, the sharp and clear soaring above of the eagle, and the gentle playfulness of the hummingbird or a gentle breeze. When my mind is balanced, it is clear of distracting and worrisome thoughts, able focus on its goal like the Eagle hunting prey, and able to soar above the noise and worry of the world. Full and deep breathing helps me to soar. Breathing fully and deeply to clear the mind and let go of whatever is clouding it, I begin to feel worries diminish and a sense of peace descend. A balanced mind is playful, and cultivates a sense of wonder, of not always knowing the answer. Play and humor have their own wisdom, and they bring joy and lightness to life, a balance to the heaviness that Earth and Water can sometimes bring. Play and laughter unlock places of angst in us and bring healing to our bodies.

Fire

Fire is the most intense of all the elements, able to burn through blockages in our energy bodies more quickly and thoroughly than any other element. Fire is creativity, passion, sexuality, and spiritual luminescence. This part of life, the creative/sexual/spiritual life, is probably the least valued part of life in my Western culture. People almost always look at this part of life as an "extra," something they can do without. And yet, without the fire inside us, the soul dies and falls into the dark ashes of oblivion. Most of my life I have been focused on this area, whether through sexuality or creativity or spirituality. These are the guiding principles of my life, and everything I do comes from this focus. From an early age I delighted in creative play, valuing above all else any play that involved making something with paint or play dough or crayon. As I grew older, I started to create stories and musical compositions, and to explore my sexuality. I also was very devoted to my connection with God, and prayer was my constant companion as a young woman. As I grew, my spirituality shifted, and I became focused on the Earth and my connection to Her. For the past 15 years I have been dancing, creating stories with my body to share with the world. I feel most alive when I am creating or making love or doing spiritual practice. Yet it must be a balance — too much time in the fire element leaves me feeling jittery and sometimes very exhausted. I have learned that this element must be in balance with my emotions, physical body, and mental state.

As the fire element has been with me from an early age, so has one of the animal guides that I associate with fire, the cat. Most often, my guide is a large cat, a black jaguar. But often it is a house cat, a regal and calm representative of the domestic animal that is so known for its affinity for heat and warmth. Cats seem to exude passion and sexuality, and I find it inspiring to watch them. Growing up with cats, I seem to have a bond with them, and they are in turn drawn to me. In the Spirit realm, I often will call on Cat for protection, for they are fierce warriors and protectors against anything real or imagined that might threaten me there.

Especially since I am on a tantric path, keeping the force of fire alive in my life brings a joy and passion to each day. For me it is a daily requirement in my life to make love or self-pleasure, to create, and to commune with Spirit through meditation or some other spiritual practice. I notice that when I am in a very creative phase, actively creating a book or dance or piece of clothing, my body begins to feel extremely energized, and my attitude toward all of life is more positive. This effect is so pronounced for me that I often use creative play as a remedy for the blues. If I find myself in pain or grieving, once I have allowed the feelings to be fully alive in me, I shift to a creative endeavor, either moving my body to release and burn through the emotions, writing to open and let go of whatever is trapped inside of me, or perhaps crocheting or sewing. These are the creative outlets that uplift me, and help to burn away and transform my pain and grief to acceptance and surrender to the will of Spirit. I find that I must surrender to be fully in the creative process, or to make love, and once I let go in that way, it becomes easier to let go of my pain and embrace the joy and ecstasy that Spirit has for me.

Water

Water is the element that is most powerful in my being, and sometimes I am afraid of being swept away by it. For me, the water element within is like the ocean, deep, cool, ever-changing, and very dark in its deepest places. This ocean lives in me, and I have become aware over time that my moods are like the tides, they come in and go out, and they don't stay the same as long as I am willing to let them change. There was a time in my early life when emotion was frozen within me, and I experienced very little of what I was feeling. It took some work to thaw the ice, and to begin to learn what I was feeling about things. Water is not just the ocean, the waters of the Earth include rivers and lakes and the rain. Once a year I like to collect water from one of each of these sources: a cool and calm lake, the Pacific Ocean near where I live, an untouched and wild river that I know, and the rain that falls during the rainy season. I learned this ritual from Starhawk's writing about celebrating the seasons as they occur in my corner of the earth (see Bibliography and Resources). Celebrating the water is powerful for me, and with this mixture of waters that I collect, I embrace the healing power water has for me. In ancient times people traveled to certain springs or rivers that were said to have healing powers. Sacred water can help to wash away the emotions that are getting in the way of living my fullest life. For me, in modern times, any water from a special place in nature can connect me to the Spirit of that place and bring the healing of that connection into my body.

In the realm of water I was first guided by the otter, who came to teach me about how joy is just as important an emotion as sadness. Otter began to teach me how to let go and swim in my emotions, rather than freezing them like ice inside me to avoid them. He taught me that joy was possible for me. In trance journeys, I would call him in and we would swim together in the rivers of the Spirit world, and I would learn how to play in the water. Even now, I love to go to the zoo and watch the otters play. In the past year, I have come to also feel the guidance of Dolphin in my life, which is not only about the lessons of joy and play, but also about community and supporting one another. Whenever I am locked in an emotional struggle, these are the guides that I can turn to for support and guidance about what steps to take to fully experience and move through any place I am stuck.

Balancing the water element in my life has increased my ability to feel pleasure. The more I let myself feel my pain when it comes, the more I am able to feel intense happiness. I have learned that my feelings are my way in to the experiences of ecstatic sexuality. Feelings are felt in the body and stored in the body. By allowing them to well up and move through me, I allow my sexual and sensual selves to unfold. I have become healthier, no longer holding as much emotional baggage in my body, baggage that was causing me to experience chronic illness and festering inner emotional wounds. Paradoxically, when I let myself feel, I am more often tranquil and serene, no longer straining with the effort of holding oceans of unexpressed feeling inside me. When I began to explore my feelings, I was astonished to find that I wasn't able to write a journal entry about my day with any feelings in it aside from "that sucked" or "I liked that." But real feelings? Despair, disappointment, disgust, respect, joy, happiness, these were a mystery to me. As time went on, I learned to write more about my feelings, and even to cry as I journaled, but I was still stuck in the deep end of the pool, in my negative emotions, and addicted to their drama, because at least when I had them I felt alive. The rest of the time I felt numb and dull and stagnant. Over time now, I have learned to embrace my positive emotions too, and to name them and see that there is as much a range of positive feeling as there is negative. And as I have begun to embrace this, I have started to see that I am coming more and more to a place where I am in the good emotions. Something about letting the bad emotions out and naming them has set me free of them, even when life isn't necessarily going the way I want it to. Learning to be in the moment is the key to emotional balance, to not be upset about something that might happen. When we stay in the present, and also out of past hurts and wrongs, things get easier.

Spirit

Spirit is the most mystical of all the elements, part of my center, the melting pot that contains all the pieces of who I am. Spirit is the space between things, the vacuum of outer space, the place in us that is waiting to be filled. I often feel this emptiness inside me that longs to be filled, and for years I tried to fill that place with food or love from men. But this emptiness is a place that can only be filled by Spirit. It is the place within us that Spirit comes into when we are open and surrendered. Sometimes I think about this center inside me as containing pieces of all the other elements, a pinch of Earth, a cup of Fire, a teaspoon of Air, a gallon of Water, and I think that is also true. In the realm of Spirit there is no right or wrong, only intuition.

I came into relationship with my animal guide at the center, my guide to Spirit, through a strange connection to an unborn fetus within me. It was my second pregnancy, and my son was 5 years old. I was unhappy in my marriage, and fairly certain that I was going to leave. And when I found myself pregnant I cried. I cried because I desperately wanted a daughter, and at the same time, I didn't want to raise a new baby alone. I felt overwhelmed and a sense of wrongness at being pregnant at that time. But I also was clear that I did not want to end the pregnancy, and I was willing to accept this child and allow Spirit to guide me in what to do. Over the next three days, I began to have powerful communications with a guide who seemed to be attached to the body of the child inside me, who seemed to be the child inside me. She called herself Raven.

I had never had contact like this with my son before he was born, and I was a little frightened. But I was also fascinated by what was happening, and I opened to the connection with her, seeing her as a powerful and vibrant young woman with flowing black hair. Ravens began to act oddly in my presence, to perch on my car and stare at me as I approached it, not flying away until I actually reached for the door. I began to wonder how I would ever parent this child, because in our conversations she seemed so much wiser than I was, so much more powerful. I felt that she really wouldn't need me at all, that she would be somehow born fully aware and be her own guide. And then, on the third day of this magnificent connection, I miscarried. I was devastated, and surprised at my upset, being so early in pregnancy. But I had already fallen in love with this darkly knowing presence I had been communicating with. My sadness was soon lifted by realizing that even though Raven had left my body, she was still connected to my heart and my spirit. I came to realize that she would never leave me, that she was my guide to the center of myself, where the elements in their magick alchemy created the essence of my soul. When I remember to call her in, that vast space within me is full, and She comes alive within me, speaking through me with a beautiful soft dark wisdom.

Having a connection to this presence within allows me to have strength and knowing in many life situations where I would crumble if left to rely on my own resources. The more I journey on my path, the more I find that balance and surrender to that balance leads to tranquility and peace. Balance does not necessarily mean that all these elements are equal in me, just that they are all present in amounts that feel healthy and right. Once I began to find this balancing point, life began to flow more easily and I noticed that many wonderful miracles began to occur in my life, little coincidences that have helped me to journey to more joy and wonder in my life. Struggle, or drama, or exhaustion are all signs that I am not in elemental balance. I feel so fortunate that my body gives me these warnings. I particularly enjoy moving through my day when I feel in balance, and can see the flow between mental, physical, emotional, and creative work. Today was a beautiful example of this, beginning with a deep meaningful talk with my lover about some things that were upsetting us and moving toward a place of resolution, then flowing into several hours of mental work answering emails, and sharing concepts about how to run our business together, then moving into some physical exercise to work the kinks out and get the blood flowing, then into writing this book, which for me is a creative task. At the end of such a day I feel whole and have a deep sense of satisfaction.

Elemental Practice

As you move through the practices in the following chapters, you will gain awareness of what the elements mean to you, and how you want to use them to weave your own journey to Spirit. Each of us is different, and each of us will have different areas of imbalance to look into as we move along our path. Wherever you journey, know that Spirit is with you, and that you cannot make a wrong choice. If you mistakenly think that you need to bring more water into your life, and you find that doing so doesn't help you feel more balanced, then you can just shift and try working with a different element. You will know if something is not working for you. Remember that shamanic tantra is an intuitive practice, and that in everything you do, you must pay attention to your inner feelings and knowledge about the work. The stronger this awareness is, the more you develop it, the more you will be able to simply know in an instant what you need, just by tuning into your inner self. The elemental practices are gateways to your healthiest, most whole expression of yourself, to be opened and explored as you discover who you truly are behind all the facades and masks of your life.

Moving to create a better life, I imagine what I want. I think about time to rest, I think about the joy of creating, I think about myself whirling and dancing and peaceful time spent doing yoga. I think about my rose garden, and my sexual partnerships. I think about the joy of being with my son and my cat. I think about playing music and reading good novels and watching movies, I think about playing with my friends and engaging in long, entertaining discussions. I think about heart-to-heart talks with my girlfriends and time to journal and meditate. As I imagine this life, I make changes, and this life comes to pass. My old work falls away, and new work rises to support me. My old creative endeavors shift and I find new levels that I never even imagined existed. In all of this, as I balance, I come into communion with the flow of all life, and Spirit itself begins to tell me how to balance, what is needed in my life, what is not needed, how to be on my center in my physical, emotional, mental, and creative/sexual/spiritual selves. Drifting in this center, I become strong, and healthy, and I grow. And most importantly of all, I am happy and free.

• Chapter 14 •

Weaving the Elements Solo

We carry within us the energy of the raging forest fire, the eternal forest, the mighty oceans, and the sweeping winds. We are clouds, mountains, lava, and waterfalls inside, embodying within our human flesh all that is true and best and good in the natural world. Through centuries of limiting culture, we have divorced ourselves from the knowledge that we are one with the natural world, and this separation creates yet another wound, yet another fragmentation of the soul. Reuniting ourselves with the world of nature is one of the tasks in shamanic tantra, to learn to live and breathe the elements into us so that they feed and nurture our sense of spiritual and sexual life. Bringing each of the elements into our lives creates a balance, and a place where we can begin to heal. Sometimes a wound requires the cleansing waters of a mighty river, other times the rest and serenity of a high quiet mountain. Each element unlocks a different place in us for healing, a different knowledge of who we are, and a different aspect of our contribution to this planet as human beings.

The solo practice of weaving the elements involves sensing in and deciding which element needs balance in you. Look at Chapter 13 for some examples of each element's energy. If you cannot decide where to start, then begin with the Earth element practices and move through Water, Fire, and Air. These practices are all best led by your intuition, which means that any choice you make is right.

Earth Meditations

Connecting to the element of earth is a powerful shamanic place to begin. We have done the practice already of connecting to the Earth Mother, and some of my students find the distinction between Earth Mother and the element of earth to be confusing. The connection to the element of earth is more abstract, and comes into your bones, tissues, and sinews. For some, the Earth meditation is felt in the body, for others, it is seen as visual imagery in the mind. Both are just as acceptable, use whichever technique works for you. As you feel or see this awareness of bones and muscle, and as you experience any place in your body that has pain, you can allow your mind to defuse that pain, to imagine moving and shifting it in the body. This is one way of healing yourself, and of healing the physical body.

Each element also has a breath that helps bring it into focus within us. Spinning around and whirling through life, so many of us lose track of how to stop, to be, and to rest. Breathing brings us back to that place of inner focus, bringing us fully present. Breathing in through the nose brings the life force into our bodies, breathing out through the mouth releases tension in the body. Elemental breath brings us fully present to the feeling and flow of a particular element within us. The Earth Breath brings you to a place of deep rest and connection with your physical body, with alignment to your center. This is a wonderful breath to do when you want to calm yourself or to fall asleep more easily. This breath is strengthening, calming, and grounding.

Practice 1: Earth Meditation and Breath

This meditation is good for cultivating centering and stillness and connecting deeply to your body. It is especially good for anxiety manifesting as tension in the body, or when you just need to calm yourself.

Sit comfortably and connect to Spirit by growing your roots in the Earth and sending your branches up to the sky. Begin the Earth Breath, breathing in through your nose for the count of 5, out through your mouth for the count of 5, then waiting 5 counts before inhaling again. Notice there is no pause between the inhale and exhale, only after the exhale. Once you have the breathing established, move your awareness into your skin, muscle, bones, and sinews. Feel into where your muscles are tight and where they are relaxed. Use your exhale to release any tension. Sink deeply into your own body with your awareness as you continue to breathe. If you feel any discomfort in your body, you may wish to place your hand there and use the exhaled part of your breath to release the pain or tightness and the inhale to draw in healing energy from the Earth.

Continue this meditation for as long as you like — 5-10 minutes is often a good amount of time to start, setting a timer so you can let go of awareness of time while you are meditating. Do the meditation as often as you need to for centering and relaxation.

Water Meditations

Flowing with your emotions without resistance is one of the goals of tantra, and the water meditation can help you begin learning this way of being in yourself. Emotions cannot be held or contained by any walls for very long. Eventually water must flow, and if it gets high enough, it will overflow any barriers or containers you put around it. Breathing in meditation allows the flow of your inner liquidity to expand until it fills you with a welter of feeling.

Flowing the sexual and emotional energies through my body is easiest for me when I use the water breath, which is simply the Circular Breath that we learned in Chapter 5. I allow the emotions to flow, opening more fully with sexual arousal and sensuality. I feel a gentle sinking into my body and into my feminine nature that is very comfortable. The water breath allows the release of emotion when you are upset, and is wonderful to use when you are in the midst of an emotional release, or to stimulate a release of things you sense you are holding in your body. The breath can also be extremely soothing when you are upset, or ill. Water is the element that soothes, calms, and cools us when we are anxious, angry or worried.

Practice 2: Water Meditation and Breath

This meditation is good for getting in touch with your emotions if you are feeling numb, and for releasing excess negative emotions like rage, grief, fear, and sadness.

Sit comfortably and connect to Spirit by growing your roots in the Earth and your branches into the sky. Now begin the Circular Breath, breathing in through your nose for 5 counts and out through your mouth for 5 counts. Do not pause between the inhale and exhale.

Once you have the breath flowing easily, turn your awareness to your emotions and to what you can feel. Breathe deeply into your belly, and notice how puffing out and in when you inhale and exhale can start to move feelings through you. Imagine your emotions are like water running through you, and let your breath move this water around in your body. Also let it flow out through your roots in the Earth. Keep breathing and allow yourself to feel all the emotions you are capable of, tuning into whatever is alive in you in this very moment.

Continue with breathing and releasing emotion for as long as you like. If you want to set a finite time for yourself to do this meditation, set the timer for 5-10 minutes so that you do not need to keep checking the time while you are meditating. You can repeat this meditation anytime you want to calm your emotions or get a stronger sense of what you are feeling about something in your life.

Fire Meditations

Writing this book, I am deeply in the creative process, letting the juices flow freely through me, without resistance. When I have things in my body and my energy field that are getting in the way, emotions that are clouding my ability to receive the writing from Spirit, or just a stuck and sleepy feeling, I know that the fire meditation will help me stay in that state of passionate and energized activity that leads to good writing. The fire meditation helps to raise your energy level and unlock your sexual energy as well as your creative passion.

The fire breath brings such an intense aliveness and vitality to my body that I don't use it too often, only wanting to bring this intensity to me in very particular situations like lovemaking, dance, or other creative work. This breath enhances creativity, and is very exciting to use when lovemaking becomes intense, or when you want to ramp up the energy of sexual passion.

Practice 3: Fire Meditation and Breath

Fire meditation and breath are fabulous for raising your general energy level, as well as arousing sexual energy and enhancing the creative spark.

Sit comfortably and connect to Spirit by growing your roots down into the Earth and branches into the sky. Now begin the Fire Breath, exhaling forcefully through your nose so that the energy can build up in your body. Make the breaths very short and quick, about 3 breaths per second. You should feel your stomach pulsing as you breathe. Focus on the exhale, letting the inhale take care of itself. Do the breath for as long as it feels comfortable. Be careful not to do this breath for too long at the beginning, as it can make you light-headed.

Now you can add a visualization of fire moving through all your body as you do a round of fire breathing, and imagine that this fire is your creative/sexual/spiritual energy. Feel this energy awaken in you as you breathe, and even allow yourself to feel aroused. Continue the visualization even if you drop out of the fire breath. Imagine the fire within warming you and waking up your body to ecstasy and creative inspiration.

You can repeat this meditation as often as you like to keep your vibrant aliveness awake in you.

Air Meditations

Opening the doors and windows of the mind takes us to a place where clarity and perspective exist. In this place where the fresh winds blow away the cobwebs that obscure our vision, we gain the ability to make clear and present decisions. We can also make decisions from a place of the emotions, but these decisions do not always serve us in the way that we hope, and I find that it is best to temper my own emotional leanings with the balance of a clear mind and its ability to open to spiritual guidance. The most beautiful use of the mind is not to analyze every situation in making decisions, but rather to come up with workable ways to implement the details of the plans that Spirit guides us to. When I first began to be drawn to teaching tantra, I found myself bogged down in a litany of reasons why it would never work. As the voice of Spirit became more insistent in me, I found that my mind's job was not to find all the ways that this could lead to disaster, but rather to create the next indicated step needed to implement the plan (everyday things like websites and business cards). In this situation, I found air meditations helpful in clearing away all the distracting thoughts within my mind and in allowing constructive and joyful planning and perception to come in.

The practice of the air breath is enlivening, bringing you into alignment with your purpose and into clarity about your course of action. It lifts the energy in your body, bringing lightness to your being, and energy. The air breath brings more oxygen into your brain and body. Air breath can also be combined with air meditation to strengthen both practices. This is a great practice to do when you need to "lighten up" a little and see the brighter side of life, to gain perspective. It is also nice when you are simply feeling tired and want more energy. The air breath is also good for clarifying the mind and blasting out the whirling thoughts, while bringing a clear mental state where studying, reading, writing, and discussing complicated subjects becomes easy. I do this breath often when I am writing late at night to shake off sleepiness, or when I have thoughts stuck in my head that I want to let go of. This breath puts me quickly into a meditative state of relaxed alertness, where I feel like the Eagle soaring over the landscape, seeing everything with its sharp eyes.

Practice 4: Air Meditation and Breath

This meditation helps to clear your mind, and is excellent to do if you need to let go of obsessive thoughts or sharpen your mental state.

Sit comfortably and connect to Spirit by growing your roots down to the Earth, and your branches up to the sky. Begin the air breath, inhaling through your nose for 5 counts, holding the breath for 5 counts, then exhaling through the mouth for 5 counts. Do not pause between the exhale and inhale.

Once you have the breath flowing, start to really focus on the movement of air through your lungs, and imagine that you are feeling lighter with each breath. Imagine your breath wafting into each part of your body and gently blowing away any heaviness, especially in your mind. Imagine that this breath flows through your mind and clears out any thoughts that are disturbing or distracting you. Let the air create space within your mind for Spirit to speak, and for you to hear.

Do this meditation for as long as you like. If you want to set a specific amount of time to meditate, set a timer for 5-10 minutes so that you are not looking at the clock while you are meditating. Repeat this meditation whenever you want mental clarity and openness to the voice of Spirit.

Dancing the Elements

A way to go deeper with experiencing and balancing the elemental energies in yourself is to add movement. I have become passionate about dropping into the ecstasy of movement, and have made it a very large part of my spiritual practice. I am often transfixed by watching it liberate things in me as I move. It is the practice that always works to balance me, free me from fear, and bring me into communion with all that is. Dancing the elements brings me into a place of visceral knowledge about my state of balance and my relationship to each element. As I move, my body speaks to me in a language of wisdom and awareness that bypasses the analytical mind. I come to know without knowing how I know.

When I dance the elements I do my best to let go of everything I think I know about dancing. I let go of the ego as much as I can, let go of worrying how my movements look. I come instead to a place of letting go and inviting a particular element to flow into my body's essence and shape my motion. I keep my connection to Spirit not only when I am moving, but also when I am choosing music to dance to, letting my intuition guide me to what will best evoke the energy of the element for me.

Dancing with the Earth, I am heavy and solid. I stamp my feet on the earth and hear the sound ring through mountains and trees. I am strong and powerful like the tallest mighty oak, like an elephant, like a buffalo. I dance myself as if I am made of boulders tumbling down a mountainside, as if I am the most solid, real, powerful creature the earth has to offer. Dancing this solidity into me, I begin to feel an earthy sensuality, a connection to my body that has in it the pleasure of receiving a massage, and the earthy feeling of my skin against the skin of my lover. It is not sexual, exactly. It is different, just a joy in experiencing the deep physicality of who I am as a human, akin to the feeling of playing in mud as a child, or feeling the sand slide between my toes. I dance Earth by putting on drum music, by breathing the Earth breath, and by letting my body do the rest. Sometimes I invoke a God or Goddess to dance with me or in me, other times I am the Goddess, feeling powerful and immeasurable in my breasts and bones and body.

Dancing Water, I flow into relationship with my emotional self, the inner child who cannot always speak, or cry, or be loved. She flows through me, as well as a deeper, darker feminine self, a mermaid who sings a siren song for me to descend into my depths and swim with her, transfixed by her beauty. Dropping into this inner ocean rift, feeling into the deepest emotions I am capable of feeling, my body flows too, making circular flowing motions like those of the water. I move in and out like the tide, or undulate like a ripple on the water. Water flows through my veins, my spine, my belly, my chest. There is no part of me that does not contain water or emotion. Our emotions shape who we are, and these emotions, trapped in our bodies, cry out for release. I dance water by choosing music that flows, with instruments like piano or voice, and moving my body in a flowing motion. Then I breathe the circular breath and let the beauty of my inner waters unfold.

Dressed in liquid gold lamé and beads, I shimmy like the Fire that dances through me as the drums swell and build to a crescendo. The crescendo of the music is in me and I become more and more filled with passion and tingling fiery energy. I feel a blazing in my soul that unlocks the core of who I am, my dragon essence. As I radiate this light, this fire, this sexual/spiritual luminescence, I send it up to the sky and out through my heart to the women who watch me, spellbound, drinking in this aura of passion. In all beings this fire exists, and in some it burns more brightly than others. Connecting to yourself to drop into a place of feeling passionate or sexual. For me the practice of playing with fire always comes with both fear and an adrenaline rush. I always have in the back of my mind the fear that one day it will consume me, and I will spontaneously combust, like the urban legends. And yet I am still here, containing more and more of the fire within my cells and my soul. The more I dance the fire, the more I drop into an easy place of creativity and sexual passion. This practice, in particular, is good for counteracting depression and stagnant energy in the body. Moving these energies out, we become free again, and our wounds, cauterized by passion, begin to heal.

Dancing Air, I bob and jump and frisk like a puppy. I start with the playful nature of air, like a breeze that picks up your papers and scatters them gently, just out of reach, teasing you. But air has other modes too — deep and still and hot, cold and piercing, direct and gently cooling. I dance all of these, searching for the mode that suits me. Am I in need of deep silent wisdom, or joyful play? I cannot tell, so I just continue what I am doing, hoping Spirit will give me some assistance. Stuck, I start to feel frustrated. What is wrong with me, that I cannot connect with Air? I used to blame it on childhood, on a lack of examples in how to be in the place of lightness and play, or even in mental clarity. So I embrace that this element is hard for me, and I move and dance anyway. If I am stuck, then I move into spinning, an activity sure to get the air juices flowing. When I am spinning, I begin to find a place of peace, because I know that my existence is no accident, and that God has a plan for me. This is part of the wisdom I gain. I love to dance to the music of flutes for this work, as they are the quintessential embodiment of air. When I finish I am floating, and I know that now I will be able to hear the voice of Spirit.

Practice 5: Elemental Movement

This exercise is a moving meditation on the elements. You can choose to do movements for an element you want to work with, or move through all the elements when you want balancing. Choose music that reminds you of each element to help inspire you. Clear out a space to move freely in, and if you are feeling self-conscious about moving your body to music, then create some privacy for yourself to move unobserved before you begin. Let go of thoughts about "doing it right," and simply let your body move to the music and express the feeling of the elements. This is truly a moving meditation, so let go of thoughts and the ego, and move fully into awareness of your body.

Stand and connect to Spirit by sending your roots into the Earth and your branches into the sky. Begin the Circular Breath and use it for each element in this practice.

Earth — Stamp your feet, move slowly and heavily, like and elephant or buffalo. Feel your body as you move.

Water — Make flowing motions with your body and arms that remind you of water. Imitate rain, ocean waves, rivers, and even whirlpools. Feel your emotions as you move.

Fire — Make shimmying motions with your hips, shoulders, hands, and feet, or any other movements that evoke a feeling of fiery passion in your body. Feel your sexual/creative energy as you move.

Air — Make ethereal, spinning, and flying motions with your body that help you feel the lightness of air within. Dance your joy and playfulness.

Balancing the Elements

Balancing the elements brings us to a place of joy and satisfaction in life, a place where we are honoring all the parts of us. It doesn't mean that each element is equal in your life, just that it is present in the amount that you need to be healthy and happy. You will know when your balance is off, because you will feel something lacking or an overwhelmed feeling in some area of your life.

One way to keep a daily awareness about your elemental balance is to bring representations of the elements into your living space, whether on an altar or in special places throughout your home. Roses adorn my main altar, which is currently on the mantel above the fireplace in my living room. Above the mantel is a painting of the Goddess, dressed in brightly colored frog skin, dancing on a Ladyslipper orchid. Nearby is a fountain with playful green frogs climbing ivy leaves over which water trickles and soothes me. There is a jar of earth from a special desert land I feel a deep spiritual connection to, and nearby are hawk feathers, a crystal globe, and several candles and crystals. I love to bring objects from nature, and artwork that represents nature, into the sacred space that is my tiny temple home. These objects remind me each day of my intention to stay balanced and to align with the will of Spirit. Each day as I dance and meditate I bathe myself in the intention to keep the balance within me. Looking around and breathing in the beauty of these objects, I sink into a gratitude for the world that I live in, and for my life. Using my imagination to create my altars and my temple is deeply joyful and satisfying for me.

Following the teachings of my Wiccan and Druid training, I place objects that represent Earth in the North, Air in the East, Water in the West, and Fire in the South. I face these directions in my meditations if I want to draw in more of that energy. In the morning, for example, I face East in meditation, to bring in clarity of mind for my writing and other creative tasks. Morning is the time associated with the element of Air for me, and I find it is the easiest time of day for me to accomplish mental tasks. I face North when I am feeling tired or when I want to reconnect with my sense of abundance in the world, West when I need to check in with my emotions or purge some unwanted feelings, and South when I want to enhance my creative or sexual fire, or connect strongly to Spirit.

Allow yourself to flow with Spirit as you create a place of meaning and magick where you can live and rest and find the balance that will heal you. Balancing the elements within is a deeper level of connecting to Spirit, of exploring all the majesty that it has to offer us through connection with our inner balance, and through connection with our guides. As you work through the elements, allow yourself to be open to receiving new guides in your meditations, guides that work together with the one you were given when first learning to connect to Spirit. In my own life, these guides are the best friends I could ever have, just as Earth Mother and Sky Father are my true parents. In the Spirit world we find deep healing of all the things in our lives that have wounded us, and the healing can be extremely gentle and joyful.

Creating a balanced life is like planting a garden. You must create a plan and use your intuition to decide what pattern to create, which colors to use, and how the whole collection of plants will work and thrive together. In the garden of your life, as in your back yard, there are no mistakes, there are only things you learn, from planting too many seeds, from placing plants together that are not compatible, but you remove what doesn't work and you try again. So in your life, allow yourself to make a magickal garden within that blooms and grows in abundance. As you cultivate your own garden, you become ready to join with the landscape of another and to manifest beauty and balance together.

· Chapter 15 ·

Weaving the Elements Together

In the two years that I have been doing tantric practice and relationship with my partner, I have never had the same lovemaking experience twice. Our connection is always new and fresh, because we stay in the moment with each other. We sink into the joy and ecstasy of the way we come together in each new moment, rather than dwelling on past hurts. The elemental practices are a part of what sustains the richness of our connection and keep us present and balanced in our connection to each other. One deeply satisfying practice involves touch. When I am present, each sensation on my body is like the first time I have ever been caressed. It is an altered state, a meditation of merging through our skins. Sacred sex is a meditation, so ecstatic sometimes, so full of love and heart-merging at others. It is a choice to be in whatever state we are present to, whether it be a peaceful, soft breeze, passionate fire, the wailing weeping of water, or the deep stillness of the earth. Giving up any expectations, giving up any control, giving up our fears, we just let go. We fall headlong into pleasure, through even deeper connection to the elements that make up Spirit. We learn to touch and connect in new ways we may never have tried before. Once learned, we let these touches, connections, and ways of making love flow.

Exploring the elements with a partner includes touch, dance, and lovemaking, and in each of these, it is important to be fully in the moment. We learn to let go of expectation, past disappointments, and habitual ways of connecting to our lovers, and release any goals about our time together. Creating a relationship of intimacy where you are truly present to your partner, and embracing all that your partner is with your whole being, while also experiencing all of who you are, is the magick of weaving the elements. When you come together with your partner, you most likely have habitual ways of relating to each other. These ways of relating tend to be on one or two of the elemental channels. Earth in relationship governs touch, sensual pleasures like food and massage, as well as creating a home and earning money. If your relationship is water-focused, you will spend time sharing feelings and listening to your partner's feelings. Sometimes you will also have unhealthy drama in the relationship, jealousy, neediness, and anger born from a need to create emotional intensity. Partners in an air relationship relate mostly on the mental channel, enjoying lengthy discussions about facts and figures and philosophical concepts. Here the relationship is often analyzed from a place of logic that forgets to include feelings as a factor. Fire relationships are founded on a strong and fiery sexual connection and/or shared creative endeavors.

You can create a fuller, healthier, and more balanced relationship by learning to relate on all the elemental channels. Your relationship need not contain exactly one quarter of each element in its make-up. Instead, you work together to find the balance of each element that feels comfortable to both of you. In a truly tantric relationship, one that allows itself to flow in the moment, the elements come into a natural balance, so that you share physical touch, emotional intimacy, intellectual communion, and a strong sexual/creative connection, all in the amounts that feel good to you. By working the elemental balancing practices together, you will begin to gain an awareness of the channels that are hard for you to relate on, and which are easy. As you do the elemental practices together with intent to balance your relationship, you allow the power of Spirit to move through both of you and create the relationship that works in your best and highest good. If there is a particular part of your relationship that you want to balance and enhance, like your emotional connection, doing a lot of water practice is a good way to do that. Similarly, do fire practice to bring in more passion and creativity. Adding these other pieces to your relationship can bring a richness and joy to your union that was previously unimaginable.

Tantric Touch

Learning to touch each other in a whole new way is the first part of weaving the elements together. New levels of pleasure and ecstasy spring into being when you are open to changing the way that you give and receive touch. When I first learned these practices from my teacher, Mellissa Seaman (see Bibliography and Resources), I was astounded by their power to evoke deep healing and awareness, in addition to the ecstasy and sexual arousal they can create. Mellissa used to tell our priestess circle that elemental touch was a way to "open all the latches" that were holding the lid of our spiritual container closed. Dropping into these practices, we open the latches one by one, until we are able to remove the lid to see all of who we are that has been locked inside.

Tantric touch takes the sexual healing modality to a deeper level, allowing us to really feel in our body how and why and when someone is touching us. Many of us need the healing that comes from loving touch, not only on our torso, legs and arms, but also on our genitals and breasts. When we allow this touch to come from a safe and sacred healing massage that includes energy healing, deep shifts in the genitals begin to happen, and layers of body armor begin to be released. Often we experience an awakening of our sexuality through regular massage, but imagine if you were to receive a massage that included loving touch on your lingam or yoni? This type of touch is important to our sexual wholeness, and I urge you to practice giving and receiving this touch with your partner. There is something magickal about receiving the gift of intimate touch from someone who does not need or even want you to touch them back or to do anything at all. For a woman receiving yoni massage, it is so beautiful to have the yoni adored without any demands to make love afterward. The yoni awakens when given this kind of touch, and especially when the touch does not insist on focusing on the g-spot. Men also benefit greatly from tantric massage that includes the lingam and the prostate without any need to be aroused. This touch on the lingam especially helps to remove armoring that stands in the way of greater sensitivity.

It is my first time with a new lover, and I am nervous about moving into physical intimacy, about how it will feel, how we will sync together. He is wise. He tells me to lie down on my belly while he massages my back. I expect a typical inexperienced back massage, but am surprised when I feel the gentle and firm touch of his hands. He is fully present to me. I hear him breathe, and I feel that he is not touching me to make some experience happen within me. Rather, he is touching me because his hands know where they are needed on my body, his hands pay attention to where they are drawn. My heart opens and I relax deeply, letting go even of feeling a head cold, charged by all the energy that is moving through me as he touches me. I am overwhelmed with the relief of being touched in such a loving way, where I can let down my guard and my boundaries, and I begin to cry, just releasing old fears and old wounds, allowing myself to receive this priceless gift of loving healing touch.

You need no formal training to do this work, only genuine desire to let healing energy flow through your hands. I first learned this work by giving healing touch to my father, who was ill with AIDS. I learned to place my hands where he had discomfort, to open my heart, and to let loving energy flow through me from Spirit and into his body. He encouraged me, saying he could feel warmth and love in my hands. Today I am a Reiki healer, but all Reiki has done is to increase the amount of energy that flows through me when I do healing touch. I encourage you to try this touch with your partner and experience how healing it is for both of you to give and receive this touch that leads toward wholeness of the body, mind, emotions, and sexuality.

There are two ways of touching on the body. One way is a very healing, loving, heart-open touch that I described above. The other way of touching the body is to create arousal. There are certain types of touch that are more arousing, and we will talk about those in detail as we explore the elemental touches. But it is mostly the intention of your touch that matters. When you touch your partner with sexual intention, you will feel aroused and your partner will feel it too. You can intentionally create a sexual touch by focusing on inhaling sexual energy up through the body. Use this arousing touch as a form of foreplay, or as a sexual experience all its own. As with any of the sexual practices, you can then flow into making love.

When you are practicing these touches, touch the other with no ego or intent about pleasing them. Rather touch to feel the texture of their skin beneath your hand, as if you were touching a lush fur rug. When you touch in this way of enjoying how your partner feels, because you feel pleasure in touching your partner, you connect directly to Spirit. This type of touch feels amazing to your partner. Breathe, and stay present to feeling your lover's essence. As you do this, feel deeply into your touching hand and slow down. The secret is to touch your partner as if you have never touched them before. It is as if you are blind, and can only know your partner's body by touch. Spend time in one role or the other, either fully giving or totally receiving, so that each of you can experience the joy of being fully present.

Practice 1: Sacred Sexual Touch

This practice teaches you a radically different way to touch your partner, one that lets you feel ecstasy in the art of giving.

To begin, decide who will give and who will receive. Do the Partnered Sacred Tree Meditation and come into connection. Start the Partnered Circular Breath. Now the receiving partner lies down and the giving partner sits comfortably next to the receiving partner. It's important to sit comfortably. If the giver is not comfortable, the touch will not feel good to the receiver.

If you are the giving partner, start by breathing love into your heart from your connection to earth and sky. When you breathe out, feel that love flow from your heart down through your arms, to your hands. Hold your hands a few inches apart and continue to breathe this love into you, and then breathe it into your hands. You may feel heat or tingling in your hands. Once you feel the love energy moving strongly into your hands, gently and slowly move into your partner's energy field and very slowly and carefully place your hands on your partner's crown chakra. Notice what you feel. Keep your hands still on the Crown chakra, staying connected to your breath and to Spirit the whole time. You may choose to slowly massage the crown chakra, and if you move your hands, move so slowly that you can still feel the warmth radiating off the receiver's body, and the energy that is radiating from them as you touch. Do not touch with the intention to make your partner feel good, but touch to feel the miracle of your partner's body and energy under your hands. Feel the texture and warmth of their skin. Touch for your own pleasure, the way you might touch an exotic piece of velvet or silk simply to experience how it feels on your skin. Keep your hands on the receiver's crown for as long as you are called, not moving until it feels intuitively right to do so. Now slowly and lovingly move your hands down through your partners chakras, spending as much time as your hands tell you to on each one. Often your partner will trance out or fall asleep during this work. Give them permission to do this as it is part of the healing work, and a way for you to show your love for them as they show their trust in you even more. When you come to the yoni or lingam, just cup the genitals with your hand and send loving energy as you have on all the other chakras.

When you are finished, you can trade places so that the giver is now the receiver. Or you can choose to trade places giving and receiving on another day. Close this practice with Reconnecting to Self.

Do this practice whenever you want to practice loving touch with your partner.

Earth Touch

Holding the hands still without moving for periods of time brings the stillness of the Earth element into your touch, and prepares you for this same practice in lovemaking. It is important for both of you to stay in the breath fully and completely with this practice, keeping a strong awareness of your hands on the body. As you touch this way, imagine that you are channeling the Earth element into your partner, its stillness and safety. If you are receiving this touch, then breathe deeply into where your partner is touching you, and imagine you are drawing the Earth element into your body. Notice what this practice evokes in each of you.

Water Touch

Water touch is heart-connected, allowing the love from your heart to spill through your hands as they flow like water over your lover's body. Oil is essential to this loving touch, allowing the hands to slide easily over the body. It is a touch that opens your heart, and lets all the emotions that you feel there to travel down through your hands and into your lover's being. It is a beautiful process of connecting in this way, to be present and to just let yourself feel the heart connection that you have with your partner. I often feel moved almost to tears when connecting with this touch, and I can feel it activate my heart and my emotions. This can be a tremendously tender practice, especially if your partner is lying on their back and you can make eye contact while giving the touch. I find that this touch brings me fully into my heart when I give or receive it.

Air Touch

When the wind blows across my naked skin, the movement of all the little hairs starts me tingling. It is this same shivery and delicate feeling that is evoked by air touch, as well as an awakening of sexual energy. This touch brings a lightness to my body, a shivery preparation for more fiery pleasures, or perhaps a soothing after lovemaking ends. When I am touched this way, my mind clears, and becomes serenely occupied only with the experience of touch and of the tingling that moves through me.

Fire Touch

The dance of fingernails across the skin brings the sexual energy higher, and is called a fire touch because of the passionate energy it usually evokes. You can also evoke the fire energy through pulling hair gently at the roots (see Elemental Touch), or gentle biting. Fire is an intense energy and can be frightening for some and intensely arousing for others. The energy of fire creates a crescendo of sexual passion in me, unlocking the full force of my inner fire and sexual passion.

Once you learn all four of these touches, you can begin to flow between them, to experience a flowing tantric massage, following your instinct and intuition to see what touch to use on the body and where. When my lover's touch weaves the elements together, I soar into ecstasy. He begins with Earth, resting his hand gently on my breast, sending a sense of calm and safety into my body. As his hands begin to move across my body I feel so loved that my heart opens, and I sink into a feeling of being deeply cherished. I feel my whole body begin to awaken, and the graze of his teeth on my neck. I become more aroused as his nails find all the places of delight on me and I purr with ecstasy. He playfully tickles and teases me, and blows his breath across my skin and I shiver all over. Now we flow into making love and he continues to touch me now, flowing between all the touches in an intuitive dance with my body's energy. I soar into multiple climaxes as my sensuality, passion, mind, and emotions come into balance and unblock my soul.

Practice 2: Elemental Touch

This is the advanced practice of sacred sexual touch, learning how different touches can create safety, transmit love, arouse passion, and create playfulness. Have massage oil handy and music playing to create a beautiful mood.

Connect with the Partnered Sacred Tree Meditation and flow into Partnered Circular Breath together. Have the receiving partner lie down and the giving partner sit comfortably. Begin touching your partner with Sacred Sexual Touch, and once you are well connected to your hands and your touch, try these different touches, holding the basic principles of touch in your awareness.

Earth/Healing Touch — Place your hands on your partner's body and hold them still at first. Imagine that your body and your hands are a grounding rod to the earth. Move into a very slow traditional massaging touch with the intention of building trust and sending healing into your partner's body. Touch with deep, peaceful, slow, and grounded hands while you continue to breathe out through your roots any tension in both your body and your partner's body.

Water/Loving Touch — Get out the massage oil and open up the connection between your hands and your heart. Massage your partner with all the feeling that you have for them, using slow, sliding, loving touch that flows like water over their body. This is a solid touch like the earth touch but with a smooth slow flowing of the hands. Imagine that your hands are water flowing slowly over your partner's body. Move your hands with loving touch over your partner's body, while being guided by the connection between your heart and your hands. Feel into the joy of the flow of love from your hands, and the feeling of your partner's body beneath them. Let your hands move where they are guided by your heart and your intuition, and let your emotions move freely.

Air/Playful Touch — Use a very light touch, almost tickling, your fingertips barely touching the little hairs on your partner's skin. Even though this is a teasing touch, move as slowly as you can. Play with tracing your partner's body without even touching it, running your hands perhaps a centimeter above it. Then switch and caress your partner with one finger as if it is a light breeze flowing over their body. Tease your partner with this touch, holding the intention to send shivers of joy, and feel joy and delight flowing back to you from your partner.

Fire/Passionate Touch — Fire Touch is similar to Air Touch, but with more passion and sexual fire added. Lightly and slowly graze your partner's skin with your fingernails, being gentle and slow in your movements at first until you feel the passion build. Send your sexual arousal into your partner with this touch. Let your hands be filled with the passion and excitement that your body feels in this intimate connection with your partner. As with all the touches, stay present in the moment by remembering to breathe and stay connected to earth and sky. If you find yourself wanting to arouse sexual pleasure with the intent to reach some goal, then stop, take a breath, and move back into the sensual pleasure of your hands on your partner's body.

Once you have learned all four of these touches, start allowing yourself to flow between them, to weave them together into a tantric massage. Or use them during lovemaking, following your instincts and intuition about what touch to use on the body and where.

Elemental Movement

Dancing the elements together is another practice to take you into an experience of deeper connection to the parts of Spirit, one that can bring deep awareness of how the passion, emotion, sensuality, and mind are operating in your relationship. The practice of moving together teaches surrender to the moment and to trust. The woman learns to trust the man to lead her in movement, and the man learns to lead the woman by trusting his connection to each element of Spirit. Together, they flow and discover new layers of bonding with each other.

Earth Dance

Because the Earth element is about our connection to the mountains and trees as well as our connection to our physical body, approaching it through dance can feel natural. When I dance earth, I feel the heartbeat of the earth beneath my lover and through the drums as we move. I sink into my body, feel my bones and muscles moving me. I feel my skin contact his, and the luscious physical sensations that brings. I feel sensual, deeply connected to my movement, my breath, and the feeling of my partner in every place he is touching me. I invite the energy of my man to come into me with my magnetic feminine self, and I feel him send the solidity of his being into me. He protects and enfolds me with his safety. I allow him to lead me to a deep sensual ecstasy through the dance.

Water Dance

Flowing from the belly, I dance with my partner and feel my emotions as we move. We dance to music that flows and ripples, evoking movement in our hearts and a flow of emotion between us. My inner self unfolds as I dance, and I let emotion flow through me and spill, letting myself cry and scream and fully feel. I let go, emptying myself as he moves me. I breathe and stay present to exactly what it is that I feel in this connection with him, and I let him see me, the real me. He supports me as I release, and I see tears well up in his own eyes. I breathe and ground his emotion. I see hidden emotions emerge in me and I accept their presence, grateful for the awareness of my inner world. I flow without judgment, I stay connected, reveling in the sharing and the knowledge that we grow closer through this dance.

Fire Dance

I dance the fire in my stomach, knowing it is a dance of power and passion, feeling myself transform into a flame that wants to merge with my lover's inner fire. I feel us share power in a way that lets us work together, and I feel relief at letting go of the struggle I've been feeling between us for weeks. I feel how we can both be powerful as I focus my fire and passion on my center and imagine his power and purpose penetrating me there, joining our creativity together. I let myself feel powerful and I follow him. I let go of needing him to do things the way I want him to. I surrender to the fire between us and let its flames consume and transform our conflict into powerful creative synchrony.

Air Dance

After the intensity of the fire, we float playfully into the coolness of air. The music reminds me of winds and clouds, a gentle flute melody that we seem to float on as I glide around the room in his arms. I feel a place of peace emerge in me, a calm after the storm. This lightness brings with it the ability to transcend all obstacles between us. I float on imaginary wings as if I am flying high over the earth and can see clearly all the creatures that inhabit its surface. I spin and twirl with my partner and let him lead me to a place where I am completely surrendered and completely in clarity and serenity about what is true for me in this loving union. We play in this place with each other, and let it bring joy to our relationship. Magickally, we find clarity in our differences.

Practice 3: Moving with the Elements

Just as you learned to move your body to the elements in the solo practice, you can move together to each element to explore how well you are connecting in the physical, emotional, creative/sexual, and mental/playful realms.

Find music that evokes the elements for you, and start it when you are ready. Stand facing each other and do the Partnered Sacred Tree Meditation. Begin the

Partnered Circular Breath. As you move through the elements, let the man lead and be active with his energy, sending it into the woman. The woman's role is to surrender, follow, and magnetically pull the man's energy to her. Be sure that you are working together in a space where you have plenty of room to move, and won't be disturbed.

Earth — Dance slowly together, staying deeply in your bodies and in your physical/sensual connection.

Water — Dance your emotional connection, using flowing and watery movements.

Fire — Dance your sexual/creative vibe together, using shimmies and other movements that remind you of fire.

Air — Dance your joyful/playful/mental bond, using light, flying, and spinning motions.

Use this practice whenever you want to balance your connections to each other or enjoy being close.

Elemental Lovemaking

Making love through the elements is the practice that touch and dance prepare us for, a journey through lovemaking that deeply explores the balance of sensuality, passion, emotion, and playfulness in our most intimate connection to our lover.

Making Love with Earth

Imitating the element of earth with our bodies, we come into a stillness and heavy presence as well as a deep connection to our sensuality. We sit in stillness, our connection embodying the slow grinding of the earth's tectonic plates and the great stillness of mountains. We breathe deeply, using an earth breath to drop into our sensual connection. We feel into each bit of deep awareness that lives in our flesh, and all the sensations that our skin can embrace. Making love slowly, we feel our bodies wholly in contact with each other. I breathe into my muscles, into the skin of my yoni and into my legs and feet. I smell the scent of my partner's skin. I embrace the beauty of being in a physical body, and feel the deep ecstasy of total presence in my flesh.

Making Love with Water

In water sex, I flow into a wide open heart, feeling deeply while making love. I feel tears, I feel grief, and I feel joy. I begin to cry, not sure if my tears are happy or sad, just a well of raw emotion rising up in me to be witnessed and then released. I let my partner see these tears, and they arouse his heart, opening the inner gates so wide that I begin to feel like I can fly. He holds space for me, marveling at the beauty of my emotional release. I breathe my intention into this opening, and let trauma, mistrust, disappointment, and abandonment be washed away and replaced with pure crystalline joy. I release the fear of my own emotion, and of being seen, and realize that I am held safe in his eyes. I feel him anchor me, and I feel the richness of this deep connection unfold.

Making Love with Air

Lightly and playfully, I drop into a sense of wonder with my beloved. We become children together, exploring each other with curiosity and joy. We try new and crazy sexual positions, and tease each other with hands, yoni, lingam, and breath. I giggle with not knowing what to expect. I tease him in turn, pushing him out of my vagina with my PC muscles, or pulling away for a moment and then playfully allowing him back into my yoni temple. We are sacred playmates in this space, exploring like two children on an adventure at a circus together, knowing there are amazing and wonderful experiences always waiting for us just inside the next circus tent. As we play, we lighten our whole relationship, and just like the air dance, I feel things unlock and loosen from my mind. I let go now into serenity and joy.

Making Love with Fire

I feel the fire rise up in me, raw animal energy and passion. I feel the force of the kundalini move through me, and I let go as it burns pleasure through my body. The more I open, the more I feel the fire move through me, shooting flames of bliss up and down my body. My passion increases and my pleasure becomes larger and larger. I give up control to my partner as we become more passionate with each other. I know I have only to utter a single word to stop if the intensity becomes too high. I begin to growl and purr, and the black jaguar in me scratches and bites. I allow myself to merge with the cat, feel it look out through my eyes, as I feel it in me. I even roar my pleasure and feel my fire and know that it has no limits. I feel my partner's fire dancing with mine, feeling the power we create together, and the magick.

Practice 4: Lovemaking with the Elements

This exercise teaches you that there can be a lot of variety in your lovemaking, and shows you some ways of making love that let you express the type of intimacy you want to create in each moment with your lover.

Sit or lie together on the bed and come into connection using the Partnered Sacred Tree Meditation. Come into the Partnered Circular Breath and flow into the elements of touch, practicing what you've learned. Stay in the breath together and let yourself totally surrender to the moment. When you are ready to flow into lovemaking, try these different types of intercourse:

Earth/Stillness — Place the lingam in the yoni and squeeze the PC muscle and breathe. Make love without moving, simply squeezing the PC muscles. Try also a very slow and deep motion of grinding the pelvises together.

Water/Loving — Make slow, gentle, flowing motions of the lingam in the yoni. Open to your love and emotion for each other. Make love with your hearts, adding the Heart Circuit practice from Chapter 6.

Air/Playful — Tease the yoni with the lingam by pulling it all the way out, then gently re-entering unexpectedly. Use the tip of the lingam to tease the labia and clitoris. Use the air touch with your hands as well to tease, play, and laugh while you make love.

Fire/Passionate — Turn up the intensity and use deeper and faster thrusting to create high levels of arousal. Practice staying connected while making love in fire. Keep your eyes open and use your breath to move the sexual energy through your whole body. Let the practice flow without any goals of orgasm and see where Spirit leads you.

Once you have tried all of these, let yourself choose whichever mode of lovemaking feels right to you in the moment, and let yourself shift between them when it feels right in the moment. Do this practice anytime when you are making love, and notice if it enhances your connection.

As you weave the elements together in new ways of touching, moving, and making love, you create the Spirit of your relationship, that mysterious fifth element that comes from a combination of the other four. Nurturing this Spirit together leads to lasting change in relationship, often through shifts in disagreements, or patterns that seem to easily resolve themselves. The more you surrender to Spirit in these practices, the more whole and complete you will feel, ready to step forward through the final gateway of the Divine Union of the masculine and feminine.

✦ The Sixth Gateway ✦

Divine Union

Chapter 16

Center, Purpose, and Polarity

Opening to my partner, I sink into the center of my inner ocean, and invite him to follow. My love dives in joyfully, with passion, groaning in ecstasy at the feeling of my yoni closing around his lingam, of our energies mingling. He plunges wildly into me, sending all his desire, all his passion into my body and my being. I feel a wave of heat and passion rise within me and I become wild, like an ocean storm, as I pull him to me. He cannot look away, his eyes are boring into mine, and I open, I receive, I pull him in. We become an endless loop of energy, two beings merged in perfect union, as Spirit flows through us, as I open to him, as he gives to me. He holds me down, and my body surrenders by gushing hot amrita over him. He cries out, and plunges his lingam deeper, feeling the waves of contraction in my yoni. My yoni grasps his lingam, pulling him deeper, milking him, craving the feeling of his essence. Time loses all meaning, and we are suspended in this wildness, exploring, biting, surrendering, breathing. I want to give all of myself to him, to surrender to whatever he wants of me, trusting deeply, releasing completely. Waves of pleasure crash over me again and again as I feel my connection to him and to Spirit expanding more and more. I am making love to God in human form, and I am surrounded by his light, his warmth, and his ravishing passion. Afterward, spent, we feel into the love that flows between us, connecting our hearts to each other and to our genitals, feeling the endless circuit of love and ecstasy, carrying that out into the world.

Finding the Feminine

True, deep womanhood, is my spiritual goal. To be all of who I am, without apology, whether I am a business owner, a healer, a dancer, a lover, or a mother. Carrying a longing within me, I yearned to express my fullness, to strip the veils away that hid me from society, those rigid roles of mother, career woman, and wife. I struggled to unleash the wild woman within me, to love deeply, to feel satisfied. As a woman I am a complex creature full of love and anger and joy. I contain a limitless sea of emotion within me, a fiery forge of creativity and passion, a crystalline clear mind, and a deeply sensual body. But how to embrace all of this and still exist within society? Shamanic tantra opened a gateway, showing me the path to a new paradigm of strength and power that emanates from being on my own axis mundi, centered, grounded, connected, and flowing. On this journey, a woman's journey, my greatest strength lies in my ability to draw in all that I need with each breath, opening to fully receive. I am learning to be magnetic, to consciously pull what Spirit tells me I need into my life, whether that thing is money, belongings, or men. I have learned to be in the great stillness, and to allow the world to travel to my sacred feet. I have learned to love myself so deeply, that I feel worthy to receive what Spirit brings to me.

At first this way of being in the world confused me. Learning what it was to be fully receptive, let alone magnetic, was profoundly difficult. I was a woman who would receive a gift or a package in the mail and not open it for days. This trait in me was a problem with the act of receiving. I learned that if I am able to receive, then I am able to unwrap the package when it arrives. I am able to receive the love and attention of a man when it is given to me. I am able to accept favors and kindness from other people. When I am truly in a place of power as a woman, I allow myself to receive these gifts. I receive not because I am weak and needy, but because I am a powerful queen and earth mother who deserves respect and admiration. This receiving is the secret to empowering men to give to me and to be strong.

I am not trying to say that women should only take from a man. In fact, the dynamic I experience, whether in life or in energy work, is that once I receive a certain amount from a man, I begin to give back naturally, without any conscious effort. In energy work, when a man is giving to me and I am fully open, there is a point where my energy begins to naturally flow back to him, without any conscious effort on my part. In life, when a man gives to me, at a certain point I start to naturally feel the desire to give back through sexual union and nurturing. This dynamic only becomes possible once I allow myself to fully receive. If I am not open to what is coming my way, then my inner sacred bowl can never be filled, no matter how much others give to me. It is up to me to learn to create the space within, where all the blessings of the world can flow.

Exploring the Masculine

Struggling to survive in a world with many demands, men often feel confused about what is appropriate or desirable behavior, especially when it comes to women. Men are supposed to be strong and sensitive, masculine and feminine. And yet, when men water themselves down, when they hold in their need to actively penetrate the world, it weakens them in all of their life. They find that sex is boring, or that they can't stay erect as much as they like, or make love as long as they want. And often male students come to me and tell me they feel there is so much more for them, but they are unsure how to access it. It doesn't help that we women give mixed messages. We want them to be strong and protect us, but we want them to be sensitive and listen to us talk about our feelings. This leaves so many men in exasperation about what women want!

Tuning into the divine masculine is a way for men to bring more aliveness and passion to life. Being fully in your masculine can activate that part of you that is electric with purpose, virility, and strength. When you pull this divine masculine energy in, it can help you to be more courageous as you penetrate the world. If you let yourself become one with this electric energy, you will hold the energy of the sky father archetype within you. As you consciously increase your connection to this power and learn to listen, it will guide you on your purpose and path. Part of this being on your masculine purpose means having the courage to take the lead with a woman, whether in life or in bed. When you let your guidance show you the path, you can fearlessly take her with you as you penetrate her life, her energy, and her yoni with your power, awareness, and love.

Cultivating Sexual Polarity

This giving and receiving between a man and a woman creates a polarity, like that between two magnets. If two magnets have the same charge, they repel each other, but if they have opposite charges, they connect. It is this same underlying pull of energies between humans that creates sexual passion and tantric spiritual union. Polarity is the key I was always looking for in creating a powerful sexual connection that lasts. In both my marriages, we prided ourselves on being equal partners and being "on the same page" with everything. For me, this often led to sex that might be fun, or even deeply loving, but not exciting or enticing or passionate. But for the past two years, as I have explored tantric partnership, I have found that each lovemaking session feels like the first time. There is a richness in it that is created by each of us consciously committing to staying polarized in masculine and feminine roles, both in our lives and in the bedroom.

As a woman, this means I am continually thinking about surrendering and opening to my partner as much as I can. This openness, this surrender, this full receiving of the man's energy is orgasmic. It allows me to feel safe because my partner moves naturally into the role of protector and container for my feminine energy. I can be soft and still powerful and centered, and know that I am completely held, so that I can let go and open even more to my feminine depths. It gives me something to push against, so that I don't have the fear of flying off the face of the Earth, or getting so big that I dissipate myself.

For men, true polarity comes from a willingness to fully penetrate a woman with their energy, to take the risk of asking her to open. Most men have yet to experience the joy of being fully received by a woman, of feeling that their partner is fully open to them, fully accepting, and joyous in following while he leads the dance of life. There is power and magick in this experience, where a man becomes willing to penetrate with his energy as deeply as a woman can take him, without fear of being swallowed up. Exchanging energy and making love with this type of woman can be an initiatory experience for a man. Whether you are doing this work as a solo practice or in partnership, to be fully received means you must trust and let go of your own fears of rejection. You must let yourself connect strongly and powerfully with a woman, or with the Goddess. Be present, but stay within her boundaries. You must not be afraid to give her all that you have, to penetrate her with your energy, your eyes, and, in lovemaking, your lingam. The key to this powerful connection is to circuit energy strongly with her, and to understand the differences between masculine and feminine sexual energy.

Masculine sexual energy is very different from the feminine. In general, the seat of masculine sexual energy is in the lingam. In tantric sex, arousal for the man begins in the lingam and rises up through the chakras in the body, opening his heart to receive from the woman, and opening his crown to divine communion. Feminine sexual energy is found living in the heart. In most women, this is where arousal begins, in the breasts, and from there it spreads downward to awaken the yoni, and upward to open the crown. One of the benefits of sacred sexual practice is that it teaches us how to bring the masculine and feminine into union, how to join these two. But paradoxically, it is the differences between men and women that create a sexual charge. As with magnets, if two have the same charge, they repel, rather than attract each other. It is the same with sexuality. Without this charge between masculine and feminine, active and receptive, there is no sexual attraction or passion. In the beginning on the path, men's work centers on learning to awaken the lingam so that he can more fully give energy to the woman. The lingam, as it wakes up, becomes a powerful transmitter of both sexual energy and love. The word "lingam" means "wand of light." The waking of the lingam also yields more sensitivity to touch and to the experience of being within the yoni, so that the man comes to experience his sexuality in a whole new way. As the lingam wakes up, the heart begins to open and learns to be vulnerable to loving energy from the woman.

A Woman's Center

A woman can learn to feel safe either by embracing a man's protection or by finding and cultivating her center. Centering in themselves, women in their true feminine power open to their vision of Spirit's will. Only through this vision can they manifest the life that is best and most growthful for them. With this centered vision also comes a clarity of their role in life, of the place within themselves from which all things emanate. My own center is my spirituality. Everything I do must come from this place in me if I am to stay aligned with Spirit's will for me. This means that I must meditate and pray and do spiritual practice daily. It means that I must walk my path in all of life, bringing my spirituality into every activity that I do, from putting gas in the car to cooking dinner. Aligned in this nexus, my life and abundance radiate out, and magnetically draw money, love, and situations to me that are beneficial. All of these things make me abundant, and as long as I sit in the center of this spider's web of connections to the world, I manifest easily any desire that is also the desire of Spirit for me.

To find this inner center and stay there requires a commitment to living life in a truly feminine way. Authentically feminine women allow things to flow without forcing or fixing. Inaction is often the best choice for a woman, whether in relationship or in work. When we trap ourselves in the need to constantly interfere in things that really don't require our hands (for example taking out the trash or mowing the lawn because we don't trust your partner to do it, or don't like the way they do it), we start to lose our femininity. Uncentered activity shifts us into a masculine way of being in the world that takes us away from our natural magnetic nature. In your life, try letting others come to you when something is needed, and only attend to those things that are officially your responsibility. You may find that your definition of what is urgent becomes more and more liberal as you embrace this practice. In this way of being, imagine yourself standing in the center of a hula hoop. Whatever is outside the hoop is not yours to worry about or interfere in. Even then, when there is need, take a deep breath and see if there is a way to do what needs to be done while staying centered and calling the solution to you through your intuition. In all parts of your life, strive to stay in the center of your web of power.

Cultivating my feminine is hard when it means I must let a man lead. All of my needs and programming for strength and empowerment scream against it, as if following the path that the masculine opens for me somehow makes me less than I am. I have learned to see following the masculine's lead as a way that Spirit provides ease for me in life, so that I can concentrate on my center. The Earth is powerful and yet she follows the lead of the sun and stars as she glides along her orbit. So too can we as women remain in our power as we follow where men go. This does not mean that we cannot make requests, that we cannot make our desires known, but that we allow the man to answer those requests in his own way. We learn to accept the yeses and nos he gives us and still stay centered and flowing with him. Raised by a matriarchal family of feminists, I find it especially hard to trust enough to follow, certain that any man will lead me someplace scary or limiting. And yet I find that if I have chosen the right man to follow by calling him to my center, I am able to let go and surrender. In this way I allow the man to have the power to lead, and somehow my power increases also. I become softer, more receptive and flowing, a magnetic power that harmonizes with the electric masculine drive. This choosing the right man to surrender to is part of the key to success in the feminine life. If you don't feel safe, it is not possible to surrender.

Staying on Center

Dance was the practice that unlocked my power to surrender more deeply to a man. In partner dance, you must have a leader and a follower, and traditionally it is the woman who follows. I learned to surrender to this, to let it be okay, even if the man was "doing it wrong." I found I was carrying so much judgment that it made it impossible for me to be a good partner. I was so convinced that I always knew the right way to do a particular step or movement. As I began to surrender more deeply to my partner in the dance, I found a lot of fear waiting for me, fear that my partner would lead me somewhere embarrassing, or that I would somehow get physically hurt. I had to learn to let my partner contain me in the dance, and this has led to an ability to let that happen in life.

Dance in general is good for the feminine soul. For me, it was my way into tantric practice, and has become part of my spiritual practice. When I notice that I am feeling down, or that I am feeling curiously empty or numb, I dance. I also dance to express my joy. Moving to feel the sensuality of my body frees my mind from worry and my body from boredom. In my journey through dance, I have found connection to Spirit, deep emotional release, and intense joy and ecstasy. This happened by degrees, over many years of first learning the technique and form of dance, then surrendering to freeform dance meant to unleash the soul. Each form of movement is a learning experience in its own right. Something about dancing frees me totally and completely from all the limitations I have let society put on me. Dance gives me a healthy way to express my feelings, and at the same time to allow Spirit to come in and seal the healing.

A Man's Purpose

The core of being masculine is to find and stay on your purpose. To do this, you need clarity of mind, which you can gain through sitting in meditation and exploring your inner world. The gateway of Divine Union is a deeper level of the Soul Gazing gateway, and only becomes possible once you have conquered your inner demons. With the space that their death leaves behind, your path is clear to fully embody the electric energy and drive of the balanced masculine. The more you call the divine masculine into you, the more you will embody it in your daily life. It is a process of absorbing it into your cells, and getting familiar with how it feels to run this energy through your body. Daily communion with the Divine Masculine, even if only five minutes per day, will bring the masculine into our body and soul, and this will be evident in both your spiritual and sexual life.

Finding your purpose is also about leading in life and in relationship. So many men are afraid to take the lead, afraid they will be labeled as macho or callous. They are afraid of abandonment by the women in their lives, who always seem to be asking for caring and compassion. And yet most women are ultimately happy to see their man take the lead in their lives and in their bed. This isn't to say that women are without choice when they are following. But as in partner dance, a strong lead makes it so much easier for a woman to relax into herself, and into her place of deeply feminine radiance and intuitive perception. It is also easier for most women to open sexually when the man is insistent and strong in his gentleness. I encourage men to allow themselves to be powerful and take charge so their women can relax and become even more juicy, alive, and sexy. I am not talking about old-fashioned macho behavior. A strong man does not make his partner weak or dominate her. A strong man is someone who can use his strength to forge a path for himself with an open heart. This is the tantric ideal of a man truly leading his partner along his path.

True divine union comes from a place of being on your purpose, led fully by Spirit in making decisions and choosing your path. To be in this place, you must let go of fear and shame and guilt, as well as the need to please your partner. All these things flow from a controlling ego, and this ego is not needed in tantric practice, where we are striving to be fully present and in the moment. Connect with your own desires and your own sensations in your fingers, hands, feet, legs, heart, and penis. Connect fully with your body and your desires, both in lovemaking and in life. Stay connected to Spirit throughout this, and allow Spirit to tell you where your path lies. Allow yourself to enjoy the journey, and to revel in these sensations. This is the path to living ecstatically, to an orgasmic life.

Staying on Purpose

When a man is on his purpose and really drawing in his masculine power, he is poetry in motion, energy and electricity flowing through his body and ready to be discharged in the service of his purpose. A man in his full masculine power breathes into Spirit and from there makes a strong plan of action. He uses his will to discipline himself to stick to whatever Spirit guides him to do. It is an awesome thing to see in action, this masculine strength on its purpose. Using this strength, men move into a place of strong charge, which carries them into connection with women, career, and life, blasting like a lightning bolt through obstacles and outside interference. Let yourself be this lightning, this pure energy in motion, and create a high expression of masculine divinity that is immanent within you.

Needs

Every human has needs. Getting in touch with these needs begins in the Soul Gazing gateway. As you travel through the gateway of Divine Union, you learn to not only tune in more sharply to what you need, but also to start asking for what you need from Spirit, from your friends, and from your partners. You learn not only to ask, but to be willing hear yes or no, to accept that your needs will not always align with your partner's. There may be so many needs bottled up insides you from years of not asking that you are afraid once you start asking, the flow of need will never stop. While it is true that there are appropriate and inappropriate needs, it may be hard to tell the difference.

One way to check whether a need is healthy is to check in with Spirit during meditation and prayer. Simply ask if the need is healthy and let that question fall into the silence of your meditation. Wait and stay present, and an answer will come to you. Another way to determine if a need is healthy is to educate yourself about healthy emotional needs and appropriate emotional expression (see Bibliography and Resources for information on NVC and CODA). With your partner, asking for support is healthy, and even asking for how that support will look is healthy. But expecting them to say yes to every request is not reasonable, because your partner's first job is to meet their own needs. If they must compromise their own needs to meet your request, then a healthy partner must say no. It is our job in healthy relationship to take no for an answer, and to celebrate the no as a sign of health in our partner. And it is also our job to keep asking for what we need, unattached to whether we hear yes or no from our beloved. It is our job to get our needs met by Spirit, our friends, or ourselves if our partner cannot met them.

Emotional sharing is a healthy need that cannot always be met by our partner. Sharing is a part of healthy intimacy, but expecting a partner to sit and listen while you spew anger and sadness at them for many long minutes is not healthy. Limit your emotional sharing to "I" statements and expressions of feelings about specific occurrences, and keep your sharing in the present, not in blaming about occurrences in the past. Get some training in healthy communication if you need help with sharing in this way. Often, when we want to blame and rage at our partner, we are acting out of feelings stirred up from our childhood, not out of feelings that are about the present situation. Use your journal instead if you need to gush out all the emotions inside you, and keep your sharing with your partner kind and loving, even when it is about difficult subjects.

Moving into our centers or onto our purposeful paths, we become men and women who are enjoying rich and satisfying lives that are more fully connected to Spirit and to each other. Our relationships become rich, our work satisfying, and we move through the challenges of life with ease. We are connected to Spirit and to the depths of our souls at the same time. As we persist in our dedication to our paths and our inner centers, we find the divine living within our own souls.

• Chapter 17 •

Divine Union Solo

So often, from so many people, I hear the question, "How can I practice tantra without a partner?" When I first began to teach the Six Gateways as a framework for tantric practice, I was mystified about how to bring divine union into a solo practice, but I trusted Spirit when it told me that it was possible — that all the gateways could be done as either solo or partnered work. Finally I was given the answer through my own practice. As I was teaching a student, I began channeling the practice of making love to the Goddess or God. When you make love to the divine, you call them in as your tantric partner. With practice, their energy and presence will feel as real to you as exchanging energy with another person. You learn to allow the God or Goddess to embrace you, to connect to you. Any tantric practice you can do with a human partner can be done with the divine.

Connecting directly to the God or Goddess allows us to pull in their energies for balance. None of us can live totally in the place of the masculine or feminine all the time without difficulty in living happy, productive lives. While we may choose to express ourselves the majority of the time as masculine or feminine, there are times when we need to tap the opposing polarity within us to accomplish certain tasks or live through certain situations with ease. The masculine is important for getting things done, holding a job, and paying the bills. The feminine has the opposite job of holding the vision, nurturing, manifesting, and creating. Together these two parts make a whole, a dance within you.

To begin to look at this balance is a tricky thing, because if we are stuck in our ways of being, we may find it hard to embrace change, and still drop into old habits. I became stuck myself, when I was a new mother. I became completely polarized in the feminine, unable to perform many of the tasks for myself that had been easy for me when I was a career woman in a corporate job. I swung too far to the feminine in searching for my balance. It took me a long while to recognize that I needed a pinch of masculine within my being so that I could take care of myself.

Let me be clear, though, that by balancing, I do not mean that we should all be genderless, perfectly in the middle between the masculine and feminine natures. In my experience on the path of sacred sexuality, it is best to commit to one or the other way of being, because they have different tasks in relationship and in the world. The masculine task is to lead, to be active, and to be on its purpose. The feminine task is to follow, to be receptive, and be magnetically and powerfully on its center. Society often moves us out of our natural place of gender balance. We must learn to let go of those influences and decide how we are going to express ourselves. We must find our own inherent polarity. If that polarity is mostly feminine, we cultivate our center. If it is masculine, then we can focus on our purpose. Relationship works best if the partners make opposite choices, to create the polarity that creates true tantric union. In this union, the masculine polarity connects and penetrates, while the feminine polarity opens, attracts, and receives.

Polarizing your Energy Field

Polarizing your energy field can be done, like all tantric work, with the power of the mind. Many years ago, I dreamed that two giant serpents were battling with each other. One snake was angular and fierce and covered with sharp diagonal designs and fiery colors. The other was velvety and flowing and covered in swirls and pastels. In my dream the snakes battled with each other for dominance, and neither could seem to win the fight. At that time in my life I was caught between the masculine and feminine. I was working as a scientist, and yet pulled to spirituality, writing, and to work with people. This dream captured perfectly my struggle, my desire to let go of my masculine side and embrace the feminine.

Cultivating Feminine Receptivity

Dance is a marvelous tool for exploring your feminine self, allowing you to dive into a place of unique sensuality. When you move your body to music that brings out the deep feminine sensuality in you, it awakens your magnetic feminine sexuality. There is a magic in movement that allows the Goddess to enter our bodies, that allows us to express ourselves emotionally and spiritually in a way no other exercise is equal to. Dance was a very important part of women's rites and rituals for ancient peoples, because it evoked the Goddess to manifest in each woman, bringing power, magic, and mystery to their lives.

Another way to cultivate your feminine is to meditate on embodying the Earth Mother, and bring Her divine energy into you. She is, earthy, sensuous, full of vitality, rich, deep, and dark. She is the height of beingness. She creates...slowly. Nothing is hurried or rushed, all comes from her monumental place of center. Connecting to this depth and richness brings women to a place of centered serenity. From this place they gain permission to really be women, not women who must keep up with men and behave like men. Women truly in their feminine wait and see rather than jumping in and doing.

Practice 1: Cultivating Feminine Energy

This exercise is wonderful for helping a woman to really experience her feminine as divine, and to gain the awareness of what the divine feminine feels like to her. Find a comfortable sitting position, and connect your roots to the earth and your branches to the sky, as you did before in the Sacred Tree Meditation. Now begin the Circular Breath. Once you feel grounded, and your breath is flowing smoothly, take your awareness deep into the earth. Start to inhale the essence of the deep and rich earth up through your roots and into your body. Breathe it up into your yoni, belly, stomach, and breasts. Let the richness of the Earth Mother flow effortlessly into you. Feel her strength, power, and sensuality fill your body, and allow the essence of her to become one with your own energy. Exhale any obstacles to allowing this energy to permeate your being, breathing down the body and out though your roots. Allow yourself to merge with the Goddess as you become Her. Feel Her sexual power fill you. Feel how Her energy drops you into your center and notice what that center is. Notice how your body feels when you are on this center.

Continue this meditation for at least 5 minutes. You may wish to write down your experience. Repeat this meditation as often as you like, whenever you want to connect with your feminine.

Finding Masculine Purpose

Men without a purpose are lost in the world, wandering aimlessly through life, letting it happen to them. Bringing purpose in allows you to experience a new level of joy, contentment, and freedom because you are creating this purpose yourself, with nobody's intervention. Focusing your will and intent will bring great rewards, as long as the will is used appropriately to do no harm and to follow the will of Spirit for you.

Men can also explore their masculine purpose through moving their bodies. Tribesmen of ancient times performed rituals of initiation for young boys, using their movements to show the boys what being a man is. Imagine the way your body would move, what you would convey, and the virile masculine feeling in your body. Movement gets you out of your ego because there is no need to stop and think too much about what you are doing, only to allow the flow of the movement, the manliness and the raw primal feeling to take you over. Let Spirit and the music you choose show you how to move. Music with a heavy drumbeat is often especially good for men. In dance the God can dance through you, recalling himself to others by using your body to take physical form just for a short time. Dance gives you a chance to be divine, and to join with the God to find the piece of Him that is you. Gain awareness of your purpose in this way, by feeling and seeing that piece of the God that holds your identical image and your path in life.

Connecting at a deeper level to the Sky Father, the Sun God, can help you to sharpen and focus your masculine self. It is also a way to bring the presence of the divine masculine alive within your body. Go out into nature and breathe in the sky, the clouds, and the raging thunderstorm. Breathe these things in so that you can embody them, so that you can feel them in each particle of your being. Breathe in to strengthen your purpose. Sit in nature, go into meditation, and put your branches into the sky. Breathe in through these branches, and draw the God into you. Breathe Him in at your branches and out through your roots. Let Him flow through you like a pounding rainstorm, or jolts of lightning. Let him wake you up, let Him show you your purpose and where it flows out from your body. Breathe strongly into the purpose that He shows you, and accept its gift, even if it seems outrageous. When you are ready, start to breathe him out your lingam as well. Activate this part of your body and own it as powerful, healthy, and the spear of your masculinity. Take some time after this meditation to write about your purpose, and to write your vision of yourself living out that purpose in your life. Let Spirit show you how to bring that into being in your life.

Practice 2: Exploring Masculine Energy

This meditation helps men to connect strongly to their masculine power and purpose.

Sit comfortably and grow your roots in the earth and branches in the sky, as you did before in the Sacred Tree Meditation. Begin the Circular Breath. Now focus your awareness on your branches in the sky, and inhale the warmth, fire, and creative energy of the sun into your crown, forehead, throat, and heart. Exhale and push that energy down through your stomach, belly, lingam, legs, and feet. Continue inhaling through your head and exhaling down the body, letting yourself imagine you are standing in a waterfall of light pouring down through your body from the heavens. Let this waterfall of light become the divine masculine energy and let it become one with you, showing you clearly your passion and purpose, your path. Continue to breathe and connect to this limitless energy, integrating it into your blood and bone so it becomes you.

Continue this meditation for at least 5 minutes, and repeat it as often as you like to keep the strength of your power and purpose alive in you. You may wish to write down any experiences that you have, especially insights or messages about your purpose.

Spirit as a Primary Partner

If you are a woman, opening to receive the God into your body can bring a connection to the masculine divine energy that can be father, lover, or even son. For me, my connection to the divine masculine is my primary relationship, outweighing all human relationships. Over time, this relationship has become more and more real, something that is always there for me. It helps me to be unafraid of any changes that might occur in my relationships with men, and has been powerful in helping me heal jealousy and fear of abandonment.

It can be hard for me to remember this relationship to the God energies when I am upset with the man in my life, and in fact these are for me the hardest times to feel the connection. But I am also aware that I am not feeling the connection because I am closing it off out of anger, that I want to isolate myself from any further upset by completely detaching from the physical man in my life, as well as the divine masculine. Now that I have been doing the practice of connecting to the masculine, I know that when I cut it off, it is out of fear, and I remind myself that opening my heart will allow me to feel better. I anchor myself into my connection with the Goddess and God, and fully drop into the feelings I am having, allowing myself to be present to the emotional storms within me. In this space of being held by Spirit, I am safe, and Spirit helps me to release what is within me, to accept the situation that I am upset about, and perhaps even to gain a new perspective on my feelings.

Practice 3: Making Love to the God

This practice is wonderful for women learning that their primary romantic and sexual relationship is to God. This is the "beloved" in Rumi's timeless love poetry. This beloved manifests in our partners, but we can always connect directly to receive love from the masculine. This practice also allows us to do almost any partnered practice with the God when a physical partner is not available.

Sit or lie down and put your roots in the earth and branches in the sky, as in the Sacred Tree Meditation. Begin the Circular Breath. Now feel into your connection to the sky, and ask the Sun God or Sky Father to flow down to where you are and partner with you. Let him come into whatever connection you are craving, whether it be sexual, moving energy as in a partnered exercise, or just holding you. If you choose a sexual connection, stay in your breath, and allow yourself to feel sexual. Stay in the relaxed tantric state without any particular goals. Fully receive the god, however you are connecting, and share your fears, your anger, your joy, your sadness, and your ecstasy. Know that he can hold space for any emotions you have and that he can help you transmute them and let go.

Do this practice for as long as you want, and repeat it whenever you want the comfort and connection to the beloved that it brings.

Men can do the same practice with Earth Mother to feel Her as their wife, their mother, their mistress, their first and most important true love who is always willing to lovingly receive them and make love to them for as long as they want. Cultivating this special relationship with the Goddess brings a man the courage to be fully powerful with a woman. With the Goddess as his partner, a man need have no fear that he will hurt her. He can be as rough and masculine as he chooses and still know what it is like to be fully received. This acceptance by the Goddess helps a man learn to open his heart, because her love and acceptance of him has no demands attached, but is only pure unconditional love.

Practice 4: Making Love to the Goddess

This practice is great for men learning to be fully sexually powerful with women. The Goddess is a sex partner who is always available and always able to fully receive you. This practice may feel a little funny at first, and it may be hard to tell the difference between fantasy and real connection with divine feminine energy, but this is natural. When you are truly connecting to the Goddess, you will feel her receiving your energy fully in her yoni and giving it back to you in the heart. It will feel different from fantasy because the connection will be ethereal and Spirit will be guiding you.

Sit comfortably and put your roots in the earth and branches in the sky, as you did in the Sacred Tree Meditation. Begin the Circular Breath. Once you have the breath flowing, call the Goddess to flow up from the Earth and make love to you. Place Her on your lap and let Her receive your lingam inside Her. Flow into the Heart Circuit, sending your sexual power to Her through your lingam and receiving the love she sends out to you in your heart. Feel the joy of being fully received and keep breathing. Make love to Her, and let yourself be fully aroused while letting go of any goals or need for orgasm. It's okay to touch your lingam with your hand, as long as you do not fall into your routine masturbation habits. Continue this practice as long and as often as you like, whenever you want to fully express yourself sexually.

Self Marriage

After years of marriage to others, therapy, and spiritual practice, it became clear to me that I needed a commitment to love myself above all others. This was so hard for me, because it seemed a very selfish thing to do. I had been taught that it was noble and spiritual to sacrifice my needs for the needs of others. Changing this pattern has been uncomfortable, and what finally persuaded me to do it was realizing how much I had left my feminine center to stay in relationship with my lovers. I was in a lot of pain because I had abandoned myself and my needs.

Finding my way back was easy, once I had the desire and willingness. My guides and the divine energies helped me, through dreams, trance journey messages, and strong intuitions received in meditation. I did the practices of Cultivating Feminine Energy and of Making Love to the God daily, and eventually I was given a ritual to anchor my marriage to Spirit and to myself. This ritual I named the Self Marriage Ceremony.

Since creating and experiencing this ritual, I have become stronger in knowing what is best for me in relationship, and in asking for that. I have received transformational healing of my abandonment fears through setting intention to release them and allowing a healer to work on me in that willing state. Her work was powerful, and released a giant shard of pain from my heart. Since that time I am calm and fearless, and I trust that Spirit will bring me the love that is best for me, because I have learned to love myself.

Practice 5: Self Marriage Ceremony

This is a powerful practice for feeling whole and complete in yourself and strong in your connection with Spirit. You may wish to find, make, or purchase a power object or special piece of jewelry to symbolize your commitment to yourself.

Light a candle, and place your power object or jewelry next to it. Also have a rock or crystal, a feather, and a small bowl of water to represent the other elements. Have a journal nearby if you want to record your insights.

Sit comfortably in front of your candle and other objects, and send your roots into the earth and your branches into the sky. Breathe the circular breath to stay present. If you are a woman, call in the Goddess energy to fill you, and the God energy to hold you. If you are a man, call in the God to fill you with strength and the Goddess to witness and receive you.

- Now bless each chakra with a rock or crystal by placing it on the chakra and saying, "I bless this chakra with the power of Earth."
- Pick up the feather and use it to bless each chakra with the power of air.
- Use the candle to warm each chakra and bless it with the power of fire.
- Pick up the bowl of water and bless each chakra with the power of water by anointing it.

Now lie down on the floor and let yourself go into a deeper meditation. Let the divine energies guide you and show you what is needed for you to be whole and complete in yourself: on purpose if you are man; on center if you are a woman.

When you have come out of meditation, begin your vows. Say these affirmations out loud while you hold your power object or piece of jewelry in your right hand:

"I commit to a lifetime love affair with myself.
I promise never to abandon myself again.
I honor my body as a sensual temple.
I remember to take care of myself first, before caring for others."

If you have a piece of jewelry, place it on your body. If you have a power object, place it on your altar or in a medicine pouch around your neck (or in some other significant place). You may wish to write out the affirmations and place them in a spot where you will see them every day.

End this ritual with some self-care (rest, food, bathing, walking), and notice in the coming days if your life perspective shifts. You can repeat this ritual whenever you want to recommit to your self-marriage, using the same power object or piece of jewelry.

Spirit wants our happiness. Balancing the masculine and feminine in us, feeling whole and complete whether or not we are alone, brings a deep joy into life. It creates us as beings who come into connection with others from a place of fullness and sharing. It leaves behind connection from a place of lack, of neediness. It is the paradox of the universe, that if we feel a lack, a neediness, then we attract more of that lack to us, because it is what our thoughts are focused on. If we instead cultivate a fullness in our hearts, then we attract more of that to ourselves. The more we fall into a love affair with ourselves, the more desirable we are to others. Buying ourselves gifts, nourishing ourselves with foods that keep the body healthy, keeping our bodies beautiful and clean, allowing ourselves to play — these are all things that create a fullness within. Being okay with pleasuring ourselves if a lover is not available, and making that act as deeply pleasurable and satisfying as a union with another liberates us from sexual dependence. This divine union, this inner wholeness, is the last gateway to re-creating ourselves as healthy, whole, and fully sexual human beings. Once we achieve this wholeness, we are ready for the final step of creating a whole that is greater than the sum of its parts, through full Divine Union with our beloved.

• Chapter 18 •

Divine Union Together

As in dance, so in life when it comes to the connection between a man and a woman. One person must lead while the other follows. If both lead, there can be no dance. There is a pull, a magnetic attraction, between a man who is on his purpose and a woman who is on her center. Centered, a woman pulls men to her who are like a key to her lock, who fit with her centered seat in the world, and who can contain her energy and harmonize with it in all of life. On his purpose, a man moves through a woman's center only if she is along his path and can receive and connect with him. He no longer wastes time trying to make connections where there is no energy or interest. Together, these two make a synergy of union, a grand siren song that is the most powerful force behind the universe, the power of sexual magnetism, life energy, and creation. This is the energy that creates all of us, and that can emanate from a union between a man and a woman to create a beautiful life. Singing within this zone of attraction, a man and a woman can accomplish anything together.

Sadly, this state is rare in our culture, because we are told that love is clinging and neediness. We are told that if we "love" someone it doesn't matter whether our centers and purposes are in alignment, that love is all we need. But it does matter. This conditional love alone is not enough to create a state of divine union. When you are in true harmony with a partner, there is a natural flow, and together you grow, making emotional, creative, and spiritual progress together. In this flow, your lives together become more and more rich and pleasant. Each of you somehow helps the other without trying to help. You may struggle against the pull of the magnetism, feel afraid of being so tightly bonded, or you may drop into old patterns of relationship that lead to power struggles. We are all human and imperfect. These struggles are simply a signal that there is more growing that you can do within yourself, to create yourself as a being who is fully centered or totally on your purpose, even when you are connected to your partner.

Divine Union is really just another word for the sacred marriage, the union that flows from the coming together of a priest and priestess of the sexual mysteries. Anyone who studies tantra can become a priest or priestess of these secrets. In divine union, magick flows. The sacred marriage with our partner brings us into a deep level of merging. This is tantric love, this desire for oneness. When we merge, as in dance, one person must follow while the other leads. In shamanic tantra, the woman takes the following, receptive role, while the man takes the leading, active part. To learn this dynamic, the woman begins by fully receiving from the man while he gives. Once she has mastered this state, both partners flow together to a place where they are giving and receiving. The woman stays in a soft magnetic state, while radiating energy back to the man from a place of fullness. The man stays in a sharply focused connecting state, and then learns to open his heart to receive from the woman. The couple practices this connection both in meditation and in lovemaking.

Surrendering and Penetrating

To fully surrender, a woman must feel safe. She must feel that no matter what happens or what she does, the man will hold her safe and not turn away from her in disgust or disinterest. Part of this safety is the man's responsibility to create by standing in his powerful ability to hold a container for the feminine swirl of emotions. And part of the safety is the woman's responsibility to create, both by choosing a suitable partner who can hold that safety, and by creating her own safety within. How do you create your own safety as a woman? You learn to hold a strong connection to Spirit and to follow the guidance it gives you at all times. Every time in my life that I have not felt safe, it has been because I didn't listen to Spirit's guidance for me, because I wanted something so badly that I grabbed at it even though Spirit was telling me no. The more I listen deeply to Spirit's guidance, the safer I feel, and the more I am able to open. The more I let go of fear, and stop expecting the worst from every situation, the more joyous my daily life becomes. In a long-term relationship that has accumulated fears and resentments from its past history, I must also learn to let go. I must decide to trust when Spirit says that it is safe. In tantra we stay in the present, we let go of the past and the future, knowing that only this moment truly exists.

The man's role is the polar opposite to the feminine. Where her role is to attract, his is to penetrate, to seek, to jolt, to pry life open, to connect.

The key to this strong masculine presence of connection is confidence, and this is built, again, by listening to Spirit. If you are continually trying to force situations with your will that are not what Spirit wants for you, you will find that life will become very hard, that your path to your purpose will often be blocked, and that you will begin to feel very beaten down and discouraged. When you are on your purpose, you surrender, but not to your partner or to defeat. Rather you surrender to Spirit's will for you. When you hear Spirit tell you to go forward, to leap off the cliff, you do so, trusting that Spirit will be there to catch you. You must trust when Spirit tells you to run, to leap, to go to someplace you don't want to go. You must learn to notice the magickal coincidences that come about when you listen to Spirit's voice in your heart and move without thinking, in whatever direction you are led. Think of Spirit as the ultimate male mentor who knows everything and can teach you all of it with an open heart and no strings attached. Who wouldn't want that deal?

When you bring this same passion and purpose into lovemaking, when you stand with confidence and strength in your ability to lead the woman into any place you feel led by Spirit, the two of you will ascend to unimaginable heights of passion and spiritual experience in your connection. Lovemaking will get better and better for you, and you will grow more and more in your relationship with each other.

Practice 1: Opening and Diving In

This is an exercise in being fully masculine or feminine and experiencing how those polarities work together.

Sit or lie down facing each other and connect with the Partnered Sacred Tree Meditation. Begin the Partnered Circular Breath, the man leading the woman in the breath.

Now the woman imagines that she is opening her energy field, like the slow unfolding of a flower bud, to become a flower in full bloom. As she opens, the man imagines focusing his energy and penetrating her, like the bee going deeply to the flower's center in search of its pollen. Continue to breath, to open and probe with each other. Use your eyes too, women softening to receive in their eyes, men penetrating with their gaze. Notice what feelings arise for you with this practice. Remember to keep breathing. Women surrender even more. Men penetrate even deeper. Continue for as long as it feels good to you, and then share with each other about your experiences. Repeat this exercise as often as you like, to practice being active and receptive with each other.

Intentional Cording

Usually we speak about creating cords with another person in life or in spiritual practice as a negative thing, something we are trying to banish. But in Divine Union, we create intentional cords of connection with each other to expand the flow of energy and engage all of the chakras in our connection. We begin with creating cords at the root and crown chakras, as in the Partnered Sacred Tree Meditation. We then progress to cording at the heart and third eye chakras, adding more bridges for the energy that you are moving between you. To create cords intentionally, you simply visualize them in your mind's eye, imagining yourself lovingly connecting to your partner. When you do this practice of intentionally creating and then disconnecting cords with your lover, you will find that it starts to bring more awareness into you about the cords that you have been creating in your life without meaning to do so. Being intentional about your connections with others is a very important spiritual practice that includes learning healthy boundaries. Cords are usually formed with people who are close to us, but there are times when others will create cords with us that we don't want or need. In these cases we are free to disconnect these cords without any guilt about doing so or worry about how it might affect the other person. Whenever anything is hooked into our energy field, we have a right to shift it.

Releasing Cords

Another very important, in fact critical, component of the divine union practice is that we learn to fully reconnect to ourselves when we are away from our partners. We connect instead to Spirit. This allows us to move through life unencumbered and undistracted by ties to someone who is not present with us in the moment. This does not mean that we do not have agreements with our partners that we honor, nor is this disconnection an excuse for irresponsible or hurtful behavior in a relationship. Rather, it is a way of creating clarity, freedom, and balance for ourselves in relationship. We learn to balance our lives between connection to our partner, connection to our friends and family, and connection to Spirit and ourselves. This practice has created profound change in my life. When I was first in relationship with my tantric partner, he needed to return home to his living space at the end of the night after our tantric practice. I honored his need, and at the same time, my need was for him to stay and to enjoy the closeness that comes for me after I have made love to someone in the tantric way. We struggled quite a bit with our differences until we created the practice of lovingly detaching intentionally from each other and connecting ourselves to Spirit. Now this practice is a cornerstone of how we practice tantra.

This practice doesn't mean that you give up any of the energy or love of the experience, or that you don't have intention to reconnect in the future. Bringing yourself back into your own space allows you to stay on your center or purpose and stay in strong connection to your own spiritual guidance. The first time I successfully did this practice, I pulled all the cords out, and then started to feel really tearful and sad without that connection. So I quickly put my roots in the earth and felt Mother Earth holding me — ahhh, that felt really good. Then I quickly put my branches into the sky and felt Father Sky kissing and containing me. Mmmmmmm. Then I pulled both the earth and sky into my heart to feel their love for me. Yes. And then I was back on my center and ready to move into my own space, separate from my lover.

Practice 2: Connecting and Releasing Cords

This practice teaches you to both deeply connect with your partner and to Reconnect to Self even more powerfully by releasing the cords between your chakras after a deep connection to another person.

Sit facing each other and begin your connection with the Partnered Sacred Tree Meditation. Now flow into Circular Breath, the man leading the woman. Imagine that in addition to the connections between your crown and root chakras, you are creating cords of energy that connect your hearts. Women, stay totally receptive and breathe in this connection. Now open your eyes if they are closed, and create a cord at your 3rd eye center. Again, women stay receptive here, while men send energy to them. Men pull from earth and sky so they are not using their own energy, but rather being a conduit for divine masculine energy. Continue forming cords at the throat, then the stomach, and finally the belly. Notice the quality of each of these cords, and the feelings that arrive with each of them. Allow Spirit to lead you into deep and full connection with each other. After a few minutes of totally receiving, women should notice a natural desire to start giving energy back to their partner. Allow this to happen, and men, allow yourselves to breathe in the energy, so that both partners are now sending energy out with the exhale and pulling energy in with the inhale, at all of the chakras.

Do this practice for as long as you like, and then practice reconnecting to self. First come out of the physical connection, women leading. Once you are no longer touching, begin the energetic disconnection by kissing each of your partner's cords and releasing them, then drawing in your own cords and letting them integrate the full experience of the connection into you. Use your hands to help disconnect any cords that are not letting go easily. Imagine at the same time that your partner is lovingly sending your own cords back to you.

Once you have kissed and released all your partner's cords, and reeled your own cords back in, disentangle your roots and branches, and powerfully reconnect to earth and sky, breathing the love of the divine Mother and Father into your heart, and breathing out to circulate that love through your heart, arms, and hands. Place your hands on your own heart and send love to yourself, feeling whole and complete in your connection to Spirit. Breath in the experience you just had and know that both you and your partner keep the whole experience. Realize that lovingly reconnecting to yourself does not mean that you have to give up any of the beautiful experience the two of you just created. In fact, now that you are whole and complete within yourself you can share the beauty of your experience with the whole world.

Share with your partner afterward about your feelings and experiences. Repeat this exercise whenever you want to create a deep and powerful connection with your partner. It is an excellent prelude to lovemaking, and the Reconnection to Self portion can be used after lovemaking, when you are both ready to move back into the world independently.

Practicing the Sacred Marriage

Call in Spirit when you are making love, and do it intentionally. Begin by creating space for your lovemaking whenever you do this practice, even if you are not planning a long tantric session. Light candles and incense, bathe, and create a beautiful mood with music that inspires you both. Begin your lovemaking with the sacred tree meditation, bringing yourself into presence. Connect your roots and branches to one another. Breathe together, and gaze into each other's eyes. Allow yourself to be transparent in your emotions, and connect deeply. Touch each other as if you have never touched each other before, using the different types of elemental touch. Join the chakras in your imagination, creating a full connection to your partner.

If you join together with the intention to hold unconditional love for each other, miracles happen as you make love. Things unlock from the soul and release that may have been stuck in your body for years. Old fears and resentments can vanish in an instant. Spirit will show you how to let go. As you make love, allow yourself to feel the connection to Spirit within you, call the God into you as you make love, if you are a man, or call in the Goddess, if you are a woman. Let yourself experience both yourself and your partner as divine while you are connecting. As you do this practice more and more often, you should notice a shift in the way your lovemaking feels to you, a shift that comes with being fully present to the gloriousness of your partner.

Stillness

Moving energy between our bodies, my lover and I shiver with passion. We sit on the bed, nude, facing each other. We warm up our energy bodies by practicing the Divine Union circuit. He sends out sexual energy through his lingam into my yoni, I breathe it in, move it up to my heart, and send it back our to his heart, creating a circle of energy between us. We are preparing to make love by awakening our sexual energy and bringing ourselves present to the sacred connection we are about to form. He draws me close to him and I surrender to his will, the first step for me in opening up and receiving the masculine fully into my body. As he draws me onto his lap and I feel his lingam come physically close to my yoni, I squeeze my PC muscle to wake up my yoni. My pulsing arouses his lingam, and I feel it bob underneath me, pressing against my yoni, asking for entrance. As we sit, he strokes my breasts, gently teasing them awake with his fully present touch. I moan and just receive him, his touch, his presence, and his body. He looks into my eyes and pins me with his gaze, an intense look that I open and receive within my own eyes, feeling now that he is coming fully into my energy field, merging with me in a mystical union of swirling life streams. I circuit my energy more intentionally now, following his breath. I breathe the light of his lingam into my yoni and pull it up to my heart, where I breathe it out into his heart. I also breathe in from his eyes, and pull that down to my heart. I breathe out from my heart into his, where he pulls my energy in and sends it up to his eyes and down to his lingam. Merging closer and closer, we are preparing for the sacred practice of lovemaking in stillness.

Looking into my lover's eyes, I breathe deeply. I breathe him into me, opening myself to be the Goddess, the lock to his key, knowing that all my inner gates can be opened just by his lingam, his wand of light. He enters me and we go into stillness, breathing together with the lingam in the yoni, both of us pulsing our PC muscles, but not otherwise thrusting or moving. We are joined by our eyes, joined by our energies and by the circuit that we are both creating. Our thoughts make real this circle of light that moves between us, pulsing out from his penis and into my vagina, snaking up my spine to my heart and radiating back out from me, permeating his chest as he absorbs my radiance, pulls it back to his lingam, and starts the cycle over again. Joy and ecstasy come into me. I feel a powerful sexual arousal. A tingling rises through my body and shoots out to the stars. The circuit of energy still runs between us, but it is only one of many energy circuits that I am feeling awaken in my body, and I surrender to them all. I feel a strong knowing that my intention and Spirit are in charge of this experience, not me. I pulse my yoni and feel him gasp, he pulses too, and my yoni responds with electric shocks of pleasure. We hold each other, me sitting on his lap, and we rock back and forth in pleasure, in stillness. Without thrusting or moving anything but our breath and our PC muscles, we are making love. We continue like this, feeling the energy build in us until we are both climaxing, my yoni pushing out streams of amrita, while after several full body orgasms he chooses to allow his lingam to pour its seed into me, brought to ejaculatory climax through the joining of these two sacred fluids creating a magic that we both feel alive in us afterward, as we rest together and hold each other.

Resolving Conflict

Practicing the sacred marriage of divine union also includes cultivating the ability to move through conflict. Conflict is natural and normal between humans, just a part of life, like feelings of sadness and grief. It is part of the full range or relationship. Call in Spirit when you are in conflict to allow new answers to your struggles with each other to present themselves, or to allow situations to shift into a place where you no longer have a struggle to discuss. Sometimes this process is quite magickal, and I have seen it work amazingly well in my own relationships. Recently I had a conflict with an old lover that had been going on for two years, and we had not been able to come to an agreement. I had tried giving into what he wanted, and that felt horrible so I couldn't do that anymore, and neither could he agree to any of the solutions I offered for the situation. Finally I decided to ask Spirit for help. I'm not sure why it didn't occur to me earlier, except that there were lawyers involved, which clouded the issue. When I tuned into Spirit, and to myself, I found that I had very clear answers about what I needed in this situation. I decided to simply state my needs calmly and clearly. I listened to my old lover's upset at not wanting to give me what I needed. I stayed centered in my feminine, and, like White Star Woman, I stated what I needed calmly again.

I was amazed at how all the emotional upset I'd been feeling about the situation was gone. I found myself held by Spirit, staying calm and serene in my discussions with him. Even without an immediate solution I felt better than I had in months. Eventually, after a month or so of these discussions, we came to an agreement that I felt good about. I can honestly say that I felt the hand of Spirit through the entire process. I felt Spirit holding me centered in the disagreement, and I saw Spirit giving my ex-lover clarity as well about what was fair, independent of his emotions about it. The best part is that we are even better friends after this resolution, because we have seen that there are new ways for us to resolve very old conflicts.

Loving Your Reality

I have seen many people come to the practice of tantra with great certainty that they cannot practice tantra with the partner who is in their life because their partner is not willing or interested. A great spiritual practice is to love the relationship you're in, and do your best to practice with that person. Even if your partner is not following the tantric path, you can still run your own energy and do your own spiritual practice when you connect with them. You can practice gratitude and acceptance of who they are, without the need to change or fix them. In partnered work, this approach can bring a shift of consciousness in you and in the relationship. I have seen old patterns of conflict and resentment in my relationships slowly change through this practice.

For many years I simply ran my own energy while making love, and did more full tantric circuits with the divine masculine while self-pleasuring. Eventually, my lover saw the positive changes in me and decided to pursue tantra for himself, not because I wanted him to. Our relationship has deepened and opened out as a result of this change. Tantra is first and foremost about unconditional love. If you are judging your partner, feeling angry with them, and wishing they would change, you are not in unconditional love. You must let go of what your partner does, and simply focus on your own heart. You must continue to love yourself. As you focus on this self-love, as it becomes a part of you, your way of being will naturally shift those around you.

Recommitting

If you are working at loving the relationship you're in, and your partner is willing, a recommitment ceremony can bring a sense of communion and ease to working through conflict. One commitment you can make to each other is to stay in the present, whether you are making love or embroiled in a conflict. Bringing the events of the past into argument serves only to perpetuate conflict. If you stay focused on the present, communicate with an open heart, let go of fear and stay aware of why you are upset right now, this will help conflict to resolve more easily. Moving through conflict with this deep sense of presence and love can allow a relationship to drop into a place of joy and satisfaction, in knowing that we need only experience our partner as they are right now. It also simplifies life immensely to focus only on the feelings that are alive in my heart in this moment. Recommitting to a relationship is very much like recommitting on a daily basis to a spiritual practice, because a relationship is a spiritual practice. Our friends and lovers are our greatest teachers in life. They are a mirror that allows us to very clearly see our emotional selves, just as a mirror that hangs on the wall allows us to look clearly at our physical selves. We can choose to use this mirror to learn and to make changes.

Practice 3: Recommitment Ceremony

This ceremony is designed to help you and your partner make an intentional commitment to unconditionally loving each other. Before doing this exercise, it is best for each partner to first do the solo Divine Union practices, especially the Self-Marriage Ceremony in Chapter 17.

The man chooses a gift for the woman to symbolize his love for her, and this becomes the center of the altar. Create the rest of the altar together, and include a rock or crystal for each chakra. Tumbled stones are fine for this purpose, and any stone the color of the chakra is fine, for example red jasper for the root chakra, carnelian for the belly, citrine for the stomach, aventurine for the heart, turquoise for the throat, amethyst for the 3rd eye, and clear quartz for the crown.

Sit facing each other in front of the altar, and connect using the Partnered Sacred Tree Meditation. Do the Partnered Circular Breath together and then intentionally connect your cords at each chakra.

Once you are in this deep connection together, the man picks up the red stone and says,

"I accept and love your physical being"

The woman replies,

"I receive your love and acceptance" and takes the stone from him, holding it in her hand.

The man picks up the orange stone and says,

"I accept and love your sexual being"

The woman replies,

"I receive your love and acceptance" and takes the stone from him.

With the yellow stone in his hand, the man says,

"I accept and love your power"

The woman replies,

"I receive your love and acceptance" and takes the stone from him.

With the green stone he says,

"I accept and love the ways that you give love to the world and to me"

The woman replies,

"I receive your love and acceptance" and takes the stone from him.

With the blue stone he says,

"I accept and love your expression of who you are"

She says,

"I receive your love and acceptance" and takes the stone from him.

With the violet stone he says,

"I accept and love your vision"

She says,

"I receive your love and acceptance" and takes the stone from him.

With the white or clear stone he says

"I accept and love your Connection to Spirit"

She says,

"I receive your love and acceptance" and takes the stone.

Now they switch roles, and she moves through the same series of statements, as he receives the stones from her.

Now they hold hands, look in each other's eyes, and say these words together:

"I, ______________, recommit to you as my beloved, to be in the moment, to accept you, and to love you unconditionally."

End the ceremony by sharing food that you prepared in advance, and if you like, seal the ceremony with tantric lovemaking. Remember to release your cords and reconnect to self when you are ready to go your separate ways.

The Divine Union Ritual

A beautiful way to bring your entire practice together and to celebrate your relationship with your partner is a day-long ritual of lovemaking called the Divine Union ritual. This ritual was inspired by the Hindu tantric Maithuna ritual. The Maithuna ritual has very strict boundaries about how it is practiced. In the shamanic tradition, we flow more into our intuition about what is needed, and we plan the ritual according to those needs. The first step is finding time. Most of us do not have a full day open without kids, work, or chores around the house. To do the Divine Union ritual, we need to consciously make the time, knowing that the rewards of doing this work are well worth it.

Practice 4: Divine Union Ritual

Do this practice whenever you want to celebrate your love for your partner with a full day of tantric practice.

For a day-long ritual, spend some time, perhaps an hour, preparing the bedroom to be a beautiful romantic and opulent space. Use candles, incense, or aromatherapy oils to create romantic lighting and scent the air. Draw the drapes if you like, to create an intimate haven. Have scented or unscented massage oils at the ready to massage each other. Put away all the clutter, and put clean sheets on the bed. Prepare some finger food that you can keep near the bed to feed to each other when you are hungry. Have towels and condoms and lubricant handy as well, so you don't have to go searching for them later. Provide everything you will want for your comfort before you begin. Make this preparation time part of the ritual. Stay present to this moment and notice how nice it can be to do these simple acts. Once you begin, take the phone off the hook, lock your pets out of the bedroom and send the kids to grandma's house or a sitter for the day. This is time for the two of you to sink into pampering each other and connecting.

Begin by clearing your energy fields and the room with smudging with sage or incense, and then drop into the Partnered Sacred Tree Meditation to center and bring the two of you into sacred space. Breathe together for a few minutes to come into harmony. When you come out of the meditation, spend an hour just talking and sharing what is alive in your mind and heart in the moment, talking in "I" statements and using compassionate communication. After that hour, move into an hour of massaging and caressing each other, not touching the genitals yet, just pampering the body. Focus on how glorious it feels to be touched by or to touch your beloved. Take a break at this point and eat. Pamper yourself with food, paying attention to how the food tastes and relishing in an unhurried meal. Get some fresh air if you can go outside in your robes. When you return, come back into touching, but now add kissing and touch on the genitals and body to your connection. Stay present to this touch with your breath and feel the energy move through your body. Do not allow yourself to climax, but rather let the energy cycle build up and flow down several times. Spend at least an hour doing this, and when the energy gets too high, stop to do some tantric spiritual practice like circuiting energy or connecting your chakras. See what it is like to let the energy cycle completely down before ramping it back up.

When you are ready, come back into connection and allow full intercourse for an hour, but do not allow the man or the woman to climax, just simply enjoy the energy and build it even higher. Use the Earth/Stillness mode of lovemaking in Chapter 15 to cycle the energy down in lovemaking. Stop and feel into not having any goals and letting Spirit guide you. Take another break to nibble your food treats and do spiritual practice.

Now come into the final union, making love for at least another hour before allowing yourselves to climax. For men, this means that you let Spirit guide the energy as high as it wants to, still without any goals for ejaculation or orgasm. See what it is like to flow through an ejaculation while breathing with your eyes locked on your beloved, fully present. When you are ready to climax, drop in and surrender, let yourself go. For women, this means that you let yourself surrender totally to your Goddess self. You pull as much sexual energy as desire from your man, without holding back for fear of bringing him to a climax. See what it is like to be fully present to this experience. Receive your man in your yoni and eyes.

Men should not be surprised if they have difficulty climaxing after this many hours of lovemaking. Sometimes the tantric state becomes too expanded for a traditional orgasm. It is often the same for women. Just relax into it if this is the case, and see where the lovemaking takes you, staying fully present in the moment by breathing together and gazing into the universe within your partner's eyes. After this very intense practice, take care of yourself by bathing, eating, and resting. Remember to release cords and reconnect to self when you are ready to go your separate ways.

Fully integrating the Six Gateways into a lovemaking practice to create Divine Union banishes boring lovemaking forever. The gateways bring infinite variety to your lovemaking. There are infinite ways to breathe, touch, and move energy between you, to connect your bodies to each other, and to merge with the God and Goddess. As you practice this union, the lovemaking becomes more and more ecstatic — it is a re-learning that all of us are capable of. Once we remember the state of sexual wholeness that is our birthright, we become free and ecstatic. We remember that the ecstatic state is always available to us, and that the only thing that stands in the way of all of life being a continual orgasm is our own resistance to that energy flowing through our body. The orgasmic pleasure energy of the universe is always available to is, whether we are making love, doing spiritual practice, painting, writing, dancing, or caring for our children. We learn to connect to all of creation, to all beings in this creation with love. We learn to be unconditional with love, to let go of judgment, and to cultivate compassion. As our sexual energy becomes reunited with the rest of ourselves, we feel less scattered, more centered, and we have more energy for our lives, more passion. Practicing tantrics often report that not only is their sex life amazing, but they also have vibrant physical health, feel happy and joyous most of the time, and need little sleep. My life has altered dramatically in the past several years, my health in particular, and I am healthier today and need less medical care than I did 20 years ago. I feel better and stronger physically, emotionally, mentally, and creatively than I ever have. In my sexual life there is no longer a sense that it is separate from any part of who I am. This strength and wholeness is available to anyone who walks this path with pure intention and commitment.

Bibliography and Resources

Books About Tantra, Sexuality, and Relationships:

Spider Woman's Web: Traditional Native American Tales about Women's Power by Susan Hazen-Hammond. Berkley/Perigee, 1st Ed., 1999.

Circle Round: Raising Children in Goddess Traditions by Starhawk, Diane Baker, Anne Hill, and Sara Ceres Boore. Bantam, 2000.

The Kama Sutra of Vatsayanna, translated by Sir Richard Burton. Standard Publications, 2004.

The Art of Sexual Ecstasy by Margot Anand. Jeremy P. Tarcher, 1989.

The Art of Everyday Ecstasy by Margot Anand. Broadway, New Ed., 1999.

Witch Crafting by Phyllis Curott. Broadway, 2002.

The Love Spell by Phyllis Curott. Gotham, 2006.

Tantric Orgasm for Women by Diana Richardson. Park Street Press, 2004.

The Heart of Tantric Sex by Diana Richardson. O Books; New Ed., 2003.

The Book of Secrets by Osho. St. Martin's Griffin; First Ed., 1998.

The Ethical Slut by Dossie Easton and Catherine A. Liszt. Greenery Press, 1997.

Loving More, The Polyfidelity Primer by Ryam Nearing. Pep Publishing, 3rd Ed., 1992.

Polyamory, the New Love Without Limits: Secrets of Sustainable Intimate Relationships by Deborah Anapol. Intinet Resource Center, 1997.

The Joy of Sex by Alex Comfort. Pocket, 1992.

More Joy of Sex by Alex Comfort. Pocket, 1991.

Wheels of Light by Rosalyn Bruyere. Fireside, 1st Ed., 1994.

Wheels of Life by Anodea Judith. Llewellyn Publications, 1st Ed., 1999.

Kama Sutra: Including the Seven Spiritual Laws of Love by Deepak Chopra. Virgin Books, 2006.

Windhorse Woman by Lynn V. Andrews. Grand Central Publishing, 1990.

The Jewel in the Lotus: The Sexual Path to Higher Consciousness by Sunyata Saraswati and Bodhi Avinasha. Ipsalu Publishing, 1994.

The Way of the Superior Man: A Spiritual Guide to Mastering the Challenges of Women, Work, and Sexual Desire by David Deida. Sounds True, 2004.

The Dance of Intimacy by Harriet Goldhor Lerner, Ph.D. Harper Paperbacks, 1990.

Intimacy and Solitude by Stephanie Dowrick. W. W. Norton & Company, 1st American Ed., 1996.

Tantra Groups Online:

(For a more complete and up-to-date list, go to www.yabyummy.com)

www.tantra.com — a listing of tantra teachers throughout the US.

www.meetups.com — lists local groups that practice tantra.

Tantra Teachers

www.yabyummy.com — Yabyummy is a shamanic teaching temple committed to unifying sexuality with spirituality. They offer many classes, events, retreats, and private tantra sessions in the San Diego and nearby areas. Contact them at kypris@yabyummy.com or steven@yabyummy.com.

www.ecstaticliving.com — Steve & Lokita Carter have been teaching Tantra workshops, Tropical Tantra vacation retreats and the Love & Ecstasy Training (LET) for couples and singles since 1999. Based in Northern California and teaching all over the USA and Central America, they are the founders of the Institute for Ecstatic Living, and the directors and senior faculty of Margot Anand's SkyDancing Tantra Institute. A committed married couple, they receive great inspiration from walking their talk and practicing their methods to enhance their relationship and their lives. Steve & Lokita are also the creators of the best-selling sacred sex DVDs *Tantric Massage for Lovers, The Breath of Tantric Love* and *Tantric Yoga for Lovers*. They can also be reached at 877-982-6872.

Shamanic Resources:

www.Heartwisdom.net — Mellissa Seaman, a powerful shamanic healer, teacher, and originator of the 16 Elements of Ecstasy, as well as one of my own teachers.

www.HandsOverHeart.com — Katie Weatherup is a shamanic healer who offers in person and long-distance soul retrieval and classes. Her book, *Practical Shamanism* is available on Amazon. She can be reached at 619-518-7658 or katie@handsoverheart.com.

Addiction and Recovery Resources:

www.alcoholics-anonymous.org — Alcoholics Anonymous.

www.na.org — Narcotics Anonymous.

www.codependents.org — Codependents Anonymous, a group for people who are codependent and want recovery.

anon.alateen.org/english.html — Al-Anon, a group for anyone affected by alcoholism or addiction now, or as a child.

Communication Resources:

www.cnvc.org — Center for Non-Violent Communication (CNVC), resources for learning healthier communication.

www.nlp-world.com — Neuro-linguistic Programming (NLP), an interpersonal communication model and an alternative approach to psychotherapy.

About the Author

Shamanic tantra is a spiritual journey into a passionate, creative life that includes a full and rich sexual connection to God. Initiated on this path by a powerful shamanic healer, Kypris has journeyed in search of spiritual wisdom, beauty, and the open heart through many places on Mother Earth: walking the witch-hunting hills of Salem, MA; bathing in the healing waters of Tahiti and Hawaii, and making love to the austere deserts of Sedona and Anza-Borrego. With the roots of her spiritual practice in Wicca, Kypris was led to tantra through visions of Aphrodite and Shiva, and transformed through solo practice of ritual, energy channeling, bellydance, and yoga. Led to her tantric partner by a powerful shamanic dream, Kypris practices tantra today in tandem, and works as a spiritual coach, healer, and teacher.

Printed in the United States
204258BV00003B/121-339/P

9 780615 199412